BELLA **SZYSZKOWSKA**

HASHTAG ENGLISH 2

ELEMENTARY

LANGUAGE BOOSTER

Pearson

MISTO
Papel | Apoiando o manejo florestal responsável
FSC® C103535

Catalogue Publication Data

Hashtag English 2 Elementary Language Booster
Authors: Bella Szyszkowska
Pearson Educación de México, S.A. de C.V., 2023
ISBN: 978-607-32-5680-3
Area: Schools
Format: 20,5 × 24,7 cm Page count: 112

Product Vice President: Marianne Lewis ■ **ELT Director:** Marjorie Robles ■ **Product Managers:** Anita Heald, Priscila Marconi ■ **Product Developers:** Renata S. C. Victor, Carolina Andrade ■ **Editor:** Elaine Mendonça ■ **Art and Design Coordinator:** Anderson Ferreira ■ **Art and Design Editors:** Andréia A. Santa Rosa, Patricia Santos, Luiz Rubio ■ **Layout:** MRS Editorial ■ **Illustrators:** MRS Editorial ■ **Cover & Interior Design:** Apis Design ■ **Cover Photo:** Shutterstock ■ **Digital Development Supervisor:** Isabel Silva ■ **Digital Content and Development Editors:** Rafaela de Mendonça, Fernanda Patucci, Lara Tasso, Mirella Armentano ■ **Digital Content Authors:** 2014 Solucões Editoriais, Ohana Editorial, Bella Szyszkowska ■ **Audiovisual Coordinator:** Lucas Domingues ■ **Audiovisual Editor:** Lucas Motta ■ **R&P Coordinator:** Maiti Salla ■ **R&P team:** Maricy Queiroz, Cristiane Gameiro ■ **Content Support:** 2014 Soluções Editoriais (Editors: Carla Maurício Coelho da Silva Vianna, Joyce Rocha Gomes, Juliana Maria Franco Tavares, Marcos Carvalho Mendonça, Rebeca Pasqua de Andrade. Assistants: Cristine Zanela Monte, Elani Souza Gomes, Juliana Aga, Pedro Zanela) ■ **Proofreading:** 2014 Soluções Editoriais, Silva Serviços de Educação ■ **Picture Credits:** Pearson Asset Library, Shutterstock, 123RF, Alamy Stock Photo

Contact: soporte@pearson.com

First published, 2023

ISBN PRINT BOOK: 978-607-32-5680-3

Printed in Brazil by Reproset RPSZ 221221

1 2 3 4 5 6 7 8 9 0 - 25 24 23 22

Avenida Antonio Dovalí Jaime #70
Torre B, Piso 6, Colonia Zedec Ed. Plaza Santa Fe
Delegación Álvaro Obregón, México, Ciudad de México, C. P. 01210

www.PearsonELT.com

Pearson

Pearson Hispanoamérica
Argentina ■ Belice ■ Bolivia ■ Chile ■ Colombia ■ Costa Rica ■ Cuba ■ República Dominicana ■ Ecuador ■ El Salvador ■ Guatemala ■ Honduras ■ México ■ Nicaragua ■ Panamá ■ Paraguay ■ Perú ■ Uruguay ■ Venezuela

LANGUAGE BOOSTER INDEX

The **LANGUAGE BOOSTER** is a separate book for you to review and practice the content of your Student's Book and engage in additional lessons in class and at home. The Language Booster is partially printed and partially worked on in the e-Language Booster, which consists of interactive consolidation activities. Each of the nine units in the print Language Booster follows the same structure as the Student's Book (Discover, Clarify, Understand, Develop, and Challenge). It also includes a page to reinforce the content covered in class (Assess). The additional pages at the end of the print Language Booster offer further practice. These are:

FOCUS ON CULTURE

This double-page section includes an authentic text, comprehension tasks, and a writing task.

TEEN TALK

This single-page section contains communicative activities to practice the grammar and vocabulary of the unit. These activities include role plays, information gap activities, interviews, and discussions.

GAMES

The game pages contain nine games, one for each unit. These games review content in a fun way.

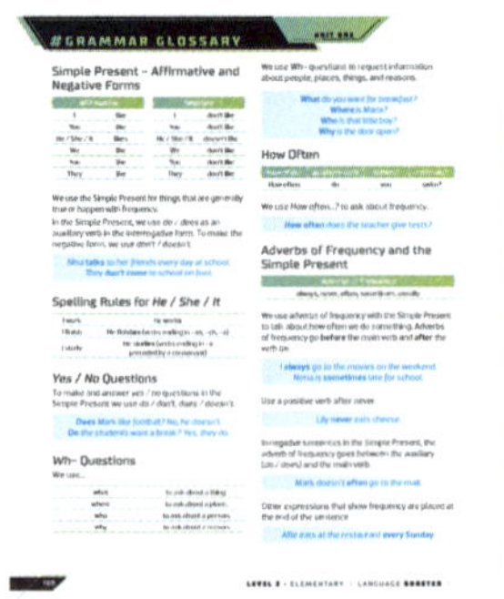

GRAMMAR GLOSSARY

The Grammar Glossary pages are designed for quick grammar reference and review.

The Language Booster also contains the audio tracks and the audio scripts from all the units.

Vocabulary

School Subjects
Adjectives

1 Read the e-mail and complete the sentences.

CANCEL SEND

TO Kirsty

FROM Ana

SUBJECT Hello!

Hi Kirsty,
Today I start school. I have my schedule... it's OK.
On Mondays I have history and music. That's an interesting day! Thursdays are bad ☹ ... I have geography. I don't like it because it's very hard! Math is on Wednesdays and Fridays... It's not my favorite subject, but it's easy.
What about you? Do you have a good schedule?
Talk to you soon,
xoxo
Ana

1. Ana likes ________________ and history.
2. Ana doesn't like ________________.
3. In Ana's opinion, ________________ is easy.

2 Complete the table with school subjects. Then write how you feel about them.

School subject	How I feel about it
m________	It's ________.
P________	________.
s________	________.
h________	________.
l________	________.
m________	________.
E________	________.

3 Think about the school subjects in your timetable. Underline the sentences that are true for you.

1. I have easy subjects.
2. My schedule is boring.
3. My schedule is bad.
4. My schedule is good.
5. I have hard subjects.
6. My schedule is interesting.

Reading

1 USING PRIOR KNOWLEDGE. Check (✓) to complete the sentences about your school.

My school is

- ☐ interesting.
- ☐ boring.
- ☐ fun.
- ☐ easy.
- ☐ hard.

2 Listen to Lucas describe his school and underline the correct sentence. 02

1. Lucas's school is boring and hard.
2. Lucas's school is interesting and fun.

3 Read the article about different schools. Which school does Lucas go to?

NEW TAB

Three Different Schools from Around the World!

1. In the U.K., some children don't have a school building. The school is the forest! This is Forest School. They learn about nature. They have classes outside every day.
2. Some children in India use the train platform as a school. There are no interactive whiteboards, desks, or chairs. But there is a teacher, so they can learn!
3. In Denmark, there is a school called the Orestad Gymnasium school. The classrooms don't have walls, desks, or chairs! Students feel relaxed and comfortable.

4 Read the article again. Match the pictures (a–c) to the schools (1–3).

a.

b.

c.

5 In your opinion, which of the three schools is the most interesting? Why?

I like the Orestad Gymnasium school because it's modern.

____

____

____

6 Record your answer to Activity 5 in a voice message and send it to a classmate.

Grammar

like / don't like / think

Why and *Because*

Giving Directions

1 **What after-school activities do you have at your school? Check (✓).**

- ☐ Sports club
- ☐ Music club
- ☐ Drama club
- ☐ Art club
- ☐ Study group
- ☐ Math club

2 **What after-school activities do you like?**

____

3 **Read the messages. What after-school activities does Reena, Emil, and Jo's school have?**

____

____

Reena: Hey! How are you?
Emil: Heya... So bored!
Reena: Oh... I'm at drama club now. I really like it! Do you like drama?
Emil: Hmm no, I don't.
Reena: What? Why don't you like it?
Emil: Haha... It's hard for me. I don't know. Is the music club today?
Reena: No. It's tomorrow.
Emil: Oh, OK.
Reena: I think today we have drama club and sports club.
Emil: Cool! I like sports!
Reena: I think Jo is at sports club now. Go meet her!
Emil: Great! Tell her I'm coming.
Reena: Sure! See you. 😃

4 **Read the text in Activity 3 again. Then complete the sentences with *like / likes / doesn't like*.**

1. Reena really ______________ drama.
2. Emil ______________ drama.
3. Jo and Emil ______________ sports.
4. Emil ______________ music.

5 **Complete the table about yourself.**

	Score the activities.	Why?
		Because it's fun. The teacher is cool. I meet my friends.
Sports	☆☆☆	
Drama	☆☆☆	
Music	☆☆☆	
Art	☆☆☆	
Math	☆☆☆	
Study group	☆☆☆	

6 **Use your ideas from Activity 6 to write a paragraph about yourself.**

I don't like sports because they're hard. I like art because it's fun and the teacher is cool.

____

____

____

7 **Send your paragraph to a classmate. Check if he / she used *like*, *don't like*, and *because* correctly.**

8 **Look at the map on page 17 of your Student's Book. Write three new sentences. Use *go straight on*, *turn left*, and *turn right*.**

____

____

____

Use of English

1 **Amie is new to her school. How do you think she feels? Check (✓) the options.**

1. ☐ happy
2. ☐ nervous
3. ☐ lost
4. ☐ confident
5. ☐ ____________

2 **Read the e-mail from the school counselor to Amie. What is the purpose of their meeting?**

____

CANCEL SEND

TO Amie

FROM Gavin Fry

SUBJECT First day introduction

Hi Amie,

I'm looking forward to meeting you tomorrow to give you information about your classes.

Please come to my office. It is on the first floor. At the entrance, you will see the administration office on the left. Go straight on and turn right after the bathroom. Turn right again after the art classroom and go straight on. You will see my office at the end of the hallway, opposite the science labs.

You can ask me any questions you want about the school.

See you tomorrow!

Gavin Fry

Student Counselor

Green Park Secondary School

3 **Look at the map. Draw Amie's route from the entrance to the counselor's office.**

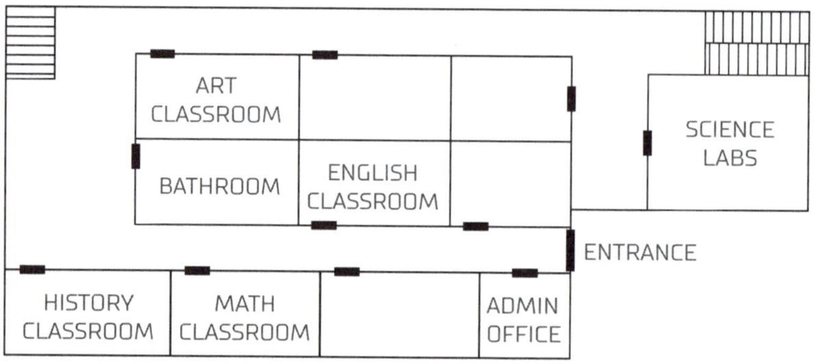

4 **Amie's first class is English. Write the directions from the counselor's office to the classroom.**

____

____

____

____

Writing

1 Read the instant message from Amie's mom. What is she curious about?

____

Mom

Today

Mom: Hi, love! How's your first day of school? I hope the school counselor helped! What classes do you have? Do you like the teachers? Love you xxxx

Prepare to Write

2 Look at Amie's schedule. Circle the school subjects.

9:00 – 9:30	Induction: Student counselor	Mr. Fry
9:30 – 10:30	English	Ms. Phillips
10:30 – 12:30	Science	Ms. Benis
12:30 – 1:30	Break	
1:30 – 2:30	Math	Mr. Gordan
2:30 – 3:30	P.E.	Ms. Ford

3 How does Amie feel about her classes? Look at the schedule in Activity 2 again and use *likes / doesn't like* to complete the sentences below.

1. Amie ______________________ English.
2. Amie ______________________ science.
3. Amie ______________________ P.E.
4. Amie ______________________ math.

Write

4 Write Amie's reply to the message in Activity 1. Remember to answer the questions Amie's mother asked her.

Mom

Amie: Hi, mom,

____

____

____

____

____

____

____

____

____

____

____

____

Check and Change

5 Check your message. Make sure you included at least three of the items listed below:

- ☐ school subjects.
- ☐ adjectives to describe school subjects.
- ☐ *like / don't like*.
- ☐ *why* and *because*.
- ☐ directions.

Publish

6 Write a clean version of your instant message.

#ASSESS

Vocabulary

1 **Use the codebreaker to find the school subjects.**

0	1	2	3	4	5	6	7	8	9	10	11	12	13	14	15	16	17	18	19	20	21	22	23	24	25
U	V	N	O	G	S	I	B	J	L	K	M	D	C	R	E	A	Q	X	Y	T	H	F	Z	W	P

1. 11. 16. 20. 21. ______________
2. 5. 13. 6. 15. 2. 13. 15. ______________
3. 9. 6. 20. 15. 14. 16. 20. 0. 14. 15. ______________
4. 25. 15. ______________
5. 21. 6. 5. 20. 3. 14. 19. ______________
6. 11. 0. 5. 6. 13. ______________

Grammar

2 **Circle the correct word to complete the sentences.**

1. He **likes** / **like** geography.
2. She **don't like** / **doesn't like** P.E.
3. We **doesn't like** / **don't like** the history class.
4. **Why** / **Because** do you like English?

Reading

3 **Read the e-mail and mark the sentences T (True) or F (False).**

CANCEL SEND

SUBJECT RE: How are you?

Hi Rosa,

How are you?

Everything is fine at school. I have math and history today. I like those subjects because the classes are fun and we always play games!

My English class is tomorrow. My English teacher is not nice this semester. I like the subject, but I can't say I like him. Why do some teachers never play games?

Hope you are good!

Lots of love,

Kim

xxx

1. ☐ Kim has math and English today.
2. ☐ She thinks the history class is fun.
3. ☐ They play games in math and history classes.
4. ☐ Kim's English teacher is nice.
5. ☐ Kim doesn't like English.

Listening

4 **Listen to Rosa's voice message. Does she feel happy or unhappy with her classes and teachers?** 03

____

Writing

5 **Write directions.**

1. From your classroom to the bathroom.

____
____
____
____

2. From the cafeteria to the library.

____
____
____
____

Speaking

6 **Record yourself speaking. Talk about:**

- Your favorite subject.
- Directions from the school entrance to your favorite place.

Vocabulary

Free-Time Activities

Collocations with *Have*, *Go*, and *Play*

Prepositions

1 **Read Brian and Alan's conversation via an instant messaging app. What are their plans for the weekend? Circle the correct option.**

Alan

Brian: Do you want to hang out on Saturday?

Alan: Yes! What do you want to do?

Brian: Maybe watch a movie at the movie theater?

Alan: Hmm, no .... There aren't any good movies on.

Brian: OK. So what?

Alan: I want to buy new football cleats.

Brian: Cool. Let's go shopping!

Alan: Yes! And I want to have lunch at the mall.

Brian: OK, sounds good 😀

1. Go to the movie theater and go shopping.
2. Go shopping and play video games.
3. Go shopping and have lunch.

2 **Match the phrases. Use go twice.**

1. do
2. go
3. have
4. play
5. take
6. use
7. watch

☐ a movie
☐ a walk
☐ community service
☐ lunch
☐ shopping
☐ social media
☐ swimming
☐ video games

3 **Which are your favorite and least favorite free-time activities? Complete the sentences.**

1. I love to ______________________________ ______________________________.
2. I like to ______________________________ ______________________________.
3. I don't like to ______________________________ ______________________________.

#CLARIFY

UNIT ONE

Reading

1 **MAKING CONNECTIONS. What do you do to avoid wasting water in your house?**

2 **SKIMMING. Listen to Kim talk about her new school project. What is it about? Underline the correct answer.** 04

1. The project is about sports.
2. The project is about sustainability.
3. The project is about fashion.

3 **MAKING PREDICTIONS. Predict what students from Kim's class are going to talk about in an online school forum about sustainability. Check (✓) the pictures.**

1. 

2. 

3. 

4. 

4 **Now read the forum posts and check your predictions.**

FORUM

Kim99: Hey! I need ideas for my class project. How can we use water wisely in our community?

Happydog: Well... I never take long showers!

Harrylove123: I often post eco-friendly ideas on my social media! Check them out later 🙂

BTSfan: In my house, we reuse water from cooking. We use it to water the plants!

Tiff: I rarely take a bath. A full bathtub requires up to 70 gallons of water. That's crazy! I do community service on the weekend. We campaign against water waste. Wanna join?

Kim99: Thanks for your ideas, guys! @Tiff Sounds good... I'm in! Text you about that later.

5 **SCANNING. Read the text in Activity 4 again and mark the sentences T (True) or F (False).**

1. ☐ Happydog always takes long showers.
2. ☐ BTSfan reuses water to wash vegetables.
3. ☐ Tiff does community service.
4. ☐ Kim accepts Tiff's invitation.

6 **Research new ideas on how to use water wisely. Then answer Kim's forum post.**

FORUM

www.forum.com

Hi, Kim! I ______________________________

____

____

7 **Record your answer to Activity 6 in a voice message and send it to a classmate.**

Grammar

Simple Present

Yes / No Questions and *Wh-* Questions

1 **How often do you do the free-time activities below? Write A for always, U for usually, O for often, S for sometimes, R for rarely, or N for never.**

1. ☐ go swimming
2. ☐ do community service
3. ☐ use social media
4. ☐ watch a movie
5. ☐ play video games
6. ☐ go for a walk
7. ☐ play soccer

2 **Listen and complete the sentences about Frida's and her family's activities.** 05

1. Frida ______________ almost every day.
2. Frida's mom ______________ cooking.
3. Frida's sister ______________ at the park after school.
4. Frida's grandfather sometimes ______________ in the park to see her sister.

3 **Make the sentences in Activity 1 true about you.**

I don't play video games every day.

____

____

____

4 **Complete the sentences with the verbs from the box in the Simple Present.**

go	have	not	watch	play	start	use

1. Ryan often ______________ social media after school.
2. Lucas and Olivia ______________ movies at the movie theater.
3. ______________ Ric ______________ soccer on the weekends?
4. I ______________ swimming with my sister.
5. Dad ______________ English classes in the evening.
6. We always ______________ classes at 7:30.

5 **What does your family do on the weekend? Complete the table.**

Name	Activities

6 **Use your answers in Activities 3 and 5 to write a paragraph about your and your family's free-time activities.**

____

____

____

____

____

7 **Read the paragraph in Activity 6 and record it. Check if you used the Simple Present correctly.**

#UNDERSTAND

UNIT ONE

Use of English

1 **Read the text and identify the genre. Check (✓) the correct option.**

1. ☐ An e-mail
2. ☐ A social media profile
3. ☐ A text message

face.com/profile

Lalo Martinez

Add Chat

Basic Info

I live in Bogota. I go to school in Chapinero. I come from Venezuela. I have a sister and a brother.

Interests

I like arts and music. I always paint on the weekends, and I visit art galleries, too.

I play the bass guitar, and I have a band. Sometimes we play in concerts.

I love to eat delicious food, but I never cook. I don't like to!

2 **Read the text in Activity 1 again and underline the verbs in the Simple Present.**

3 **Based on the text in Activity 1, write about Lalo. Remember to change subject pronouns, possessive adjectives, and verb forms.**

Lalo lives in Bogota ____________________

____

4 **Rewrite the sentences below according to the text. Change the adverbs of frequency.**

1. Lalo never paints on the weekend.
   ____
2. Lalo and his friends rarely play in concerts.
   ____
3. Lalo often cooks.
   ____

5 **Complete the sentences about yourself with the adverbs from the box.**

always never often rarely sometimes usually

1. I ________________ paint on the weekends.
2. I ________________ visit art galleries.
3. I ________________ go to concerts.
4. I ________________ cook.

Writing

1 **Read Lalo's e-mail. What is it about?**

____

CANCEL SEND

Hi, ____________________

How are you? My name is Lalo, I'm from Venezuela, but I live in Bogotá, and I'm here to invite you to join my community project. Do you know the Sustainable Development Goals (SDGs) by the United Nations? The objective of the program is to call people to action to end poverty, protect the planet, and guarantee peace and prosperity by 2030. My community program this year is to address SDG#6: "Ensure availability and sustainable management of water and sanitation for all." Did you know that billions of people around the world don't have access to safe drinking water and sanitation? For that reason, my group and I have the mission to help people from my neighborhood use water wisely. That's why I need your help. How often do you think about the sustainable use of water? What do you do to use water wisely at home and at school? What don't you do? What about people in your family and your classmates? Write to me!

Bye!

Lalo

Prepare to Write

2 **You are going to answer Lalo's e-mail. Complete the mind map with your ideas.**

Sustainable use of water

Write

3 **Write an answer to Lalo's e-mail. Use the information in Activity 2 and the text in Activity 1 as a model.**

Check and Change

4 **Read your e-mail and make sure you included:**

- ☐ a greeting and personal information.
- ☐ things you do / don't do to use water sustainably at home and at school.
- ☐ verbs in the Simple Present.
- ☐ adverbs of frequency.

5 **Edit your message. Make sure all the elements in Activity 4 are included.**

Publish

6 **Write a clean version of your e-mail.**

Vocabulary

1 **Create an icon for each free-time activity below. Then add two other activities and their corresponding icons.**

use social media	take a walk	go swimming
play video games		

Grammar

2 **Check (✓) the correct sentences. Rewrite the incorrect ones.**

1. ☐ Brian and Alan go shopping.

____

2. ☐ Does they watch movies on the weekends?

____

3. ☐ Frida do community service.

____

4. ☐ My grandpa loves to be outdoors.

____

5. ☐ Lalo doesn't like cooking.

____

6. ☐ He live in Bogota.

____

Reading

3 **Read the social media profile. What does Annie do on the weekends? Write complete sentences.**

Annie Milan

Basic Info
I live in London. I go to school in Muswell Hill. I have two sisters.

Interests
I like sports. I always play football on Saturdays. On Sundays, I relax, listen to music, or watch movies with my friends.

____

____

____

____

Listening

4 **Listen to Awlad talking about himself and complete the sentences.** 06

1. Awlad has _______________.
2. He really _______________ music.
3. He _______________ after school.
4. He usually _______________ with his friends.
5. _______________ he does community service.

Writing

5 **Write a profile for yourself. Use the text in Activity 3 as a model.**

Speaking

6 **Record yourself. Talk about your favorite free-time activities, where you do them, who you do them with, and how often you do them.**

Vocabulary

Food Items and Food Adjectives

1 **Read the e-mail from Ayari to her friend Jorge. Why is she e-mailing him? Check (✓) the correct option.**

CANCEL SEND

TO Jorge

FROM Ayari

SUBJECT recipe

Hey, Jorge!

How are you? I have a new recipe for you. It's an orange and chocolate cake! It's a perfect mix of sweet and bitter.

Here is the link to the recipe: www.sweettoothrecipes.com. I often add an extra egg and more chocolate – it's perfect!

Let me know what you think 🙂

Ayari

xoxo

1. ☐ To ask for healthy food recipes.
2. ☐ To meet him for dinner.
3. ☐ To give him the link to a new recipe.

2 **Label the pictures.**

1.

____

2.

____

3.

____

4.

____

3 **Use the words from the box to complete the chart. Then add a new word to each category.**

beets bread cake carrots
coffee fries jam juice meat
milk soda tea water

Foods	Drinks

4 **Match the adjectives to the food and drink items.**

1. bitter
2. sweet
3. savory

☐ sugar, apple pie
☐ cheese pie, fries
☐ coffee, green tea

Reading

1 **Listen to Robin talking about the local market in his neighborhood. What does he buy there?** 07

____

2 **What other kinds of food can you buy at local markets? Make a list.**

____

____

____

3 **MAKING PREDICTIONS. Which markets are these? Label the pictures.**

Floating market in Jahlokathi, Bangladesh
Street market in Mexico City, Mexico
Borough Market in London, U.K.

1.

____

____

2.

____

____

3.

____

____

4 **Now read Kay's blog posts about this week's top 3 markets and check your predictions in Activity 3.**

The Adventurer Blog

This week's top 3 markets:

Jahlokathi is a floating market in Bangladesh. Local people go there to buy fruit, vegetables, and coconuts from the boats on the river. It's a fascinating experience!

There are street markets everywhere in Mexico. My favorite one is in Mixcoac because it's full of colorful kinds of fruit, vegetables, and chili peppers. It's a delicious experience!

Borough Market in London is a great market. They sell the usual kinds of fruit, vegetables, and meat. They also have lots of snacks like cakes, savory pies, and amazing kinds of cheese. It is a good place to meet friends!

5 **SCANNING. Read the text again and answer the questions.**

1. What foods do they sell at the market in Jahlokathi?

   ____

2. What kind of market is the one in Jahlokathi?

   ____

3. Why is the street market in Mixcoac Kay's favorite?

   ____

4. Which foods do they sell at Borough Market, in London?

   ____

6 **Research the top markets in your city or neighborhood. Then write a small post about one of them.**

7 **Record your post in Activity 6 in a voice message and send it to a classmate.**

Grammar

Countable and Uncountable Nouns
Definite and Indefinite Articles

1 **Listen to Diego and Lily's conversation. What are they talking about? Underline the correct alternative.** 08

1. Their favorite food.
2. Their dinner.
3. A good recipe.

2 **Look at the picture of Lily and Diego's refrigerator and label the food items.**

3 **Complete the table with some food and drink items from the refrigerator in Activity 2. Then add two new words to each column.**

bananas carrots cheese juice
peppers tomatoes water yogurt

Uncountable	Countable

4 **Complete the sentences with definite or indefinite articles.**

1. Is there ______ apple in Lily's refrigerator?
2. We need to follow ______ recipe to make that delicious chocolate cake.
3. There's ______ jar full of olives in Lily's refrigerator.
4. ______ tomatoes on the top shelf are fresh.

5 **Look inside your refrigerator and make a list of the foods and drinks you can see. For each item write U (Uncountable) or C (Contable).**

____

____

____

____

____

6 **Use your answers in Activity 5 to write a paragraph about what you can find in your refrigerator. Use countable and uncountable nouns, and definite and indefinite articles correctly.**

____

____

____

____

7 **Read the paragraph in Activity 6 and record yourself.**

Use of English

1 **Read Pete's recipe. What does he want to make? Check (✓) the correct picture.**

Ingredients
2 eggs
100ml cream
150g ham
200g pasta
1 onion
1 clove of garlic

Directions
Cook some pasta for 10 minutes.
Fry a clove of garlic and an **onion** in a pan. Add the pasta, **ham**, and cream. Add the **eggs** and cook until soft. Mix it all together and add **salt** and pepper.

1.

2.

3.

2 **What do you think about Pete's recipe? Underline the statement you agree with.**

1. It's delicious!
2. It isn't healthy.
3. It seems OK.
4. It's awful.

3 **Read the directions to the recipe in Activity 1, pay attention to the words in bold, and use them to complete the box below.**

1. countable nouns: ____________, ____________
2. uncountable nouns: ____________, ____________

4 **Write the list of ingredients to your favorite recipe. Record a voice message to a classmate explaining what he / she will need for the recipe. Remember to use definite and indefinite articles.**

To make this chocolate cake, you need...

Writing

1 **Read the e-mail from Perla and write a suitable subject line.**

CANCEL SEND

TO Mike

FROM Perla

Hi, Mike,

As you know, it's Amny's birthday on Thursday. I want to treat her with her favorite food. This is the menu:

Snack: salty onion sticks and cheese

Lunch: fresh, healthy salad with chicken

Dessert: bitter coffee cake

Drink: sweet apple juice

I think we need a vegetarian option. What do you think?

Perla

x

2 **Read the e-mail again and circle the adjectives that are used to describe foods or drinks.**

Prepare to Write

3 **You are going to write a menu for a friend's special breakfast. Make a list with your ideas.**

____

____

____

____

____

____

Write

4 **Write a menu for a friend's special breakfast. Use the information in Activity 3, the text in Activity 1, and the texts in your Student's Book as models.**

MY FRIEND'S SPECIAL BREAKFAST MENU

Meals

Desserts

Drinks

Check and Change

5 **Read your menu and make sure you included:**

- [ ] 2-3 different options for foods.
- [ ] adjectives to describe the foods.
- [ ] 1-2 different options for drinks.
- [ ] 1-2 healthy options.

6 **Edit your menu. Make sure all the elements in Activity 5 are included.**

Publish

7 **Write a clean version of your menu.**

Vocabulary

1 **Write five foods or drinks you can see in the shopping cart.**

____

____

____

____

____

Grammar

2 **Which food and drink items in the shopping cart in Activity 1 are countable? Which ones are uncountable?**

____

____

____

____

Reading

3 **Read Pedro's and Emel's messages and mark the sentences T (True) or F (False).**

1. ☐ Emel wants to have something sweet for dinner.
2. ☐ Pedro needs to buy peppers and potatoes.
3. ☐ The supermarket doesn't have any peppers today.
4. ☐ Pedro wants to buy some cheese.

Pedro: What do you want for dinner?

Emel: I want something healthy!

Pedro: OK.... How about pasta and vegetables?

Emel: Yes, that sounds good. We need to buy peppers and tomatoes, too.

Pedro: I am at the supermarket. They don't have any peppers today.

Emel: Oh, no! What about onions?

Pedro: Yes, I can buy onions, tomatoes, and maybe some ham?

Emel: Yum! Yes 🙂

Pedro: OK... See you at home.

Listening

4 **Listen to Emel's voice message to Pedro and answer the questions.** 09

1. Who wants to have dinner with Emel and Pedro?

   ____

2. Why doesn't she eat meat?

   ____

3. What does Emel ask Pedro to buy to go with the pasta and vegetables?

   ____

4. When does Emel want to eat eggs?

   ____

Writing

5 **Look at the shopping cart in Activity 1 again. What meal can you cook with those ingredients? Write today's menu.**

Speaking

6 **Record yourself. Talk about your favorite healthy meal.**

Vocabulary

Jobs
Prepositions Related to Work
Teach and *Learn*

1 Read the text. What is Mel's job? Check (✓) the correct picture.

NEW TAB

worklifeinfo.com

Work life

Today we're interviewing Mel, from Birmingham, U.K.

Mel, tell us about your job

I work at a hospital and also at a school. I start working at school at 2 p.m. It's my daughter's school so I sometimes see her in the hallways. At 7 p.m. I go to the hospital and work the night shift. I come home at 5 a.m.

What are the best and the worst parts of your job?

I don't like the uniform or the long hours I need to work, but I love my coworkers. They always make me smile.

1.

2.

3.

2 Unscramble the letters to write jobs.

1. olpit ____________
2. eheactr ____________
3. cauminis ____________
4. ndsetti ____________
5. eubrpml ____________
6. ubs riedvr ____________
7. tcsitesni ____________
8. ealrwy ____________
9. cyetsarer ____________
10. nerclea ____________

3 Complete the sentences with *as*, *at*, *in*, or *for*. Use each preposition only once.

1. They work _____ education. They're school principals.
2. Larry works _____ the Riksbank, Sweden's central bank.
3. I'm a nurse, but I'm currently working _____ a secretary _____ a private hospital.

4 Answer the questions using the verbs *teach* and *learn*.

1. What's an important lesson you can teach your friends?

____

____

2. What are you learning at school now?

____

Reading

1 Label the pictures with the jobs from the box.

designer pilot plumber scientist

1. 

____

2. 

____

3. 

____

4. 

____

2 **Listen to David's voice message to his friend and underline the correct statement about it.** 10

1. David has a new job as a plumber at a school.
2. David has a new job as a scientist at a laboratory.
3. David has a new job as a designer at an office.

3 **USING PRIOR KNOWLEDGE. Write two sentences about what designers and scientists do.**

____

____

____

____

____

____

4 Read the text and check your answers to Activity 3.

Work life

Today we're interviewing David from Guadalajara, Mexico and Vanessa from Buenos Aires, Argentina.

David, tell us about your job.

I work in an office. My job is stressful because the clients are demanding. I design ads, and the clients change their minds very often. I have a lot of meetings every day!

What are the best and worst parts of your job?

I use a lot of creativity, and I like designing and making beautiful things. The worst thing is the number of meetings.

Vanessa, tell us about your job.

I go to the laboratory every day. I work on experiments most of the time. I work alone for long hours, and I have to be good at math to do my job. I love it!

What are the best and worst parts of your job?

The best part? Well, I love my job because it is important! Now I am developing new medicines to help people. One thing I don't like very much is that I am the only woman at the laboratory. My colleagues are men, and sometimes I feel isolated.

5 **MONITORING COMPREHENSION. Read the text again and answer the questions.**

1. Why is David's job stressful?

____

2. What does he like about his job?

____

3. What is Vanessa developing at work now?

____

4. How does she feel at work sometimes?

____

6 **Which job do you prefer: Mel's, David's, or Vanessa's? Why?**

I prefer Vanessa's job because I like to work alone.

____

____

Grammar

Present Continuous Simple Present and Present Continuous Prepositions with Time Expressions

1 **Match the pictures to the descriptions. Then underline the ongoing actions in the sentences.**

- ☐ She's cleaning the floor.
- ☐ She's having a meeting.
- ☐ He's doing an experiment.
- ☐ He's helping the patient.

1. 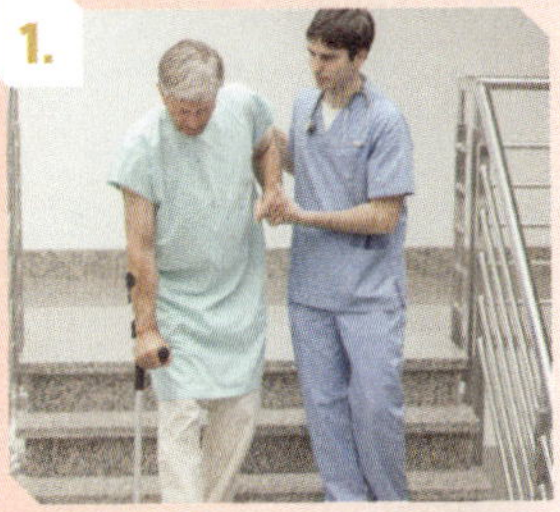

2. 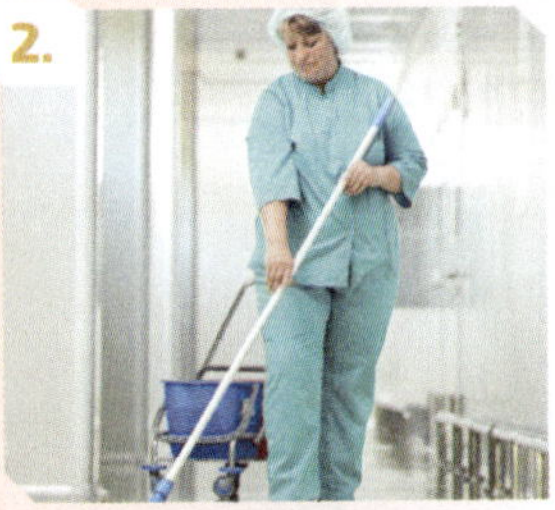

3. 

4. 

2 **Listen to Hans talk with his friend Mel about his day. What is his job? Check (✓) the correct answer.** 11

1. ☐ doctor 2. ☐ nurse 3. ☐ scientist

3 **Listen again and answer the questions. Use the Present Continuous.** 12

1. What is Hans doing now?
____
2. What is Mel doing now?
____
3. Why does Hans finish the call?
____

4 **Use the verbs in parentheses in the Simple Present or the Present Continuous to complete the sentences.**

1. My friend Leila ______________ (swim) three times a week.
2. ________ your dad ________ (cook) lunch for the whole family on Sundays?
3. The students ______________ (have fun) in the school yard now.
4. Carl ______________ (not study) in his room right now, he ______________ (watch) TV.
5. Our classes ______________ (start) at 7:30 on Mondays and Fridays.

5 **Complete the questions using the prepositions from the box.**

at	in	on

1. What do you always do ______ Saturdays?
2. Where do you and your family prefer to be ______ Thanksgiving?
3. Which classes do you have ______ the afternoon?
4. Why are you leaving the classroom now? Doesn't your class finish ______ 3 p.m.?

6 **Answer the questions in Activity 5. Use the Present Continuous or the Simple Present and the correct prepositions.**

1. ______________________________
2. ______________________________
3. ______________________________
4. ______________________________

Use of English

1 Look at the text. Is it an e-mail or a discussion on an online forum?

____

NEW TAB

layla2005: I'm looking for a summer job. Do you have any ideas?

FreddaFrog: @layla2005 I work at a café on the weekends. They're looking for a server there. Let me know if you are interested 🙂

pingpongwhat: They're advertising a job at the bakery!

letsdance: They're looking for a new Queen of the World.

layla2005: LOL! @letsdance @fredafrog and @pingpongwhat text the information, please! Thanks guys... 🙂

2 Read the text is Activity 1 and answer the questions.

1. What is Layla looking for? ______________________
2. Where do her friends suggest she looks? ______________________

3 Read the text is Activity 1 again and find two examples of the Present Continuous and two examples of the Simple Present. Write them in the table below.

Simple Present	Present Continuous

4 Complete the paragraph with the correct prepositions.

Layla is working at the bakery now. She works there [1] ______ Saturdays and Sundays. She starts [2] ______ 7 a.m. and finishes [3] ______ 4 p.m. [4] ______ lunchtime, she eats with her friends. She plans to go back to college [5] ______ September 5th. But we are still [6] ______ August, and she has a lot of work to do!

Writing

1 Look at the picture. Then read the picture caption for an online post on a social media campaign and write what you think the campaign is about.

I teach preschoolers. Men and women can teach all levels!

2 Read the picture caption again and write two other ideas of captions to use.

Prepare to Write

3 You are going to choose a picture and write a caption to post on a social media campaign to address the issue of gender equality at work. Make a list with your ideas.

Write

4 Search for a picture and write a caption for a post on a social media campaign for gender equality at work. Use the information in the previous activities and the texts in your Student's Book as models.

maryellen
posted 3 hours ago

#genderequailtyatwork

Check and Change

5 Read your caption and make sure you included:

- [ ] an appealing picture.
- [ ] a welcoming message.
- [ ] a verb in the Simple Present or in the Present Continuous.

6 Edit your caption. Make sure all the elements in Activity 5 are included.

Publish

7 Write a clean version of your caption.

#CHALLENGE

UNIT THREE

Vocabulary

1 **Find and circle 11 jobs in the wordsearch below.**

A	U	U	T	H	D	T	D	N	S	R	K	H	F	R
S	U	B	N	R	O	E	I	V	O	E	R	E	I	Z
D	Y	Q	I	T	M	S	T	I	E	N	A	V	L	E
P	D	V	R	E	N	A	E	L	C	G	P	Y	T	X
U	E	A	D	S	R	P	M	I	E	I	L	R	A	A
R	F	E	D	E	D	A	I	P	T	S	U	A	O	D
V	R	F	Y	H	T	B	L	L	A	E	M	T	G	Q
N	Z	W	A	C	A	P	L	F	O	D	B	E	C	W
T	A	M	U	S	I	C	I	A	N	T	E	R	B	W
L	S	T	S	I	T	N	E	I	C	S	R	C	O	T
S	T	I	E	E	T	C	A	R	B	I	E	E	Z	R
F	E	R	T	T	E	A	C	H	E	R	S	S	F	A
P	I	K	E	N	K	B	M	M	G	B	A	G	J	I
U	B	I	D	Q	E	G	T	M	G	X	V	Y	I	N
P	B	M	R	B	N	D	Q	U	K	M	P	W	A	F

Grammar

2 **Check (✓) the correct sentences. Rewrite the incorrect sentences.**

1. ☐ She's working as a nurse at a hospital now.
____
____
2. ☐ They don't work at Mondays and Wednesdays.
____
____
3. ☐ I often work on the weekends.
____
____
4. ☐ I am starting working at 9 a.m.
____
____
5. ☐ **A:** What is he doing?
B: He's a musician.
____
____

Reading

3 **Read the e-mail and mark the sentences T (True) or F (False).**

TO

Hi, Rosa!

Hope you are well.

I'm writing to update you! I'm working in an office now. I have a job as a secretary at a design company. It's really cool. The people are very friendly, and the job is not stressful. Sometimes I work late, which is annoying. But in general, I'm very happy! 🙂

What are you doing these days? Are you still working at school?

Hope to hear from you soon.

Love,

Ben.

1. ☐ Ben is a designer.
2. ☐ He likes the people at work.
3. ☐ His new job is stressful.
4. ☐ Ben sometimes has to work late.
5. ☐ He likes his new job.

Listening

4 **Listen to Sandy talk about her job and complete the table.** 13

Job	
Advantages	
Disadvantages	

Speaking

5 **Talk to a family member about his / her job. Then record yourself talking about the person's job. Mention the advantages and disadvantages of the job.**

Vocabulary

Adjectives of Appearance and Personality

1 Read the description of Joanne and her friends. Label the picture with their names.

I have two best friends. We are very close. Liam is medium-height and very funny. He has dark hair and wears glasses. Liam loves dancing and electronic music. My other best friend is Dan. He is tall and he has straight, blond hair. He is hard-working. He likes basketball and pop music. I'm short. I have long brown hair. I think I'm kind and friendly. I like playing soccer and the guitar.

2 Go back to the text in Activity 1 and identify 12 adjectives. Write them below.

1. ____________
2. ____________
3. ____________
4. ____________
5. ____________
6. ____________
7. ____________
8. ____________
9. ____________
10. ____________
11. ____________
12. ____________

3 Complete the table with the adjectives from the box. Use a dictionary if, necessary.

beautiful blond boring friendly funny hard-working interesting kind lazy overweight serious short smart tall ugly unfriendly

Appearance	Personality

4 Add two more adjectives to each column of the table in Activity 3.

5 Think about your best friend. Write sentences describing him / her. Use at least four adjectives. Use the text in Activity 1 as reference.

____

____

____

#DISCOVER

UNIT FOUR

Reading

1 **Listen to the radio announcement. What is happening on Saturday? Check (✓) the correct option.** 14

1. ☐ There is an athletics competition.
2. ☐ There is a fundraising event.
3. ☐ There is a shopping event.

2 **MAKING PREDICTIONS. Look at the picture and read the heading of the blog post. Then circle the words you think you are going to find in the text.**

1. boring	**3.** competition	**5.** skating
2. celebrate	**4.** sad	**6.** wheelchair

NEW TAB

www.site.com

Gold For Mateo!

Mateo is a talented and hard-working para athlete. He uses a wheelchair, but that doesn't stop him from winning gold medals. During his excellent performance on Monday in the para athletics competition, he won six gold medals. He says he likes to celebrate every gold medal with his friends, playing basketball or eating pizza.

3 **CONFIRMING PREDICTIONS. Read the text in Activity 2 and check your predictions.**

4 **SCANNING. Read the text again and mark the sentences T (True) or F (False).**

1. ☐ Mateo is unfriendly and serious.
2. ☐ He wins a lot of gold medals.
3. ☐ He likes to celebrate with his family.
4. ☐ Mateo is an athlete.

5 **Research into para athletes. Write the names of three sports people and events they participate in. Use adjectives in your description.**

Stephen Miller is British. He competes in the fields of Paralympic club and discus throwing. He is tall and has red hair.

6 **Read your sentences from Activity 5 and record yourself.**

#CLARIFY

UNIT FOUR

Grammar

Comparatives and Superlatives

1 **Read the feedback survey from the school fundraising event. Check (✓) the correct statement about how the students feel.**

1. ☐ The students like the event.
2. ☐ The students don't like the event.

Thank you for coming to our fundraising event. Please complete the feedback survey.

Name: Gemma **Age:** 13

Mark 1, 2, or 3 for each sentence.

1 = Disagree 2 = Somewhat disagree 3 = Agree

The fundraising event was good.	2
The games were fun.	2
The food was delicious.	3

What games do you want to see in the next event? Underline your preference.

soccer volleyball basketball

Thank you for coming to our fundraising event. Please complete the feedback survey.

Name: Sam **Age:** 14

Mark 1, 2, or 3 to each sentence.

1 = Disagree 2 = Somewhat disagree 3 = Agree

The fundraising event was good.	3
The games were fun.	3
The food was delicious.	2

What games do you want to see in the next event? Underline your preference.

soccer volleyball basketball

2 **Read the feedback surveys again and complete the sentences with comparatives. Use the adjectives in parentheses.**

1. Sam is ________ (happy) Gemma with the event.
2. Gemma thinks the food was ________ ________ (delicious) Sam does.
3. Sam thinks volleyball is ________ ________ (interesting) soccer.

3 **Read the table with the 100m race times from the fundraising event. Then answer the questions.**

Gemma	38 seconds
Sam	45 seconds
Claude	35 seconds
Naomi	34 seconds
Fatima	42 seconds

1. Who is the fastest? ________.
2. Who is the slowest? ________.
3. Who is faster than Gemma? ________.

4 **Check (✓) the correct sentences and rewrite the incorrect ones.**

1. ☐ Gemma is the fastest than Sam.
____
2. ☐ Fatima is slower than Claude.
____
3. ☐ Naomi is the faster.
____
4. ☐ Sam is the slow.
____

#UNDERSTAND

UNIT FOUR

Use of English

1 Write a sentence with each adjective comparing two people in parentheses.

1. Hard-working (two friends)
   Lisa is **more hard-working than** Laura.
2. Friendly (two classmates)
   ____
3. Serious (two celebrities you like)
   ____
4. Happy (two teachers)
   ____
5. Young (two aunts)
   ____
6. Tall (you and your best friend)
   ____

2 Think of your best friends. Give each person a gold medal for his / her personality. Write complete sentences using the superlative form.

1. For being funny.
   Hugo is **the funniest** *friend I have.*
2. For being kind.
   ____
3. For being happy.
   ____
4. For being smart.
   ____
5. For being friendly.
   ____

3 Read your sentences in Activities 1 and 2. Did you use comparatives and superlatives correctly? Read, compare, and check (✓).

1. Comparatives in Activity 1:
   a. ☐ I used *than* after the adjective.
   b. ☐ I used *-er* for short adjectives.
   c. ☐ I used *-ier* for adjectives ending in *y*.
   d. ☐ I used *more* before long adjectives.
2. Superlatives in Activity 2:
   a. ☐ I used *the* before the superlative.
   b. ☐ I used *-est* for short adjectives.
   c. ☐ I used *-iest* for adjectives ending in *y*.
   d. ☐ I used *most* before long adjectives.

Writing

1 **Read the post on the fundraising blog *Showusthelovelove*. Why does Kaleb need money?**

____

NEW TAB +

www.site.com

#Showusthelovelove

Player number 5 is Kaleb. He is 14 years old, and he is the best soccer player we know! He is hard-working and very serious about playing soccer. He is trying to raise $500 to go to a soccer training camp this summer. Help Kaleb train to be faster and better than before so his dream can come true!

Please help. Donate now.

DONATE NOW

Prepare to Write

2 **You are going to write a blog post about a friend. The post is for the fundraising blog *Showusthelovelove*. Make notes.**

1. Your friend's personal information:

____

2. Adjectives to describe your friend:

____

3. Reason why you are fundraising for this person:

____

4. How much your friend needs:

____

Write

3 **Write the post. Use the post in Activity 1 and your notes in Activity 2 as models.**

NEW TAB +

www.site.com

____

____

____

____

____

____

____

____

____

____

____

____

Check and Change

4 **Read your post and make sure you included:**

- [ ] your friend's personal information.
- [ ] adjectives to describe your friend.
- [ ] the reason for the fundraising.
- [ ] the amount of money your friend needs.

5 **Edit your post. Make sure all the elements in Activity 4 are included.**

Publish

6 **Write a clean version of your post.**

Vocabulary

1 Solve the cryptogram to find adjectives of appearance and personality.

A	B	C	D	E	F	G	H	I	J	K	L	M
25		13			7		3				5	

N	O	P	Q	R	S	T	U	V	W	X	Y	Z
9					23	14			11			

H	A	___	___	–	W	___	___	___	___	N	___
3	25	6	20		11	26	6	16	24	9	21

S	H	___	___	T
23	3	26	6	14

S	___	___	___	___	___	S
23	17	6	24	26	22	23

___	L	___
26	5	20

F	___	___	___	N	___	L	___
7	6	24	17	9	20	5	15

___	___	A	___	T	___	F	___	L
8	17	25	22	14	24	7	22	5

L	A	___	___
5	25	4	15

___	___	N	___
16	24	9	20

T	A	L	L
14	25	5	5

Grammar

2 Complete the paragraph using comparatives or superlatives. Use the adjective in parentheses.

Lily is [1] ________________ (good) me at math, but Dani is [2] ________________ (bad) me. Luca is [3] ________________ (good) in the class. In science class I feel [4] ________________ (happy) in math class, but I'm [5] ________________ (happy) student at school doing P.E. I'm [6] ________________ (fast) the other students. Maybe I'm [7] ________________ (fast) in the class. I think P.E. is [8] ________________ (interesting) history and other subjects. [9] ________________ (interesting) thing about P.E. is learning about the body.

Reading

3 Read the e-mail from Kaleb and mark the sentences T (True) or F (False).

Hi Mom,

How are you?

I'm really happy at the training camp. It is the best experience! The other players are really friendly. I'm worried that they are better than me. There is one kid called Walid. He is the fastest player. He is faster than me!

I have a new friend – Mattia. He is not so fast, but he is more confident than me. He is very good!

I miss you!

Lots of love,

Kaleb xx

1. ☐ Kaleb loves the soccer camp.
2. ☐ The other players aren't friendly.
3. ☐ Kaleb thinks the other players are worse than him.
4. ☐ Walid is the fastest player.
5. ☐ Mattia is more confident than Kaleb.

Listening

4 Listen to the voice message from Kaleb's mom and write complete answers to the questions. 15

1. How does Kaleb's sister feel without him?

____

2. How does his mom describe Kaleb?

____

3. What does his mom tell him about working on a team?

____

Writing

5 Choose three celebrities. Write a short description about each one, comparing them. Use adjectives of appearance and personality.

Speaking

6 Read your sentences from Activity 5 to a classmate.

Vocabulary

Types of Schools

1 Listen to Maria's message to her friend Adam and answer the question. 16

What language does Maria have to speak in her new school? ____________________

2 Listen again and complete the sentences. 17

1. Maria goes to an ____________________ school.
2. In Maria's school, there are students from ____________________ and Cameroon.
3. Some facilities Maria mentions about her school are a ______________ room with computers and tablets and a ______________ ______________ with lots of books.

3 Complete the sentences below with the words from the box.

fail	pass	take

1. In my school, students can't ______________ more than two exams.
2. I am very nervous because I need to ______________ two tests today.
3. My parents told me that if I don't ______________ my next math exam, they're going to get me a private teacher.

4 Complete the puzzle with different types of schools.

Down

1. The school that teaches an international program.

Across

2. When learning happens at home.
3. The school that you need to pay for.
4. The school where you study and sleep.
5. The school that is paid by the government.

5 Talk about the kind of school you go to. Audio record your message.

I go to a public school. We have our classes in English and in Spanish.

#CLARIFY

UNIT FIVE

Reading

1 ESTABLISHING A PURPOSE FOR READING. Read the posters below. What are they about?

___

Greenwood School

New Admissions Open!

Students in our modern facilities

Why our school?

- We accept students from all over the world.
- We have excellent facilities such as our new media center.
- We have experienced and talented teachers.
- We have the best technology program in the region.
- Alternative methods – no testing!

For more information contact us at greennwoodsschool@admissions.com

FOREST HILL SCHOOL

Welcome to Forest Hill School!

- The most comfortable dormitories to sleep in.
- Our excellent teachers can support your child.
- We are famous for our excellent sports program.
- A new and modern sports center for our student athletes.
- Vegetable gardens for students to grow fruits and vegetables.
- Our Arts Program is famous for the excellent Drama course.

Our happy students

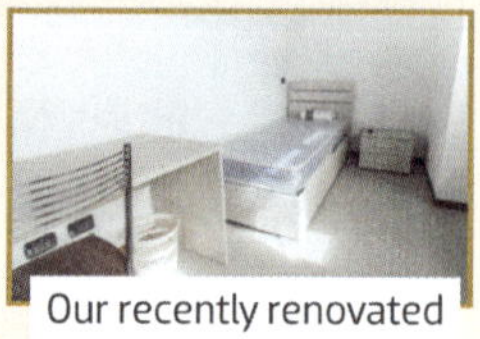

Our recently renovated dormitories

Contact us now at foresthillsschools@admissions.com

2 SCANNING. Read the information from the posters in Activity 1 and complete the table below.

	Greenwood School	Forest Hill School
Type of school		
Teachers		
Facilities		

3 Read the text again and answer the questions with the name of the best school.

Which school should you go to...

1. if you don't want to take tests?
2. if you like arts and gardens?
3. if you want to get better at playing a sport?
4. if you love computers?

4 Read the text in Activity 1 again. Which school is similar to and which one is different from your school? Why? Justify your answer using parts of the text.

5 Which school would you like to go to: Greenwood or Forest Hill? Write down your answers. Then record a voice message with your answer.

I would like to go to Forest Hill School because it has a vegetable garden and an Arts program.

Grammar

Must / Mustn't
Should / Shouldn't
Making Requests with *Can and Could* Have to / Don't Have to

1 **Read the chat. What does Emma want? Check (✓) the correct option.**

1. ☐ She wants information about a language club.
2. ☐ She wants information about joining a sports team.

Emma: Hey! How are you? I want to try the soccer team at school. Can you tell me more about it?
Matt: Hey, that's great news. What do you want to know?
Emma: I have a lot of questions! How do I join?
Matt: You should ask Mr. Jennings. He's the coach.
Emma: OK! And do you have games on weekends?
Matt: Sometimes. We play once a month. You must go to all the games, or you are out!
Emma: Oh, I know...
Matt: You should join. It's so much fun!
Emma: Cool! Could you help me talk to Mr. Jennings tomorrow?
Matt: Sure, no problem.

2 **Read the conversation again and find the requested information.**

1. A sentence that indicates an obligation:
____
2. A sentence that indicates a suggestion, a piece of advice:
____
3. A sentence that indicates a request:
____

3 **Complete the rules for the soccer team. Use *must* and the verbs from the box.**

be	bring	have	play	wear

1. You _______________ on Saturday.
2. You _______________ on time.
3. You _______________ soccer cleats.
4. You _______________ the team uniform.
5. You _______________ a team spirit.

4 **Look at the Class Rules poster. Then write two new class rules using *must and mustn't*, two pieces of advice using *should* and *shouldn't*, one necessity using *have to*, and one non-requirement using *don't have to.***

CLASS RULES

- Listen when someone else is speaking
- Work quietly at your desk
- Raise your hand when you need help
- Treat others with respect
- Play safely – make good choices
- Respect the personal property of others

1. _______________
2. _______________
3. _______________
4. _______________
5. _______________
6. _______________

Use of English

1 **Read Leo's e-mail to Julia. What type of school does Leo go to?**

____

CANCEL SEND

TO Julia (Julia.spektorr@uhu.com)

FROM Leo (leojoness@the-mail.com)

Hi, Julia!

How are you?

I am very happy in my new school. It's cool, and our teachers are great. We have in the morning and in the afternoon. I'm learning a lot. I also have lots of friends; they are from different parts of the world. The only problem is that we have to take exams every week and I don't like that very much, haha. I hope I don't fail my exams! I am studying a lot, so I think I will pass them. Come and visit me sometime.

We should meet up soon.

Love,

Leo

2 **Read the statements and mark the sentences T (True) or F (False).**

1. ☐ Leo and Julia go to the same school.
2. ☐ Leo likes his teachers.
3. ☐ Leo thinks he will pass his exams.
4. ☐ He has to take exams every day.
5. ☐ Leo's friends come from different countries.

3 **Listen to Leo talk to his friend Nicole about his language club at school. What does Nicole want? Check (✓) the correct option.** 18

1. ☐ She wants to improve her French.
2. ☐ She wants to learn more English.
3. ☐ She wants to make a YouTube© video.

4 **Listen again and complete the sentences according to what you hear.** 19

1. ______________ me some advice?
2. ______________ the language club.
3. ______________ also ______________ out our channel.
4. ______________ every day!

5 **Order the words to make correct sentences.**

1. the / language / Could / tell me about / you / club / ?
____
2. shouldn't / You / making / worry about / mistakes / .
____
3. You / must / in / participate / class / .
____
4. laugh / You / students / shouldn't / at other / .
____
5. every / don't / You / week / have to / come / .
____
6. a notebook / You / bring / have to / .
____

6 **Write Nicole three new pieces of advice about learning a language.**

You should use language apps to practice.

1. ______________________________
2. ______________________________
3. ______________________________

Writing

1 **Read the sentences and check (✓) the ones that are correct about e-mails to request information.**

1. ☐ They are concise.
2. ☐ They must have pictures.
3. ☐ They are logically organized.
4. ☐ They don't require an action by the reader.
5. ☐ They are clear.

Prepare to Write

2 **You are going to write Leo an e-mail to request information about the language club. Think about what you would like to ask him and make notes.**

Write

3 **Write your e-mail to Leo. Use the information in Activity 2 and cover the items below.**

1. Explain why you are writing.
2. Request information.
3. Ask about where the meetings happen.
4. Ask about the days and times.
5. Ask for advice on how to do well in the club.

CANCEL SEND

FROM Leo

SUBJECT Info about the language club

Check and Change

4 **Read your e-mail and make sure you included:**

- ☐ a greeting.
- ☐ the reason why you are writing.
- ☐ *can / could* for requests.
- ☐ *should / shouldn't* for advice.
- ☐ a sign off.

5 **Edit your e-mail. Make sure all the elements in Activity 4 are included.**

Publish

6 **Write a clean version of your e-mail.**

Vocabulary

1 Complete the sentences with the different types of school.

1. I am 17 years old. This year I'm finishing ____________________ and going to university.
2. It is the first year my sister goes to school. She is only three years old, and she is in ____________________ now.
3. My cousin is 12 years old, and she is in her last year of ____________________ school.
4. Leo finished elementary school and now he is ready to start ________________________.

Grammar

2 Look at the pictures and complete the sentences with *must*, *mustn't*, *have to*, *don't have to*, *should*, or *shouldn't*. Sometimes more than one answer is correct.

1. You ____________________ turn off your phone in class.

2. You ____________________ wear a uniform.

3. You ________________ talk to your friends in the library.

4. You ____________________ be careful on the stairs.

5. You ____________________ wait in line in the cafeteria.

Reading

3 Read the e-mail and underline the correct statements about it.

CANCEL SEND

Hello, Tam!
How are you?
Here is the information about our Spanish Club.
We meet every Wednesday evening, from 7:00 to 8:30 p.m. You must e-mail me and confirm your attendance by Tuesday. You don't have to pay, but we accept donations.
You should look at our website www.hiltonhighspanishclub.org. There you can find ideas about how to practice and improve your Spanish.
I hope to see you there soon!
Best wishes,
Rob.

1. To be part of the club, Tam should be free every Wednesday evening.
2. The club is free.
3. Tam can make a donation to be part of the club.

Listening

4 Listen to the message Tam sent to her sister and write complete answers to the questions. Use your notebook. 20

1. What does Tam have to practice more?
2. What is Rob's advice to Tam?
3. Do they have to do homework?
4. What does Tam think about the homework?

Writing

5 Think of a club you want to start. Write the rules for your new club.

Speaking

6 Read the rules of your club and record yourself to send the audio to a friend. Ask your friend for advice on other rules you should add and request his / her help.

Vocabulary

Sports
Play a Sport vs. *Practice a Sport*

1 **Read the chat between Silvya and Camila. What are they planning to do on Sunday? Check (✓).**

Silvya

Today

Silvya: Hey! Do you want to play volleyball at the beach tomorrow?

Camila: Hi 🙂 I can't tomorrow. I have gym practice.

Silvya: Oh, yeah! I forgot... Your competition is coming up, right?

Camila: Yes. I'm so nervous!

Silvya: Don't be... you are the best 🙂

Camila: Aww thanks. I want to go swimming. Maybe we can go to the beach on Sunday.

Silvya: Sure, sounds good... we can go swimming and play volleyball afterwards.

Camila: I know there is a new basketball court near the beach, too.

Silvya: Cool! We can ask Andrea to come with us. She loves basketball!

Camila: Good idea. Speak later then!

Silvya: Can't wait!

1. ☐ They're planning to buy new sports clothes.
2. ☐ They're planning to play different sports at the beach.
3. ☐ They're planning to have a party on the beach.

2 **What sports do Silvya and Camila talk about? Write them down. Then circle them in the picture.**

____

3 **Now list five other sports you know.**

____

____

4 **Complete the sentences with the correct forms of the verbs *play* or *practice*.**

1. At the moment, my brother is ______________ for tomorrow's competition.
2. Why don't you ______________ volleyball at the beach with us on Sundays? It's good to exercise on the weekends, too.

5 **Which are your favorite and least favorite sports? Complete the sentences.**

1. I love **playing** ______________.
2. I sometimes like to **go** ______________.
3. I don't enjoy **doing** ______________.

#CLARIFY

UNIT SIX

Reading

1 **Listen to Martin. What sport does he do?** 21

____

2 **USING PRIOR KNOWLEDGE. What do you know about judo? Underline the sentences you think are true.**

1. Judo comes from Japan.
2. A black belt shows a person is skilled at judo.
3. A judo athlete can kick their opponent in a match.

3 **MAKING PREDICTIONS. Read the title of the text. What do you think it is about? Check (✓).**

1. ☐ A brief history of judo.
2. ☐ The benefits of judo.
3. ☐ Tips to improve your judo skills.

4 **CONFIRMING PREDICTIONS. Read the text and check your answers to Activities 2 and 3.**

What Can Judo Do For You?

Emily is 13 years old, and she has one year's experience doing judo. We interviewed her to find out more about the sport.

Interviewer: Why did you start doing judo?

Emily: My brother started classes, and then I decided to start, too. I've always liked the history of the sport. It is very old and comes from Japan. The sport is a mix of physical and mental strength and agility. It keeps my body and mind healthy.

One day I want to have a black belt. That's reaching the top! But now I just want to keep practicing and improving my skills.

Interviewer: What was your best judo experience?

Emily: It was my last competition. My opponent kicked me during the match and that is illegal, so I received the trophy! I really love my judo classes. They help me build more confidence. Everyone should do judo!

5 **SCANNING. Read the text again and mark the sentences T (True) or F (False).**

1. ☐ Emily says judo is only good for her physical health.
2. ☐ Emily and her brother do judo.
3. ☐ She wants to get a black belt.
4. ☐ Her opponent received a trophy in her last competition.

6 **Research into a sport you want to start and answer the questions below.**

1. How old is the sport?

____

2. Where does the sport come from?

____

3. Why does the sport look interesting to you?

____

____

7 **Record a voice message about the sport you researched into in Activity 6. Use your answers to the questions to help you.**

Judo is over two hundred years old. It comes from Japan. I think judo is interesting because it is a mix of physical and mental strength.

Grammar

Simple Past: *Was / Were*
Simple Past: Regular Verbs – Interrogative and Negative Forms

1 **Listen to Aaron talk about his weekend. Check (✓) the sports or activities he did.** 22

1.

2.

3.

2 **Listen again and complete the sentences about Aaron's weekend activities.** 23

On Saturday, Aaron [1] *visited his grandma*, [2] ________ about school, [3] ________ for lunch, and [4] ________ with his friends in the park.

On Sunday, Aaron [5] ________ home. He [6] ________ his homework, [7] ________, and [8] ________ a pizza with his dad.

3 **Complete the sentences about Aaron's weekend. Use *was, were, wasn't,* or *weren't.***

1. Aaron ________ with his grandma on Saturday.
2. He ________ with his dad on Saturday.
3. On Sunday, Aaron ________ tired.
4. Aaron's step-mom and sister ________ at home on Sunday.
5. It ________ a lovely weekend.

4 **What did you do last weekend? Complete the sentences. Use the Simple Past.**

1. On Saturday, I ____.
2. On Sunday, I ____.

5 **Talk about your weekend and audio record yourself. Listen and pay attention to what you said. Make sure you used the Simple Past correctly.**

#DEVELOP

UNIT SIX

Use of English

1 **Complete the questionnaire about yourself.**

1. Which sports do you enjoy? Check (✓) them.
   - [ ] swimming
   - [ ] basketball
   - [ ] gymnastics
   - [ ] volleyball
   - [ ] tennis
   - [ ] judo

2. Think about the last sport you played.
   a. Did you play with friends? Who did you play with?
   ____
   ____
   b. Where did you play?
   ____
   c. How long did you play?
   ____
   d. Were you tired after playing it?
   ____
   e. How often do you play this sport?
   ____

2 **Which questions in Activity 1 are in the Simple Past?**

____

3 **How do we make questions with regular verbs in the Simple Past? Write the parts from the box in the correct order.**

did	subject	verb (without -ed)

__________ + __________ + __________

4 **Rewrite the questions correcting them.**

1. Did you played football?
____
2. You arrived late?
____
3. Was you tired?
____
4. You were with friends?
____

5 **Make questions about last weekend activities to ask a friend or a family member.**

1. **A:** *Did you have fun last weekend?*
   B: ______________________________
   ____
2. **A:** __________ you go out?
   B: ______________________________
   ____
3. **A:** __________ you with friends or family?
   B: ______________________________
   ____
4. **A:** ______________________________
   B: ______________________________
   ____
5. **A:** ______________________________
   B: ______________________________
   ____

6 **Interview a friend or a family member. Complete the questionnaire in Activity 5 with their answers. You can ask the questions in your language but remember to write the answers in English!**

Writing

1 **Look at the picture and read the event description written by Will. What was the event? Check (✓). Then listen and read.** 24

1. ☐ A birthday party.
2. ☐ A music festival.
3. ☐ A wedding.

It was a marvelous day. My sister was in a white dress. Her husband was in a gray suit. The ceremony was at the local registry office. There were about ten family members and friends there. After the event, we all were ready to celebrate their love with a big party. We headed to a local restaurant and ordered lots of different dishes to share. We danced and shared our happiness with them. I was very happy for my sister!

Prepare to Write

2 **You are going to write a description of an event. Think about a wedding or a special party you attended recently and make notes. Answer the guiding questions below.**

1. What was the event?
2. When was it?
3. Where was it?
4. Who was there?
5. What was special about the event?

____

____

____

____

____

____

____

Write

3 **Write a description of an event. Use the text in Activity 1 and your notes in Activity 2 for help.**

____

____

____

____

____

____

____

Check and Change

4 **Read your text and make sure you included answers to the guiding questions in Activity 2 and verbs in the Simple Past.**

5 **Edit your text. Make sure all the elements in Activity 2 are included.**

Publish

6 **Write a clean version of your text.**

Vocabulary

1 Draw an icon for each sport.

cricket	gymnastics

volleyball	judo

Grammar

2 Order the words to make sentences in the Simple Past.

1. last weekend / practice / I didn't / gymnastics / .
2. golf / last week / I / played / .
3. Did / to football practice / you / go / ?
4. Helen / do / Did / yesterday / karate / ?

Reading

3 Read the social media post. What did Nusrat do last weekend?

nusrat

I was so proud last weekend! My best friends played so well in the volleyball competition at #GalesHighschool. I was sad I didn't play, but my ankle wasn't better. But happy to see my team win! We obviously celebrated the victory with ice cream and a movie marathon. Next game is in 2 weeks. I hope I can play then!!

5 comments

Listening

4 Listen to Graham talk about the volleyball competition and check (✓) the correct sentences. 25

1. ☐ Graham was surprised the team won.
2. ☐ He thinks they played well.
3. ☐ He noticed Nusrat wasn't there.

Writing

5 Write a social media post about an event last weekend. Use the text in Activity 3 as a model. If possible, add a picture to your post.

Speaking

6 Talk about your last birthday and audio record yourself.

1. What did you do?
2. Who was with you?
3. Where were you?
4. Did you receive any gifts?
5. What was the best part of the day?

Vocabulary

Vacation Activities

Types of Accommodations

1 **Listen and match the types of accommodations (1–6) to the pictures (a–f).** 26

1. ☐ youth hostel
2. ☐ hotel
3. ☐ tent
4. ☐ vacation rental
5. ☐ room
6. ☐ house

a.

b.

c.

d.

e.

f.

2 **Complete the sentences with *book*, *make*, or *visit* in the Simple Past tense.**

1. Leila ____________ the Great Wall of China last year.
2. Marco ____________ a comfortable rental near tourist places.
3. Lena ____________ a boat trip reservation.

3 **Write a description of each vacation activity below.**

1. go sightseeing: ____________
2. sunbathe: ____________
3. go hiking: ____________
4. check in: ____________

4 **Write sentences about your vacation activities with the verbs in Activity 3.**

1. ____________
2. ____________
3. ____________
4. ____________

Reading

1 Read Rafik's message. Check (✓) the picture that best shows his vacation accommodation.

Rafik

Hey Kara,

How are you? I'm enjoying my vacation in the Alps so much! It's very cold, but the mountains are amazing!

Yesterday we went to the Swiss National Park. We went hiking and saw the wild animals near us. It was really cool! I took a lot of pictures.

Today my mom wants to read a book and relax. I don't want to do that! We have a comfortable vacation rental near tourist places. I decided to visit a cool medieval town near here.

And Mom booked a boat trip for tomorrow... Anyway, enough about me.

Tell me about your trip to Egypt!

Talk to you soon,

Bye.

1.  ☐

2.  ☐

3.  ☐

2 SKIMMING. Read the text again and write *Rafik* or *Rafik's mom* to complete the sentences.

1. ____________ took lots of pictures.
2. ____________ wanted to read a book and relax.
3. ____________ decided to visit a medieval city.
5. ____________ booked a boat trip.

3 What do you think a staycation is? Underline the sentence you think is true.

1. It's when people stay in expensive hotels on vacation.
2. It's when people have a vacation at home.
3. It's when people stay on vacation for a long time.

4 Read about Steven's staycation. Check your predictions from Activity 3.

Hi, I'm Steven!

Last year, I participated in a school project about the damage that tourism causes to the environment. The carbon footprint of tourism is very high. Almost 8% of the world's carbon emissions come from travel abroad. For that reason, this year I decided to stay home.

On my staycation I discovered local areas without the expense and environmental damage of a trip abroad.

5 Read again and mark the sentences T (True) or F (False).

1. ☐ Steven is worried about the carbon footprint of tourism.
2. ☐ Vacations abroad are good for the environment.
3. ☐ 5% of the world's carbon emissions come from vacations to different countries.
4. ☐ Steven chose to spend his vacation at home.
5. ☐ Staycations are cheap and good for the environment.

6 Think about three ideas of activities for a staycation. Write them in your notebook.

Grammar

Simple Past: Irregular Verbs
Present Perfect for Personal Experiences

1 **Complete the dialogue with the verbs from the box in the Simple Past.**

do	eat	fly	go	see	spend	swim

Alex

Alex: I can't believe the summer vacations are over

Mina: I know... too fast. What [1] ________ you [2] ________ ?

Alex: I [3] ________ to the USA to visit my family.

Mina: [4] ________ you [5] ________ your cousins?

Alex: Yes, we [6] ________ two days at their house in Houston. Then we [7] ________ to Miami and stayed at my grandma's house for five days. We just [8] ________ in the pool and [9] ________ fast food, basically. Haha!

Mina: Sounds perfect

2 **Check (✓) the correct sentences about the text in Activity 1.**

1. ☐ Alex visited his family.
2. ☐ Alex went to three different places.
3. ☐ He spent seven days on vacation.
4. ☐ He didn't have time to see his cousins.

3 **Rewrite the sentences in the interrogative (?) or negative (-) forms.**

1. You spent two days at their house in Houston. (?)
   ____
2. We flew to Miami to see Grandma. (-)
   ____
3. We have been to the United States. (-)
   ____
4. He has gone sightseeing with his mom. (?)
   ____
5. Have you made a reservation at the hotel? (-)
   ____

4 **Write about the last time you visited your extended family.**

I visited my aunt in Houston. We had a BBQ.

____
____
____
____

5 **Complete the questions with the Present Perfect form of the verbs in parentheses.**

1. ________ you ever ________ (travel) alone? If so, how was it?
2. ________ you ________ (have) driving lessons before?
3. ________ you ________ (be) to Europe?
4. ________ you ever ________ (do) volunteer work? If so, how did you feel?
5. ________ you ________ (take) a selfie at a tourist monument?

6 **In your notebook, write short answers to the questions in Activity 5.**

Use of English

1 **Match the columns to make verb phrases related to traveling. Then listen and check.** 27

1. go on	☐ a hotel room
2. book	☐ a bus tour
3. visit	☐ at the reception
4. travel	☐ by plane
5. issue	☐ of historical buildings
6. check in	☐ a museum
7. reduce	☐ a passport
8. take pictures	☐ our carbon footprint

2 **Write five questions about life experiences with *Have you ever*. You can use the verb phrases from Activity 1.**

Questions	Answers
Have you ever *been to an ecological reserve?*	*Yes, I have.*

3 **Interview a family member and ask him / her your questions from Activity 2. You can ask the questions in your language, but remember to write the answers in English.**

4 **What have you learned about your family member's life experiences? Write a short paragraph.**

My sister has been to a lot of ecological reserves. She has traveled with friends to the beach.

Writing

1 **Read the e-mail from Felix. Answer the questions.**

1. Who is he writing to?

____

2. Why is he writing?

____

CANCEL SEND

TO

SUBJECT

Dear Sir / Madam,

I am writing to complain about the food at Mama Mia Restaurant.

I went there with my family on December 10 at 8 p.m.

My daughter's lasagna was cold, and my chicken was overcooked. The soup was salty, and the salad plate was dirty.

I've been your costumer for a long time, and I want to continue eating at your restaurant. But I would like to ask you for a refund of our meals.

Please consider my complaint as an opportunity for improvement as you are a great restaurant franchise.

Looking forward to your reply.

Kind regards,

Felix Wendel

2 **Read the e-mail again. Mark the sentences T (True) or F (False).**

1. ☐ Felix didn't enjoy the food.
2. ☐ The lasagna was overcooked.
3. ☐ The chicken was cold.
4. ☐ The waiter solved his problem.

Prepare to Write

3 **Think about a time you had a bad experience at a restaurant / snack bar / cafeteria and make notes.**

____

____

____

Write

4 **Write an e-mail of complaint using the information in Activity 3 and the text in Activity 1 as a model.**

CANCEL SEND

TO

SUBJECT

Check and Change

5 **Read your e-mail and make sure you included:**

- ☐ the reason why you are writing.
- ☐ irregular verbs in the Simple Past.
- ☐ Present Perfect for personal experiences.
- ☐ your complaint.
- ☐ a request.

6 **Edit your e-mail. Make sure you included all the elements in Activity 5.**

Publish

7 **Write a clean version of your e-mail.**

#ASSESS

Vocabulary

1 Match the columns.

1. go	☐ tourist attractions on foot
2. go	☐ at a youth hostel
3. stay	☐ a flight
4. take	☐ hiking
5. book	☐ sightseeing
6. visit	☐ pictures

Grammar

2 Rewrite the sentences correcting the mistakes.

1. I spended one week on vacation.
____
2. I didn't made a reservation.
____
3. My uncle didn't knew the directions.
____
4. Have you ever be to another country?
____
5. I have no seen a dolphin.
____
6. She taked pictures on vacation.
____

Reading

3 Read the e-mail. What did Rosa do on vacation?

CANCEL SEND

TO

Hi Grandma,

How are you?

I'm sorry I didn't see you this summer. I went camping with my friends. We spent three days in the mountains. It was really fun. We swam in a river and went hiking.

Lots of love,

Rosa XOXO

Listening

4 Listen to Magda talk about her eco-camping vacation. Mark the sentences T (True) or F (False). 28

1. ☐ Magda enjoyed her vacation.
2. ☐ The staff at the campsite were friendly.
3. ☐ They used a lot of plastic at the campsite.
4. ☐ They bought food from the supermarket.
5. ☐ In the evening they played video games.
6. ☐ Magda wants to go back.

Writing

5 Write an e-mail to your best friend describing your last vacation.

CANCEL SEND

TO

SUBJECT

Speaking

6 Change your e-mail from Activity 5 into a voice message and record yourself.

Vocabulary

Geographical Features
Underwater Animals

1 Read the article about an animal sanctuary. Answer the questions.

NEW TAB

The Sea Animal Sanctuary in Cornwall, in the U.K., has 50 animals. The sanctuary helps sick animals and returns them to the ocean.

Amanda Warner, the manager, said that people bring them animals from the beach. People worry because there are a lot of boats that can harm the animals in the area. They have saved lots of sea birds that were tangled in fishing lines, and they even had an octopus.

Lots of people visit the sanctuary in the summer and pay five pounds for the entrance fee. All the money pays for medicine and care of the animals. The Sanctuary also gives Friend of the Ocean classes. They also have a touch pool, where people can hold sea stars. The Sea Animal Sanctuary is a great experience.

1. What type of animals does the sanctuary help?
____
2. What harms the animals?
____
3. How does the sanctuary pay for the medicines?
____

2 Underline the animals mentioned in the text.

3 Besides the ones mentioned in the text, which other sea animals can you name? Complete the mind map below.

Underwater animals

1 ______________
2 ______________
3 ______________
4 ______________
5 ______________
6 ______________

4 Complete the table with the words from the box.

cloudy continent desert foggy
island lake mountain ocean rainy
river sea snowy stormy sunny windy

Geographical Features	Weather

Reading

1 **Listen to the introduction of a podcast episode. What is the episode about? Check (✓) the correct option.** 29

1. ☐ Deserts. 2. ☐ Lakes. 3. ☐ Oceans.

2 **Research into the gray whale migration route on the Internet. Then complete the notes below.**

The gray whale migration route...

1. Start: ______
2. Finish: ______
3. Distance: ______

3 **Read the text. Check your answers in Activity 2.**

NEW TAB

The Great Migration

Gray Whales swim every year from Baja California, off the coast of Mexico, to the Arctic. They prefer the warm water of the Pacific Ocean to have their babies. The Arctic is their favorite place to eat.

Every year they swim around 20,000 kilometers. This is the longest migration of any animal on Earth. The journey usually takes two to three months, and they travel in groups or *pods*.

There are around 25,000 gray whales, but they are in danger. Global warming means they have less food in the Arctic and the whales are very hungry.

4 **Read the text again and answer the questions.**

1. What do gray whales do in the Pacific Ocean?
______
2. What do they do in the Arctic?
______
3. How long does the migration take?
______
4. What is a group of whales called?
______
5. Why are the whales in danger?
______

5 **Write two questions you would like to ask Dr. Mauricio Lopez about the gray whales. Then research on the Internet and find the answers to your questions. Audio record your questions and answers as part of the podcast in Activity 1.**

______

Grammar

Future with *Will*
Future with *Be Going to*

1 **Would you like to be a marine biologist? Why or why not?**

____

____

2 **Listen to an interview on Our Planet podcast. What will Dr. Lopez learn? Check (✓) the correct option.** 30

1. ☐ The size of the whales and the distance they travel.
2. ☐ The number of baby whales that survive their migration.
3. ☐ The route the whales travel and how many of them there are.

3 **Read the interview script and use the verbs in parentheses in the future with *will* or *be going to*. Then listen again and check your answers.** 31

I: Interviewer **D: Dr. Lopez**

I: Hello, Dr. Lopez. Welcome and thank you very much for joining us today!

D: Hello! It's great to be here.

I: So, you'[1] ______________ (spend) three months with the gray whales.

D: Yes, I am. I'm very excited. I'[2] ______________ (travel) with the whales on their migration route up to the Arctic. I'[3] ______________ (tag) the baby whales – we call them calves. A tag is a tracking device, so we know where the whales are.

I: Oh, OK. And why do you do that?

D: Well, the gray whales[4] ______________ (be) extinct very soon if we don't do anything to help. So we need to count how many gray whales there are. We [5] ______________ (learn) how many calves survive their migration.

I: That sounds very interesting and useful.

D: Yes, I hope it[6] ______________ (tell) us more about these beautiful animals.

4 **Imagine you are a marine biologist. You will study penguins in Antarctica. Write three sentences to plan your research trip.**

I'm going to study penguins in Antarctica. The trip is going to be...

____

____

#UNDERSTAND

UNIT EIGHT

Use of English

1 **Read the dialogue. What are Robin and Fay going to do?**

____

____

____

Robin: Hey, are we going to meet later?
Fay: Yes! I'm going to meet Pia to talk about the school project. Will you help us?
Robin: Sure, I'll come now.
Fay: Cool!
Robin: Do you have any ideas for the project?
Fay: Yes... We're going to start a clean water campaign. We're going to make some posters, too.
Robin: OK, that sounds good. I'll bring my *markers*.
Fay: That'll be great. So, see you at Pia's house.
Robin: I'll be there in a few minutes!

2 **Read the dialogue again and underline the verb forms about the future.**

3 **Read the sentences. Decide if they are correct or incorrect. Rewrite the incorrect sentences correctly.**

1. Are you go to see Pia?
____
2. I not going to meet you later.
____
3. We're going to talk about a project.
____
4. Will you bringing your markers?
____
5. I'll make a poster.
____
6. We no will be late.
____

4 **Write a phone conversation between Robin and Pia. Use *will* and *be going to*.**

Robin: Hello, Pia. This is Robin. I'm going to come to your house later.

Pia: ______________________________
____

Robin: ______________________________
____

Pia: ______________________________
____

Robin: ______________________________
____

Pia: ______________________________
____

Writing

1 Read Karl's social media stories sequence. Then go online and research into an endangered animal. Make notes in your notebook.

Prepare to Write

2 Plan your social media stories sequence in your notebook. Write a sentence for each topic. Use Karl's stories sequence to help you.

- **Story 1:** What animal is your story about?
- **Story 2:** Where do they live?
- **Story 3:** How many remain in the wild?
- **Story 4:** Why are they endangered?
- **Story 5:** What can we do to protect them?
- **Story 6:** What are you going to do to help?

3 Choose some pictures for your stories sequence.

Write

4 Choose a template on a graphic design platform and create your stories sequence.

Check and Change

5 Read your stories sequence and make sure you included:

- ☐ information about the endangered animal.
- ☐ information about how people can help.
- ☐ pictures to make your sequence more eye-catching.
- ☐ *will* and *be going to*.
- ☐ correct spelling and grammar.

6 Edit your stories sequence to make sure all the elements in Activity 6 are included.

Publish

7 Prepare a clean version of your social media stories sequence.

Vocabulary

1 Unscramble the letters and form words.

1. sae ________
2. ecnoa ________
3. amnnuoti ________
4. cnttionne ________
5. sdalnie ________
6. sedter ________
7. ealk ________
8. eirrv ________
9. ydulco ________
10. ainry ________
11. srtmoy ________
12. gogyf ________

Grammar

2 Complete the sentences with *will* or *be going to*. Use the verbs in parentheses.

1. The mountain is very high. It ________ ________ (be) difficult to climb it.
2. On Thursday we ________ (take) surfing classes at the beach.
3. ________ you ________ (help) with our clean beach campaign?
4. The sun is really hot today. I ________ (put on) more sunscreen lotion.
5. I ________ (jump) into the lake when everybody is ready.

Reading

3 Read the message and write complete answers to the questions.

Chat

Hey, Alf! Hope you are well! I'm going to the beach with Paul and Liz on Saturday. You have to come! We're going to have a picnic and go surfing. So, I'm going to bring my board. Bring yours! Will you bring your camera, too?
I think it'll be sunny and hot, so remember to bring your sunscreen! Let me know!

1. What are Caleb's plans for Saturday?
____
2. Are they going to have a picnic?
____
3. What is Caleb going to bring to go surfing?
____
4. What will the weather be like?
____

Listening

4 Listen to Alf talk about his weekend plans and mark the sentences T (True) or F (False). 32

1. ☐ Alf is going to visit to the aquarium with his brother.
2. ☐ Alf's sister is going to work on a school project.
3. ☐ Alf will try and meet Caleb at the beach later.
4. ☐ Alf is going to go to the aquarium in the afternoon.

Writing

5 You are going to have two friends over at your house on the weekend. Write a paragraph about your weekend plans with them.

____

Speaking

6 Imagine Caleb invited you to go the beach on Saturday. Record an audio message to him saying why you are or aren't going to accept his invitation. Remember to use *will* and *be going to*.

FOCUS ON CULTURE

1 **ACTIVATING PRIOR KNOWLEDGE. Look at the pictures and describe them. What do they represent? How can the conditions in these school environments become better? Discuss your ideas in groups and present them to your classmates.**

2 **MAKING PREDICTIONS. Read the title of the text below. What information do you expect to find? Read the text and check your answers.**

NEW TAB

"The Rich Access Quality Education as the Poor Suffer": Learning Crisis as Filipino Schools Stay Closed

The Philippines is one of only five countries in the world that has not started in-person classes.

Education experts have predicted children are going to be behind and it will have a great impact on their future.

In a survey by the United Nations children's agency in May, 84 percent of parents said that their children were learning less in distance learning than in traditional in-person learning.

"The rich are accessing quality education and the poor have to suffer with this problematic education programme," Raymond Basilio, secretary general of the Alliance of Concerned Teachers (ACT), said.

Two of the major challenges were internet connectivity and the lack of access to electronic devices, he explained.

"As parents, we are told not to protect our children from the problems of the world. But we have to expose them and teach them how to cope with these issues and keeping them in their houses is a way of protecting them also from the realities that we have," Ms Sibal, lead official education specialist said.

"In looking for solutions to make our community and our country safer and healthier, we should also consider the mental health, social wellness, and emotional health of everyone as well, especially our children."

Source: https://www.telegraph.co.uk/global-health/climate-and-people/rich-access-quality-education-poor-suffer-filipino-schools-close/. Accessed on February 12, 2022.

3 **READING FOR DETAILS. Read the text in Activity 2 again and answer the questions.**

1. According to the survey carried out by the United Nations, what did most parents observe?

___

___

2. As Filipino schools stay closed, how is education different between the rich and the poor?

___

___

3. Since the coronavirus pandemic began, what are the major challenges in education in the Philippines?

___

___

4. What is important to consider when making choices about education?

___

___

4 **In groups, list two ideas to boost the education quality in your school.**

5 **Resume the discussion about the pictures in Activity 1. Then read the text again and answer the question below in pairs.**

What can we do in our city, in our school, and at home to make sure everyone has access to quality education?

___

___

___

___

6 **Present the ideas discussed in Activity 5 to the class. Vote for the most feasible ones.**

1 ACTIVATING PRIOR KNOWLEDGE. Look at the pictures below. What can you see? What is making the people in the pictures happy or sad? What do you like doing in your free time that makes you happy? What makes you sad? Discuss your ideas in groups and present them to your classmates.

1.

2.

3.

4.

2 MAKING PREDICTIONS. Read the title of the text below. What information do you expect to find? Can you guess some of the reasons why Dutch teens are happy? Read and check your answers.

NEW TAB

Why Dutch Teenagers Are Among the Happiest in the World

Teens in Netherlands are regularly at the top life satisfaction tables, with schooling playing a big role.

In a biology class at a secondary school near Rotterdam, Gerrit the skeleton is not the only one with a permanent smile.

The Groen van Prinstererlyceum school, which first started happiness lessons ten years ago, teaches some of the happiest teens in the world.

So why is this country so good at giving young people an optimistic outlook?

Dr Simone de Roos, a researcher, says life satisfaction among teenagers has been high since 2013.

"I think Dutch children have generally positive interactions in all their social surroundings," says De Roos. "They have a supportive environment at home, with friends, and also at school. Dutch parents give a lot of support and have mild control. There's an equal climate, teachers are not authoritarian but accept the feelings of pupils, and pupils trust teachers."

According to that report, young people in the Netherlands were also in the top five for eating breakfast on weekdays, watching more than two hours of weekday television, and being kind and helpful. They generally found it easy to talk to parents.

Source: https://www.theguardian.com/world/2018/jun/17/why-dutch-bring-up-worlds-happiest-teenagers. Accessed on February 15, 2022.

3 **READING FOR DETAILS. Read the text in Activity 2 again and mark the sentences T (True) or F (False).**

1. ☐ Schooling plays a big role in life satisfaction for Dutch teens.
2. ☐ Dutch teens are happy because they spend a lot of time doing what they want.
3. ☐ There are happiness lessons at Groen van Prinstererlyceum.
4. ☐ Dutch children don't have a supportive environment at school.
5. ☐ Dutch teens have healthy routines and habits such as having breakfast on weekdays, watching TV, and being kind and helpful.

4 **Relate the pictures in Activity 1 to the text and discuss the question below in pairs. Make notes.**

How can we change low levels of happiness into high levels of happiness and have happier teenagers?

____

____

____

5 **In groups, discuss and make notes of some activities that can create positive interactions in your social surroundings, at home, and at school. Prepare slides or posters showing your ideas. Use illustrations to make them more appealing.**

6 **Present the ideas discussed in Activity 5 and the posters or slides you prepared to the class. Vote for the best ideas.**

1 **MAKING PREDICTIONS. Read the newspaper headlines below. What do you think the text you are going to read is about? Discuss in groups and present a list of foods you expect to find in those texts to your classmates.**

NEW TAB

Celebrating World Vegan Month this November? Try cooking these meat and dairy free recipes

Extracted from https://www.telegraph.co.uk/health-fitness/nutrition/celebrating-world-vegan-day-month-november-meat-dairy-free-recipes-food-cook-2021/. Accessed on February 15, 2022.

NEW TAB

Diana Henry's brilliant alternative festive desserts to a Christmas pudding in 2021

Extracted from https://www.telegraph.co.uk/food-and-drink/features/diana-henrys-brilliant-alternative-christmas-puddings-festive-desserts-winter-season-2021//. Accessed on February 15, 2022.

NEW TAB

"My kids only want chocolate or chips": the reason teenagers crave junk food and what to do about it

Extracted from https://www.telegraph.co.uk/health-fitness/body/kids-want-chocolate-chips-reason-teenagers-crave-junk-food-do/. Accessed on February 15, 2022.

2 **MONITORING COMPREHENSION USING DETAILS. Read the text below and explain how it is related to the last headline in Activity 1.**

____

____

It seemed to happen from one day to the other. One day my two boys came home from school and snacked on fruit and toast, and then next it was chocolate and bags of chips, bought with their money at the store on the way home. As a parent who's always worked hard to feed my children healthy food, it came as a real shock.

"Teenagers are growing and need lots of energy," Priya Tew, director at Dietitian U.K., explains. "Often they don't eat much at school so they're pretty hungry when they come out – mid-afternoon hunger is pretty normal for all of us – and so they'll go into the shops near school where there's easy access to high-sugar, high-fat foods."

Source: https://www.telegraph.co.uk/health-fitness/body/kids-want-chocolate-chips-reason-teenagers-crave-junk-food-do//. Accessed on February 15, 2022.

3 **READING FOR DETAILS. Read the text in Activity 2 again and answer the questions below.**

1. Why was the parent shocked to notice the change in the boys' eating habits?

____

____

2. What exactly was the change in the boys' habits?

____

____

3. According to Priya Tew, why does this change happen?

____

____

4 **Discuss the questions below in pairs. Refer back to the text in Activity 2, if necessary. Make notes.**

How do people's eating habits change? Does that change happen only in adolescence? Are eating habits related to the culture we live in? If so, how? If not, why not?

____

____

____

5 **In groups, create a healthy recipe. Make a list of ingredients and describe the instructions.**

6 **Present the recipe you created in Activity 5 to the class. Vote for the healthiest recipe.**

1 The pictures below are related to uncommon professions. Can you guess which professions they are? Discuss in groups.

1. 

____

2. 

____

3. 

____

2 MAKING PREDICTIONS. Work in pairs. Read the title of the text and answer the question posed. Then read the text and discuss your ideas.

NEW TAB

Will Jobs Exist in 2050?

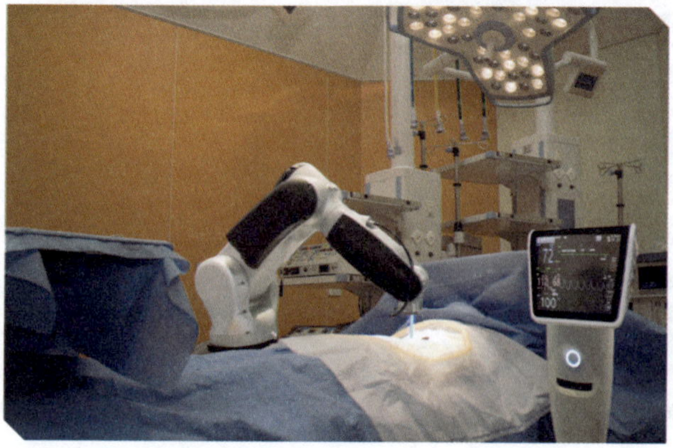

Complex machines are doing several jobs. What does this mean for the future of work? And if there are no jobs, what are we going to do with our time?

The future of work will soon become "the survival of the most adaptable", says Paul Mason, emerging technologies director for Innovate UK. As new technologies change the way we work, the jobs that remain will be complex and not regular.

"Workers of the future will need to be very adaptable and do three or more different jobs at a time," says Chopra-McGowan, responsible for new markets for the General Assembly. So continuous education will play an important role in helping people develop new skills.

The cheapest and most productive thing to do will be to automate the workers.

The future of work is unclear, but they all agree that one thing is for certain: "The nature of work is going to change – the jobs of tomorrow won't be the same as jobs of today."

Source: https://www.theguardian.com/careers/2016/oct/13/will-jobs-exist-in-2050. Accessed on February 15, 2022.

3 **READING FOR DETAILS. Read the text in Activity 2 again and underline the correct alternatives to complete the sentences.**

1. Jobs will exist **in the same way** / **in a different way** in the future.
2. In the future, jobs will be **easier** / **more complex**.
3. It will be important for people **to develop new skills** / **to learn how to work with robots**.
4. Automating the workers is **very expensive** / **very productive**.
5. The nature of work **will change** / **will be the same**.

4 **MONITORING COMPREHENSION USING DETAILS. Relate the pictures in Activity 1 to the text in Activity 2 and discuss the questions below in pairs. Make notes.**

Do you believe that robots are going to replace humans in professions such as the ones in the pictures? How can humans keep their jobs?

____

____

____

5 **In groups, make a list of professions or activities where robots can't replace humans. Choose three of those professions to describe. Make notes.**

6 **Present each profession you described in Activity 5 to the class without mentioning the profession itself. Have your classmates guess which professions you are describing. Finally, vote for the profession you think will not disappear in the future.**

1 Look at the pictures and tell your classmates what you see. Then read the statements and discuss them in groups.

1.

2.

1. A person's appearance is very important.
2. Your clothes say a lot about you.
3. Fashion is part of a teen's life.
4. You can wear whatever you want at school.
5. Going on social media is more interesting than watching TV.

2 **MONITORING COMPREHENSION USING DETAILS. Work in pairs. Answer the question posed in the title of the text. Then read the text and compare Charlotte's opinions to yours.**

NEW TAB

How Would You Feel If You Became an Overnight Instagram Sensation?

Charlotte D'Alessio is 16 and she accidentally becomes a social media influencer. The teen from Canada moves to Los Angeles with her family and, in the spring of her first year in LA, she decides to go to the music festival Coachella with a few of her new friends.

While at Coachella, Charlotte and her friend Josie change outfits several times, taking a few pictures of themselves in dresses and different jackets and post them on social media. So far, so normal. But when the successful LA photographer Bryant Eslava takes some photos of the girls and tags them on his account, their images begin to go viral. Soon the girls are seeing themselves everywhere, in photos of the festival and in the "popular" galleries of Tumblr and Instagram. They are getting hundreds and thousands of followers by the minute and being followed by strangers.

For Charlotte, a quiet, studious girl from Canada with ambitions to attend UCLA, it is entirely surreal. "I am honestly freaking out," she says. And given what happened to her life after that, it is an appropriate reaction.

Source: *https://www.theguardian.com/technology/2018/jul/22/what-would-you-do-if-your-teenager-became-an-overnight-instagram-sensation*
Accessed on February 16, 2022.

3 **READING FOR DETAILS. Read the text in Activity 2 again and answer the questions.**

1. How old is Charlotte?

2. Where is the music festival Coachella?

3. How do Charlotte and her friends become famous?

4. What happens after that?

5. How does Charlotte feel about all this?

4 **Discuss the questions below in pairs. If necessary, read the text in Activity 2 again. Make notes.**

Social media brings a lot of attention to our appearance. How easy or difficult do you think this situation is for Charlotte? Why?

5 **In groups, decide what you think happened to Charlotte after her picture went viral. How do you think her life changed after that event? Make notes.**

6 **Present your ideas to your classmates explaining the changes in Charlotte's life. Consider all the ideas presented by the groups and vote for the most interesting ones.**

1 ACTIVATING PRIOR KNOWLEDGE. Work in pairs. Read and discuss the statements below. Justify your opinions.

1. Quality education includes technology.
2. Teachers are an important part of quality education.
3. School rules are often very strict.
4. The best way to learn is in a classroom.

2 MAKING PREDICTIONS. Look at the picture and read the title of the text. How do you think they are related? Read the text and find out.

NEW TAB

Teens Are Making Historical Events Go Viral on TikTok – What Does a History Teacher Think?

There is a stereotype that teenagers spend a lot of time online, not interested in real life events.

People who say that clearly haven't seen them on TikTok, where they are engaging in the unexpected: teaching history lessons.

I asked a history expert, Izzy Jones, to watch the videos and comment. She is happy to see teenagers use the platform this way. "The ones that I really liked were the ones on international relations in the 20th century," says Jones, adding: "I can use some of those videos in class."

She explains how the most powerful videos use human beings to personify world actors – such as countries – in major historical events.

In one video, a TikTok user personifies the German empire in 1914, aggressively telling Belgium: "I didn't push you, I moved you out of the way because you wouldn't move when I asked you to move three times." It tells about the military invasion of Belgium by Germany.

"A 15-second video is probably most effective in getting across one key point. Of course, it's not the complete story," says Jones.

Source: https://www.theguardian.com/technology/2019/nov/05/teens-are-making-historical-events-go-viral-on-tiktok-what-does-a-history-teacher-think. Accessed on February 16, 2022

3 **READING FOR DETAILS. Read the text in Activity 2 again and answer the questions.**

1. What is one stereotype about teenagers mentioned in the text?

____

2. What is surprising about some teenagers on TikTok?

____

3. What are the most powerful videos according to Izzy Jones?

____

4. Does the video mentioned by Izzy Jones tell the whole story about the military invasion of Belgium by Germany?

____

4 **MONITORING COMPREHENSION USING DETAILS. Go back to the statements in Activity 1, read the text again, and discuss the statements below in pairs. Make notes.**

Online platforms can be used to teach various school subjects and engage students more actively. Traditional classrooms have to change.

____

____

____

5 **In groups, decide on three points you can teach in 15 seconds. Make notes. Then record your three 15-minute teaching videos.**

6 **Show the videos to your classmates. Vote for the best ones.**

1 ACTIVATING PRIOR KNOWLEDGE. Work in pairs. How can we promote good health? Discuss your ideas and complete the mind map below.

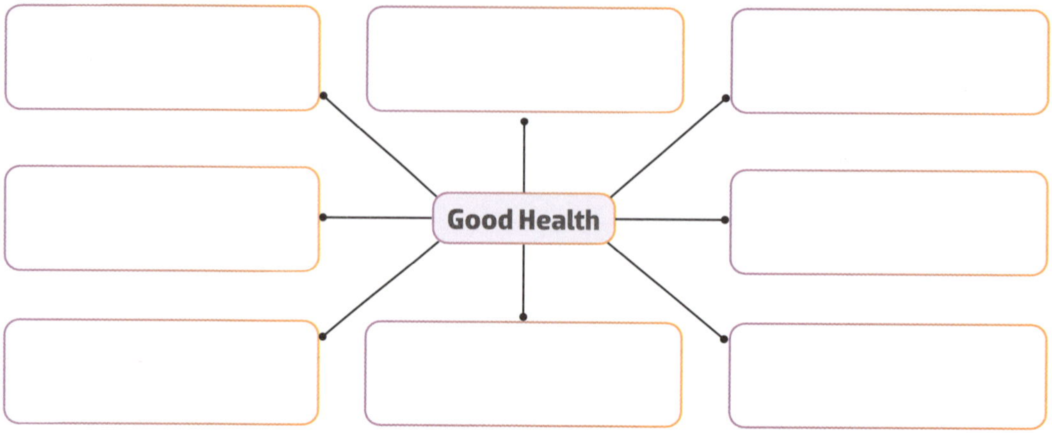

2 MAKING PREDICTIONS. Look at the picture and read the title of the text. How do you think they are related? Read the text and find out.

NEW TAB

Exercise Off-limits for 75% of Teens

More than three quarters of British children between 11 and 16 take no exercise every week, according to a new survey that will fuel the debate about child obesity.

More than half of all teenagers agreed that young people are fat, lazy, and addicted to computer games, but blame school and councils for failing to give them opportunities to exercise.

In the survey of more than 300 children and Youth Debate panels held across the country, teenagers said they spent their time surfing on the web and playing computer games, but claimed they had no other choice.

"I don't think it's an issue of kids being lazier than children before us,' said Alexandra, 16, at a north London Youth Debate panel. 'Sport isn't accessible enough. There aren't enough sports centers for us."

Teenagers complained that local sports centers and green areas were lost to building projects while the gyms appearing in their place were expensive and far from home.

Almost 70% of the teenagers surveyed agreed that young people today are more obese than they used to be.

Almost all teenagers criticized how P.E. lessons were run. "They are completely useless: we got just two hours every two weeks in years 10 and 11," said Nico, 16. "We don't get a say in what sport we play, so three quarters of the class don't bring their kit because they don't like the sport chosen."

Source: *https://www.theguardian.com/uk/2003/nov/02/health.schoolsports.* Accessed on February 16, 2022.

3 **READING FOR DETAILS. Read the text in Activity 2 again and answer the questions.**

1. How many British children between 11 and 16 take no exercise every week?

____

2. According to teenagers, who is to blame for their lack of opportunities to exercise?

____

3. Why don't teenagers exercise?

____

4. What do teenagers think about P.E. classes?

____

4 **MONITORING COMPREHENSION USING DETAILS. Go back to the mind map in Activity 1, read the text again, and discuss the statement and questions below in pairs.**

Good health and well-being starts at school. Do you agree or disagree? Why?

____

____

____

5 **In groups, decide on some actions schools can take to improve P.E. classes. Make notes. Then organize your notes and make a slide presentation.**

6 **Present your slides to your classmates and explain how the suggested actions can encourage teenagers to do more sports at school. Vote for the best presentation.**

1 **ACTIVATING PRIOR KNOWLEDGE. In pairs, brainstorm ideas and use keywords to complete the chart below.**

Tourism

Positive effects	Negative effects	Plans for the future

2 **SKIMMING. Read the text quickly and find out what it is about.**

____

NEW TAB

Top Breaks for Teens

Family travel expert Joanna Moorhead recommends three breaks to keep teenagers happy – from harmonious family vacation to go-it-alone adventures

Whatever your formula for family vacation with young kids has been, you need a rethink when they turn into teenagers. Everyone needs more space – you need more space from them, they need more space from you – and you'll need to ensure there are plenty of activities, especially the kind that can be done independently. That said, don't forget the need for family time: there's nothing more wonderful than getting together with your happy-but-tired teenagers at the end of a long day to swap stories.

1. Riviera Maya, Mexico

This is a vacation with great teen appeal. Riviera Maya is south of Cancun and has a range of spacious hotels set in tropical gardens. You can swim with dolphins, scuba dive, kayak across the Black Lagoon, and walk along jungle paths once used by the Mayans.

2. Canvas Holidays

This year Canvas Holidays expands to youngsters aged 12 to 18. This means that you get social activities, ball games, karaoke nights, and pizza evenings, as well as off-site activities such as trips to local waterparks.

3. Paris, France

Paris is a great place for a short break with teenagers: my girls, aged 15 and 13, prefer the laidback train trip from Waterloo to the hassle of going to the airport and hanging around waiting to board. The best time to go is June if your kids have just taken their exams and have finished school.

Source: *https://www.theguardian.com/travel/2007/apr/20/familyholidays.uk.paris. Accessed on February 16, 2022.*

3 **READING FOR DETAILS. Read the text in Activity 2 again and mark the sentences (T) True or (F) False.**

1. ☐ Kids and teenagers have similar needs concerning their vacations.
2. ☐ In the Riviera vacation, you can swim with the dolphins.
3. ☐ You have to be at least 18 to go on the Canvas vacation.
4. ☐ Trips to local waterparks are included in the Canvas vacation.
5. ☐ Paris isn't considered an interesting destination for teens.

4 **MONITORING COMPREHENSION USING DETAILS. Discuss the questions in pairs. If necessary, read the text in Activity 2 again. Make notes.**

What are the positive and negative effects of tourism in the areas the texts talk about? Do you think there are ecotourism options in these areas? Why?

____

____

5 **In groups, talk about some actions the places mentioned in the text should take to promote sustainable tourism. Make notes.**

6 **Present your ideas listed in Activity 5 to your classmates and explain how these tourist places can become more eco-friendly. Vote for the best ideas.**

1 **ACTIVATING PRIOR KNOWLEDGE. Work in small groups. Look at the pictures below and discuss what you see. What kind of problems do they represent? Where do these problems start?**

1.

2.

3.

4.

2 **MAKING PREDICTIONS. Read the title of the text below. What message does it convey? Brainstorm ideas with your classmates. Then read the text and check if your ideas are correct.**

____

"The Future of Life on Earth Lies in the Balance"

Overfishing

"We are overfishing our oceans very fast and choking them with plastic and other pollutants. If we want to see healthy seas that will continue to provide us with food, we need to stop this over-exploitation, protect our incredible marine environments, and make sustainable fishing the norm, as we see here."

Hugh Fearnley-Whittingstall, chef and vice-president of Fauna and Flora International

Plastic pollution

"Nature is our life support system and without it our lives on this earth would be impossible and unimaginable. We have to stop seeing the natural world as something to be exploited and taken for granted. Nature matters to me and it should matter to you. We need to put more value on our natural assets and stop destroying our precious planet."

Chris Packham, TV presenter, naturalist, and founder of Wild Justice

Source: *https://www.theguardian.com/environment/2019/may/07/the-future-of-life-on-earth-lies-in-the-balance-a-picture-essay.* Accessed on February 16, 2022

3 **READING FOR DETAILS. Read the text in Activity 2 again and underline the correct alternatives to complete the sentences below.**

1. Our oceans are full of **fish** / **plastic**.
2. Healthy seas provide us with **food** / **entertainment**.
3. We have to make sustainable fishing the **norm** / **the problem**.
4. Nature is **a life support system** / **the gray areas around us**.
5. Nature should matter **to some people** / **to everyone**.
6. We need to stop destroying **our planet** / **our lives**.

4 **Go back to the pictures in Activity 1 and resume your discussion. Then read the text in Activity 2 again and discuss the statement below in groups.**

- The future of life lies in the balance.

5 **In pairs, discuss how to illustrate the text in Activity 2 in two pictures. Use the space provided below for your illustrations.**

6 **Present your illustrations to your classmates and have them guess what they represent. Vote for the best illustrations.**

TEEN TALK

1 **Discuss in groups.**

Your school asks you to suggest one subject to add to the list of your curriculum subjects. What subject do you suggest? Why?

2 **In pairs, choose one of the pictures below and describe the school subject it represents. Under each picture there is a word you can't use to describe the subject. What are the school subjects?**

1.

numbers

____

2.

sports

____

3.
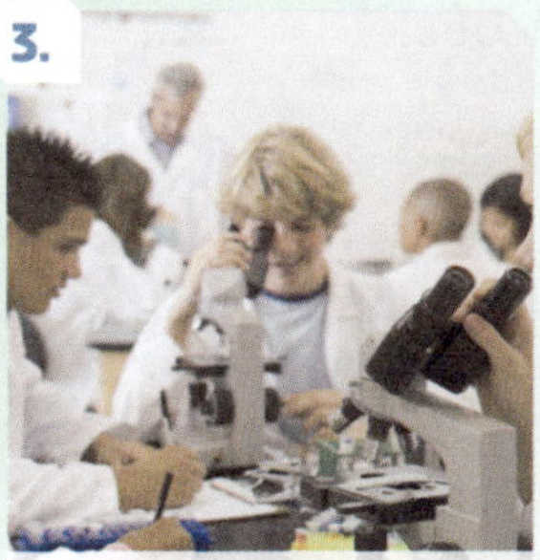
laboratory

____

4.

maps

____

3 **Draw a map of your school in your notebook. In pairs, give directions to each other to get to the different places in your school.**

Hi! I want to go to the lab. How can I get there?

Turn left after the school cafeteria and go straight on.

4 **Imagine you are a comic book hero that can fly around and talk to teens everywhere in the world. Make a list of five questions you would ask to people your age about education and the improvements they would like to see. What's wrong now? How can we make it better? Ask them about their likes and dislikes and their vision for the future.**

What is your school like?
Which subjects do you like?

5 **Work in pairs.**

Student A: You're unhappy with your education. Tell Student B three reasons why.

Student B: You're a teacher and you're unhappy with your job. Tell Student A three reasons why.

My name's Mark. I'm unhappy with the education in my school.

Really? Why?

6 **Self-evaluation. Reflect on the tasks in this section and cross out the stars that correspond to your performance.**

Learning Objectives	Rating
Did I express my ideas well?	☆☆☆
Did I use the language structures from the unit?	☆☆☆
Did I use the vocabulary from the unit?	☆☆☆
Did I pronounce new words correctly?	☆☆☆
Did I correct any mistakes?	☆☆☆
Was I collaborative in the conversations?	☆☆☆

1 **Discuss in groups.**

What would you give up to make more time to do what you like in your free time?

2 **Complete the statements below so that they are true for you.**

1. On rainy days, I like to ________________________________.
2. Once a week, I ________________________________.
3. My family and I never ________________________________.
4. In my free time, I like to ________________________________.
5. I like to play ______________ whenever I have some time.

3 **In pairs, look at the cards below. Use the Simple Present to talk about the teens and their free time.**

Name: Jose
Occupation: student
Free time: around three hours a week
- **Usually:** plays video games
- **Sometimes:** watches movies
- **Never:** plays soccer

Name: Adan
Occupation: student
Free time: very limited
- **Usually:** does community service
- **Every day:** plays with little brother
- **On weekends:** goes for a walk

4 **Work in pairs. Interview your classmate using *Wh- questions* and complete the card about him / her.**

Name: ________________________________
Occupation: ________________________________
Free time: ________________________________
____
____
____

5 **Work in pairs.**

Student A: You are an activist. You believe the world can be more sustainable, and you want to help keep the water in your city clean. Try to convince Student B to help.
Student B: You don't believe you can help, after all, what can kids do? Make notes of your arguments in your notebook.

Mark, we can help keep the lake clean.

Really? How?

6 **Self-evaluation. Reflect on the tasks in this section and cross out the stars that correspond to your performance.**

Learning Objectives	Rating
Did I express my ideas well?	☆☆☆
Did I use the language structures from the unit?	☆☆☆
Did I use the vocabulary from the unit?	☆☆☆
Did I pronounce new words correctly?	☆☆☆
Did I correct any mistakes?	☆☆☆
Was I collaborative in the conversations?	☆☆☆

1 **Discuss in groups.**

Do you agree that food is culture and culture is food? Why? Why not?

2 **You are making dinner for your friends tonight. What are you cooking? What are the ingredients? Make a list of items you need to buy at the supermarket.**

3 **In pairs, look at the picture below. Use *some*, *any*, *the*, or *a / an* to describe the food and drink items you see. Which items are healthy and which are unhealthy?**

4 **In groups, make a poster with foods that are bitter, sweet, or savory. Use food containers for your foods. Then present your poster to the other groups.**

This is a bar of dark chocolate. It's bitter.

5 **What can you do to end world hunger? In groups, complete the table below and share your ideas with other groups.**

	Advantages	Disadvantages
Give food to the poor		
Give money to charity		
Start a blog		
Make a social media post		

6 **Self-evaluation. Reflect on the tasks in this section and cross out the stars that correspond to your performance.**

Learning Objectives	Rating
Did I express my ideas well?	☆☆☆
Did I use the language structures from the unit?	☆☆☆
Did I use the vocabulary from the unit?	☆☆☆
Did I pronounce new words correctly?	☆☆☆
Did I correct any mistakes?	☆☆☆
Was I collaborative in the conversations?	☆☆☆

1 **Discuss in groups.**

Jobs will probably be very different in the future. Some jobs won't exist anymore. Do you know any jobs that don't exist anymore? Which jobs do you think won't exist in the future?

2 **In pairs, look at the people below. Think of questions to ask them. Make notes in your notebook. What are their jobs?**

Where do you work? Do you wear a uniform?

1.

____

2.

____

3 **Choose one of the occupations from Activity 2. Ask and answer the questions you have prepared with your classmate. Add extra questions in the Present Continuous to ask about things that are happening now.**

Hi, my name's Greg. I'm an IT engineer.

Hello, Greg, how are you? Are you working right now?

4 **Write an occupation on a piece of paper and tape it on a classmate's back. Go around the classroom and talk to a different classmate about the occupation taped on his / her back, but don't say what his / her occupation is. Then change roles. When you guess your profession, sit down.**

Talking to a student with the word doctor on his / her back: *Hi, I'm not feeling very well. Can you help me?*

5 **Role play the situation below in small groups.**

It's career day at school and one of the boys wants to become a professional ballet dancer. When he makes his presentation, his classmates start laughing at him and make him cry.

When the role playing is over, discuss the following questions.

1. How does each of the characters feel?
2. What makes each of the characters behave like this?
3. What are some possible solutions to this situation?

6 **Self-evaluation. Reflect on the tasks in this section and cross out the stars that correspond to your performance.**

Learning Objectives	Rating
Did I express my ideas well?	☆☆☆
Did I use the language structures from the unit?	☆☆☆
Did I use the vocabulary from the unit?	☆☆☆
Did I pronounce new words correctly?	☆☆☆
Did I correct any mistakes?	☆☆☆
Was I collaborative in the conversations?	☆☆☆

1 This is Ramon's social media profile picture. In groups, describe the picture.

2 Work in groups. Choose a classmate and describe him / her with as many appearance adjectives as possible. You can use personality adjectives, too. Have the rest of the group guess who you are talking about.

He / She is tall and has long legs.
He / She is very serious.

3 In groups, discuss how people see appearance in your country and how important it really is. How do young people deal with body positivity? Then present your ideas to the other groups. How do you feel about this subject?

4 Complete the sentences below to make them true to you. Then compare your answers with a classmate and justify them.

1. I am ______________ than my classmate.
2. Apples are ______________ than oranges.
3. Comedies are ______________ than drama.
4. K-pop is ______________ than jazz.
5. ______________ is the most important school subject.
6. ______________ is the most beautiful country.
7. ______________ is the friendliest classmate we have.
8. ______________ is the best teacher!

5 Work in pairs. What would you do if you had $50 billion?

Student A: You want to spend all this money helping yourself and your family.
Student B: You want to help reduce inequality with this money. Discuss.

6 Self-evaluation. Reflect on the tasks in this section and cross out the number of stars that correspond to your performance.

Learning Objectives	Rating
Did I express my ideas well?	☆☆☆
Did I use the language structures from the unit?	☆☆☆
Did I use the vocabulary from the unit?	☆☆☆
Did I pronounce new words correctly?	☆☆☆
Did I correct any mistakes?	☆☆☆
Was I collaborative in the conversations?	☆☆☆

1 **Discuss in groups.**

In developing countries, one in four girls is not at school. How do you feel about that? What does it say about our future?

2 **You are going to role play a school interview. Work in pairs.**

Student A: Make a list of questions to ask Student B about his / her school and school rules. Use *Wh-* questions, *must*, *should*, and *can*.
Student B: Answer Student A's questions. Change roles.

3 **Look at the pictures of two different classrooms. Compare the classrooms and talk about the quality of education you think they provide.**

Classroom 1

Classroom 2

Classroom 1 is a very simple classroom.
Classroom 2 has a lot of technology.

4 **In groups, look back at the pictures in Activity 3 and make up the classroom rules for each of the two classrooms. Make notes in your notebooks and present the rules to the other groups.**

In classroom 1, students must copy from the board.
In classroom 2, students shouldn't speak to their classmates during class.

5 **Work in pairs.**

Student A: You are convinced that education in your school can be better. Use *should*, *must*, and *can* to convince Student B you are right.
Student B: You don't think students can change things at school. You believe everything is OK, and there's no need to improve.

The school should pay teachers better salaries.

We can't change the system, we're just students.

6 **Self-evaluation. Reflect on the tasks in this section and cross out the number of stars that correspond to your performance.**

Learning Objectives	Rating
Did I express my ideas well?	☆☆☆
Did I use the language structures from the unit?	☆☆☆
Did I use the vocabulary from the unit?	☆☆☆
Did I pronounce new words correctly?	☆☆☆
Did I correct any mistakes?	☆☆☆
Was I collaborative in the conversations?	☆☆☆

1 **Discuss in groups.**

What do you know about the Olympic Games? Do you like to watch the Olympics? Why? Why not? What sports do you prefer?

2 **The picture below shows some sports. Which ones do you recognize? In pairs, search online for the ones you don't know.**

3 **Complete the table below and compare it with a classmate.**

Sports we play with a ball	Sports we play in the summer	Sports we play in the winter

4 **In pairs, look at the situations below and choose a card. Ask each other questions about your day yesterday.**

You are Sam and you are a student at the local high school. You don't like sports and you prefer to play video games or watch TV. You don't want to go out a lot. Everything seems boring to you.

You are Sally. You're strong and very athletic. You love to go out and play sports at the sports center or at the park. Your favorite sport is volleyball, but you also do yoga and volunteer to train younger kids.

What did you do yesterday, Sally?

I went to the sports center to play volleyball. What about you, Sam?

5 **Role play the situation below in pairs.**

It's a regular day at school and you find one of your classmates crying in the classroom. He / She doesn't want to talk about it and most students are ignoring him / her anyway. You try to talk to the teacher, but no one is listening. How can you help your classmate?

When the role playing is over, discuss the following questions.

1. How does each of the characters feel?
2. What makes each of the characters behave like this?
3. What are some possible solutions to this situation?

6 **Self-evaluation. Reflect on the tasks in this section and cross out the number of stars that correspond to your performace.**

Learning Objectives	Rating
Did I express my ideas well?	☆☆☆
Did I use the language structures from the unit?	☆☆☆
Did I use the vocabulary from the unit?	☆☆☆
Did I pronounce new words correctly?	☆☆☆
Did I correct any mistakes?	☆☆☆
Was I collaborative in the conversations?	☆☆☆

1 **Look at the picture below. Where do you think it was taken? What do you know about this country and its language? Have you ever been there?**

2 **Complete the sentences below so they are true for you. Compare your answers with a classmate and talk about your preferences.**

My last vacation

1. I traveled by ______________.
2. I went to __________ with __________.
3. Some of my vacation activities were __________ __________, __________, __________ and __________.
4. I have never been to ______________.
5. My friends and I always talk about going to ______________.
6. ______________ is the best vacation destination in my opinion.
7. I love to stay at ______________ because ______________.

3 **Use the verbs in parentheses to complete the questions below. Then take turns asking and answering them in pairs.**

1. Have you ever ______________ a hotel room? (book)
2. Have you ever ______________ a mountain? (climb)
3. Have you ever ______________ to another country? (be)
4. Have you ever ______________ the ocean? (see)
5. Have you ever ______________ alone? (travel)

4 **Look at two popular tourist attractions. Where are they? Which one would you choose to visit and why? What would you do there? Discuss in pairs.**

I want to visit New York because I can go shopping and take pictures.

5 **Your city council has a meeting about building a new hotel in a green area. In groups, make a poster showing the problems this construction can cause to the animals that live in that green area. Present your poster to the other groups. Vote for the best poster!**

6 **Self-evaluation. Reflect on the tasks in this section and cross out the number of stars that correspond to your performance.**

Learning Objectives	Rating
Did I express my ideas well?	☆☆☆
Did I use the language structures from the unit?	☆☆☆
Did I use the vocabulary from the unit?	☆☆☆
Did I pronounce new words correctly?	☆☆☆
Did I correct any mistakes?	☆☆☆
Was I collaborative in the conversations?	☆☆☆

1 Discuss in groups.

Our oceans are facing a very big plastic problem. What kind of problem is it? What are the consequences for the animals that live underwater? What are the consequences to our lives and health?

2 In pairs, look at the pictures below, identify the places, and talk about the animals you might find living there.

1.

____

____

____

____

2.

____

____

____

____

3 Work in pairs. Look at the pictures in Activity 2 again and talk about the weather in each picture.

4 Complete the table with weather predictions and talk about your plans for the future using *be going to*.

Monday	*rainy*	*I'm going to stay home to study.*
Tuesday		
Wednesday		
Thursday		
Friday		

5 In groups, make a list of everything you have used today that is made of plastic. Make a poster with the items on your lists. Look online for the number of years each item needs to disappear if not recycled. Present your poster to the other groups. Vote on the best poster! Reflect on how you feel about the use of plastic now that you have new information about plastic pollution.

6 Self-evaluation. Reflect on the tasks in this section and cross out the number of stars that correspond to your performance.

Learning Objectives	Rating
Did I express my ideas well?	☆☆☆
Did I use the language structures from the unit?	☆☆☆
Did I use the vocabulary from the unit?	☆☆☆
Did I pronounce new words correctly?	☆☆☆
Did I correct any mistakes?	☆☆☆
Was I collaborative in the conversations?	☆☆☆

#GAMES

1 Do you like to play games? What kinds of games do you like? List some games you play.

2 Play the *Snakes and Ladders Game* in groups.

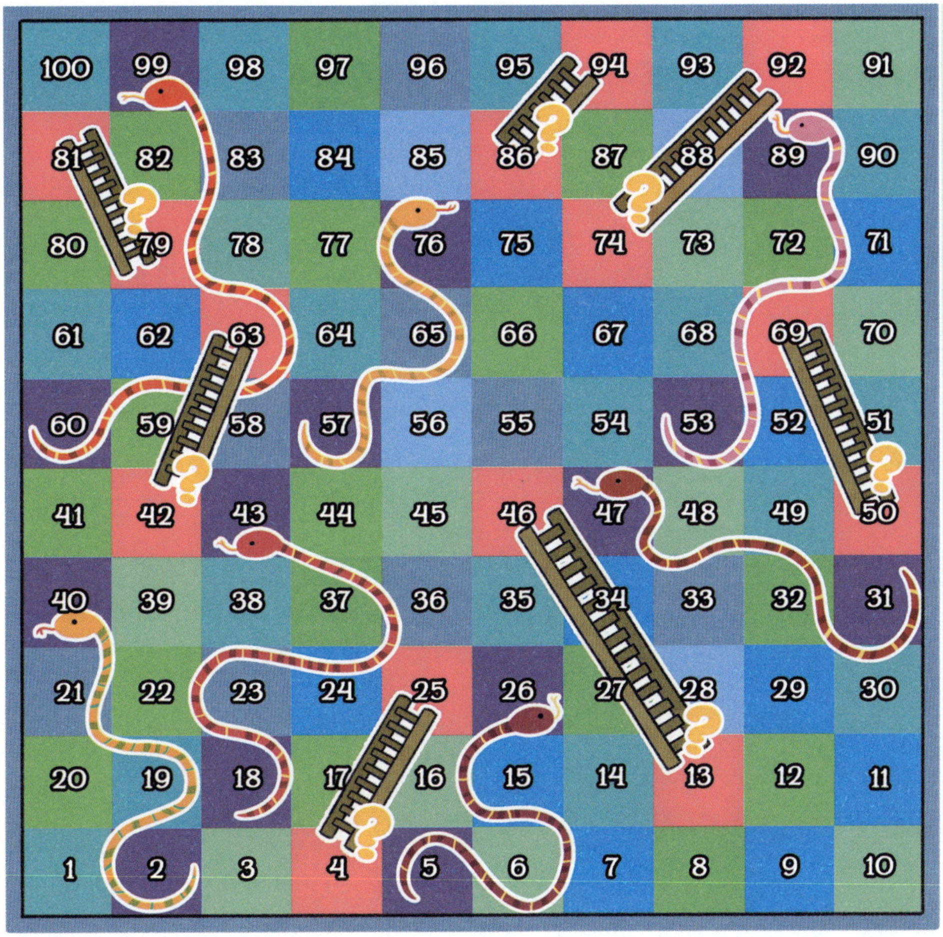

Instructions

1. Take turns to roll the die and move along the path. Move your counter forward the number of spaces shown on the die.
2. If your counter lands at the bottom of a ladder, your group chooses a question for you. Answer the question to climb the ladder. If you can't answer the question, you have to wait for your turn to roll the die again and move on.
3. If your counter lands on the head of a snake, you must slide down to the bottom of the snake and wait for your next turn.
4. The first player to get to the end is the winner.

Questions

1. What's your favorite subject at school?
2. Why do you like (subject)?
3. How can I get to the (school place) in our school?
4. Make a sentence with *I like* (school subject) *because...*
5. Make a sentence with *I don't like* (school subject) *because...*
6. What's an ideal day at school for you?
7. Complete the sentence: *Math is* (adjective).
8. Make up a question for the following answer: *Because it's fun.*

3 In groups, answer the questions about the game.

1. Was the game easy or difficult to play?
2. What was easy? Why?
3. What was difficult? Why?
4. What did you learn from playing the game?

1 **Do you like to play word games? What word games do you play?**

2 **Play the Category Game in groups.**

Things I like	Things I dislike	Free-time activities	Countries and nationalities	Places at school

Instructions

1. One student in the group will cite the alphabet silently and another student will say *Stop*.
2. Complete the grid with words starting with the letter of the alphabet that was chosen.
3. Say *Stop* if you finish first.
4. Get one point for each correct answer.

3 **In groups, answer the questions about the game.**

1. Was the game easy or difficult to play?
2. What was easy? Why?
3. What was difficult? Why?
4. What did you learn from playing the game?
5. What other categories can you add to the grid to make the game more interesting?

1 Do you know any game about food? Which one(s)?

2 Play *the Food Game* in groups.

Instructions

1. Take turns to roll the die and move your counter.
2. Every time you land on a block, your classmate will ask you one of the suggested questions.
3. If you do not answer the question correctly, you lose your turn next round.

Questions

1. Name a food item that looks like a tree.
2. This food comes from the sea.
3. You can buy fresh vegetables in this place.
4. They are crunchy and yellow.
5. People who don't eat meat are...
6. Name a dessert.
7. Give two examples of healthy food.
8. Give me one example of unhealthy food.
9. You have to break them to make an omelet.
10. They are orange and bunnies like to eat them.
11. Say three bitter foods or drinks.
12. Say three savory foods.
13. Say your favorite food and drink.

3 **In groups, answer the questions about the game.**

1. Was the game fun to play?
2. Do you think you had enough time to answer the questions?
3. Did you find the questions relevant to what you learned in this unit?
4. Which other questions would you add to the list?

1 In pairs, ask each other about professionals and their work.

What does a plumber do?

2 Play *the Jobs Game* in groups.

Instructions

1. Place your counter in the **START** tile.
2. Take turns rolling the die and moving your counter along the path. If your counter lands on a picture tile, identify the profession and say what the professional does. If your counter lands on instruction tiles, follow the instructions (go back, go forward, etc.).
3. If you can't identify the profession and / or describe the work, you lose your turn in the next round.
4. The player who arrives at the **FINISH** tile first is the winner.

3 In groups, answer the questions about the game.

1. Was the game easy or difficult to play? Why?
2. Were you able to identify the professions?
3. Were your classmates able to explain what each professional does?
4. What did you learn from playing the game?

1 In pairs, name as many clothes as you can in 60 seconds. How many did you manage to name?

2 Play the *Category Game* in groups.

Clothing & accessories	Personality adjectives	Appearance adjectives	Important events

Instructions

1. One student in the group will cite the alphabet silently and another student will say *Stop*.
2. Complete the grid with words starting with the letter of the alphabet that was chosen.
3. Say *Stop* if you finish first.
4. Get one point for each correct answer.

3 In groups, answer the questions about the game.

1. Was the game easy or difficult to play?
2. What was easy? Why?
3. What was difficult? Why?
4. What did you learn from playing the game?

1 **Some people say that games are a waste of time. What is your advice to them?**

2 **Play the *What should I do? Game* in groups.**

	1	2	3	4	5
1	I failed my exam.	My family wants to move to another country.	Mathematics is very difficult for me.	I want to study abroad.	My friends don't respect me.
2	I have to sit an exam next week.	My brother always argues with me.	One of my classmates doesn't like me.	I want to learn another language.	I need help to study for the science test.
3	My teacher is very strict.	I must wake up very early every morning.	My friends make fun of me.	I want to practice English.	I don't have time to have fun.
4	My school is closing.	I don't want to study any more.	I want to be online all day, but my family doesn't like it.	I must wear a uniform at school and I don't like that.	I mustn't talk to people during class, but I feel lonely.
5	I skipped class and my mom is angry.	I have three exams to sit for tomorrow.	Schools close for the summer and I don't know what to do with my time.	I have to speak to my teacher tomorrow about my exam.	I have to win this game.

Instructions

1. Take two dice for this activity or you will have to roll the same die twice.
2. A classmate rolls the two dice. Each die shows a number: one represents a horizontal number and the other a vertical number. The classmate has to read the sentence that is where the numbers meet and give advice depending on the situation. For example, if you roll 3 and 5, you land on one of the following: *Schools close for the summer and I don't know what to do with my time*, or *I don't have time to have fun*.
3. Every time you give meaningful advice you get a point. The winner is the student that gives the most meaningful pieces of advice after a few rounds.

3 **In groups, answer the questions about the game.**

1. Did you like playing this game?
2. Did you find it creative?
3. Was it difficult? Why?
4. What did you learn from playing the game?

1 **What do you do to improve your health?**

2 **Play the *Find Someone Who Game* in groups.**

Find someone who...

always has breakfast in the morning.	relaxes watching TV.	brings healthy snacks to school.	plays soccer.	loves nature.
exercises 30 minutes a day.	enjoys nature on the weekend.	plays a lot of video games.	goes swimming.	listens to loud music.
does yoga.	eats a lot of candy.	has more than three meals a day.	has a good relationship with his / her parents.	is very tired.
plays basketball.	likes to eat fruit.	is very stressed with tests at school.	listens to music to relax.	does aerobics.
does judo.	doesn't like to drink water.	doesn't like to hang out.	is anxious.	sleeps eight hours per night.

Instructions

1. Go over the grid with your groupmates asking, for example, *Who always has breakfast in the morning?*, *Who relaxes watching TV?*, etc.
2. Make notes of your classmates' answers writing their names in the boxes.
3. When you have finished asking and answering, go over the answers and decide on the healthiest and the unhealthiest classmate in the group.

3 **In groups, answer the questions about the game.**

1. Was the game fun to play? Why? Why not?
2. What would you change in this game?
3. Did you find the questions relevant to what you learned in this unit?
4. Would you add any more questions? Which ones?

#GAMES

1 In groups, think of a name for your group and get ready to play the *Category Game* with the rest of the class.

2 In groups, play the *Category Game* with the class.

Travel destination	Means of transportation	Places to visit	Local foods	Accomodation types

Instructions

1. Play in groups.
2. Take turns choosing the letter of the alphabet everyone will play with. Letters Q, U, V, Z, Y should not be used as they can make the game frustrating.
3. After choosing the letter of the alphabet, you and your group have one minute to fill the grid.
4. One point is scored for each word the other groups did not think of.
5. The group with the most points is the winner.

3 In groups, answer the questions about the game.

1. Was the game easy or difficult to play?
2. What was easy? Why?
3. What was difficult? Why?
4. What did you learn from playing the game?

1 How well do you know your classmates?

2 Play the *Find Someone Who Game* in groups.

Find someone who...

likes to go to the mountains.	likes to go to the lake.	likes boiling hot weather.	can draw a fish.	knows the name of an island.
is going to spend his / her vacation next to a river.	knows the name of a desert.	likes clear skies.	swims in the ocean in the summer.	saw snow last winter.
has a pet turtle.	saw a starfish at the beach.	knows the name of a lake.	can make the sound of a dolphin.	likes cloudy days.
saw dolphins last vacation.	can tell you the names of the continents in English.	can make the sound of a seal.	knows the name of a mountain.	can draw a shark.
likes to eat octopus.	likes the rain.	can name two oceans.	can name two continents.	knows the name of a river.

Instructions

1. Go over the grid with your groupmates asking, for example, *Who likes to go to the mountains?*, *Who likes to go to the lake?*, etc.
2. Make notes of your classmates' answers and write their names in the boxes.
3. When you have finished asking and answering, go over the answers and decide on the classmate that is the closest to nature in the group.

3 In groups, answer the questions about the game.

1. Was the game fun to play? Why? Why not?
2. What would you change in this game?
3. Did you find the questions relevant to what you learned in this unit?
4. Would you add any more questions? Which ones?

GRAMMAR GLOSSARY

like / don't like

I / You / We / They	like	to + verb
He / She / It	likes	
I / You / We / They	don't like	
He / She / It	doesn't like	

We use the Simple Present to talk about our likes / dislikes.

***I like to eat** ice cream.*
*Mark **doesn't like to play** football.*

think – Stating an Opinion

I / You / We / They	think
He / She / It	thinks

We use the Simple Present to state our opinions.

*We **think** the game is really difficult.*
*What does Mary **think** about the movie?*

Giving Directions

Turn left / turn right / go straight on

When we are giving directions to someone, *turn left* tells them to turn to the left side.

Turn right indicates that the person should turn to the right side and *go straight on* tells the person to keep going in the same direction up to a specific point.

***Turn left** at the traffic light, **go straight on** on Fifth Street, and **turn right** at the sports center.*

Why and *Because*

We use *why* to start a question and ask for the reason something is happening. We can also use *why* to state *the reason why.*

***Why** is Sofia here?*
(= What is the reason she is here?)
*Maria understands **why** we have to go home now.*
(= She understands the reason why something needs to happen.)

We use *because* to express the reason or cause of something.

*The Harrisons are going home **because** it's a school night.*

Simple Present – Affirmative and Negative Forms

Affirmative	
I	like
You	like
He / She / It	likes
We	like
You	like
They	like

Negative	
I	don't like
You	don't like
He / She / It	doesn't like
We	don't like
You	don't like
They	don't like

We use the Simple Present for things that are generally true or happen with frequency.

In the Simple Present, we use *do / does* as an auxiliary verb in the interrogative form. To make the negative form, we use *don't / doesn't*.

Nina ***talks*** *to her friends every day at school.*
They ***don't come*** *to school on foot.*

Spelling Rules for *He / She / It*

I work	He work**s**
I finish	He finish**es** (verbs ending in *-sh, -ch, -o*)
I study	He stud**ies** (verbs ending in *-y* preceded by a consonant)

Yes / No Questions

To ask and answer *yes / no* questions in the Simple Present we use *do / don't, does / doesn't.*

Does *Mark like football? No, he doesn't.*
Do *the students want a break? Yes, they do.*

Wh- Questions

We use...

what	to ask about a thing.
where	to ask about a place.
who	to ask about a person.
why	to ask about a reason.

We use *Wh-* questions to request information about people, places, things, and reasons.

What *do you want for breakfast?*
Where *is Maria?*
Who *is that little boy?*
Why *is the door open?*

How Often

How often	auxiliary verb	subject	main verb
How often	do	you	swim?

We use *How often...?* to ask about frequency.

How often *does the teacher give tests?*

Adverbs of Frequency and the Simple Present

Adverbs of Frequency
always, never, often, sometimes, usually

We use adverbs of frequency with the Simple Present to talk about how often we do something. Adverbs of frequency go **before** the main verb and **after** the verb *be*.

I ***always*** *go to the movies on the weekend.*
Nena is ***sometimes*** *late for school.*

Use a positive verb after *never*.

Lily ***never*** *eats cheese.*

In negative sentences in the Simple Present, the adverb of frequency goes between the auxiliary (do / does) and the main verb.

Mark doesn't ***often*** *go to the mall.*

Other expressions that show frequency are placed at the end of the sentence.

Allie eats at the restaurant ***every Sunday****.*

Countable and Uncountable Nouns

Nouns in English can be countable or uncountable.

Countable nouns are the ones we can count. These nouns can be in the singular or the plural, e.g. *orange*, *orange***s**.

Uncountable nouns are nouns we can't count. These are usually liquids, powders, or made of small particles, and are usually found in the singular, e.g. *water*, *sugar*, *rice*. We use other types of measurements to count the quantity of uncountable nouns, such as *grams*, *kilograms*, *cups*, *spoons*, etc.

There are five **chairs** in the classroom.
(chairs - countable)
This cup of **water** is cold.
(water - uncountable)

How much / How many / Some / Any

We use *How much...?* to ask about the quantity of an uncountable noun.

How much sugar do you want?

We use *How many...?* to ask about the quantity of a countable noun.

How many eggs do you want in your omelet?

We use *some* with plural nouns and uncountable nouns in affirmative sentences.

I want **some** ice cream.
Maria has **some** flowers to give.

We use *any* with plural nouns and uncountable nouns in negative and interrogative sentences.

There aren't **any** students in the gymnasium.
There isn't **any** milk in the carton.
Do we need **any** onions?
Does Lily want **any** coffee?

A / An / The

There is **a** lemon in the bag.
Lily wants to eat **an** omelet.

We use *a / an* with countable nouns in the singular when we talk about something in general. We use *an* before nouns that start with a vowel sound.

Give me **an a**pple. I'm hungry.

We use *a* before nouns that start with a consonant sound.

There's **a u**niversity near my school.

We use *the* when we want to talk about something specific. We use it with countable nouns both in the singular and the plural and uncountable nouns.

The snack Tina is eating is very tasty.
The water in this glass is very cold.

Compare:

Mark needs **a** glass of water. (water in general)

Mark needs **the** glass of water on the table. (talking about a specific glass of water)

Present Continuous

Formation:

be* + verb + *ing

Affirmative
I'm playing.
You're playing.
He / She / It is playing.
We're playing.
They're playing.

Interrogative
Am I playing?
Are you playing?
Is he / she / it playing?
Are we playing?
Are they playing?

Negative
I'm not playing.
You aren't playing.
He / She / It isn't playing.
We aren't playing.
They aren't playing.

We use the Present Continuous to talk about things that are happening at the time of speaking / now / at the moment.

*Look! It'**s** rain**ing**.*

Short Answers

Is Lily eating in the kitchen?	Yes, she is. No, she isn't.

Spelling Rules

cook – cooking play – playing	add *-ing* to the verb
bake – baking	remove *-e* and add *-ing*
stop – stopping	double last consonant when there is the sequence consonant – vowel - consonant

Prepositions *on / at / in*

We use *at* with time and expressions such as *midnight*, *midday*, *night*, *lunchtime*, etc. and festive dates.

We use *on* with the days of the week, dates, and the weekend.

We use *in* with months of the year and parts of the day, such as *morning* and *afternoon*, for example.

*We go to the movies **at** night.*
*The test starts **at** 8 o'clock.*
*The restaurant opens **on** Monday.*
*We always have fun **on** the weekend.*
*The boys prefer to play soccer **in** the morning.*
*Their birthday is **in** July.*

Comparative

adjective + *er* + *than*	James is old**er than** Mary.
more + adjective + *than*	Tunisia is **more** beautiful **than** Egypt.

We use the comparative to compare two people, things, etc.

To form the comparative, we add *-er* to short adjectives. If the adjective is more than two syllables long, then we use *more + adjective*.

Sam is **shorter than** Jim.
A tiger is **more dangerous than** a chicken.

Spelling Rules

old - old**er**	One syllable adjective + *-er*
big - bi**gg**er	Adjectives ending in consonant – vowel – consonant double the last consonant and add *-er*
happ**y**- happ**ier**	Adjectives ending in *-y* preceded by a consonant, remove the *-y* and add *-ier*
good - better bad - worse far – farther / further	Irregular comparatives

Superlative

the + adjective + *est*	James is **the** old**est** in his class.
the most + adjective	Tunisia is **the most** beautiful country.

We use the superlative to say which is the biggest / best, etc. in a group.

To form the superlative of short adjectives, we use *the + adjective + est*. If the adjective is more than two syllables long, then we use *the most + adjective*.

Sam is **the shortest** boy in class.
A tiger is **the most dangerous** animal you can see at the zoo.

Joanna is **the tallest** girl on the team.

Must / *Mustn't*

must + verb (infinitive without *to*)	**mustn't** + verb (infinitive without *to*)
You must go to class now.	You mustn't open this door.

We use *must* to talk about an obligation.

We use *mustn't* to talk about a prohibition or something that is not allowed.

Mark **must** study more. He has exams this week.
Tina **mustn't** play video games until late at night.

Should / *Shouldn't*

should + verb (infinitive without *to*)	**shouldn't** + verb (infinitive without *to*)
You should go to class now.	You shouldn't open this door.

We use *should* to give advice to someone about what to do.

We use *shouldn't* to give advice to someone about what **not** to do.

You **should** talk to Mari, she's really friendly.
Jacob **shouldn't** call you at this time. It's very late.

Making Requests and Suggestions with *Can* and *Could*

Can + subject + verb	Can you come in, please?
Could + subject + verb	Could you bring me some water?
Subject + *could* + verb	The teacher could give us an easier test.

We use *can* + *subject* + *verb* or *could* + *subject* + *verb* to make a polite request.

We use *subject* + *could* + *verb* to make a suggestion to someone.

Can I have some soda, please?
Could you get me the phone?
You **could** try to be more polite.

Have to / *don't have to*

have to + verb
don't have to + verb

We use *have to* to talk about something that is an obligation.

You **have to** tidy your room.

We use *don't have to* to talk about something that is not necessary to do.

We **don't have to** pay to get in.

Must vs. *Have to*

Must is used to express specific obligations while *have to* is used to express general obligations.

He **must** do this for me.
I **have to** brush my teeth every day.

You mustn't ride your bike in this area.

Simple Past: *was / were*

Affirmative
I was
You were
He / She / It was
We were
They were

Interrogative
Was I?
Were you?
Was he / she / it?
Were we?
Were they?

Negative
I wasn't (was not)
You weren't (were not)
He / She / It wasn't
We weren't
They weren't

We use *was / were* to talk about the past. They are the forms of verb *be* in the Simple Past.

Short Answers

Was she at the mall yesterday?	Yes, she was. / No, she wasn't.
Were they home last night?	Yes, they were. / No, they weren't.

Simple Past: Regular Verbs

Affirmative
I worked
You worked
He / She / It worked
We worked
They worked

Interrogative
Did I work?
Did you work?
Did he / she / it work?
Did we work?
Did they work?

Negative
I didn't work
You didn't work
He / She / It didn't work
We didn't work
They didn't work

We use the Simple Past to talk about finished actions in the past. We form the affirmative form of the Simple Past by adding *-ed* to the end of regular verbs. The verb remains the same for all persons (I , he, they, etc).

We use *did / didn't + verb* to form the interrogative and negative forms of the Simple Past of regular and irregular verbs.

I **played** soccer yesterday.
Did I **play** soccer yesterday?
I **didn't play** soccer yesterday.

Spelling Rules

work – worked	add *-ed* to the end of most verbs
smile – smiled	add *-d* to the end of verbs ending in *-e*
stop – stopped	double the last consonant and then add *-ed* to one-syllable verbs ending in consonant – vowel - consonant
study – studied	remove the *-y* and replace it with *-ied* in verbs ending in consonant + y

Simple Past: Irregular Verbs

Base form	Simple Past form
eat	ate
go	went
know	knew
leave	left
see	saw
spend	spent

The Simple Past affirmative form of irregular verbs doesn't follow any rules. Consult your irregular verbs list to find out the form of irregular verbs in the Simple Past. The irregular forms of the verb are used only in the affirmative form. We use *did / didn't + verb* to form the interrogative and negative forms of the Simple Past of regular and irregular verbs.

I **went** to the doctor this morning.
They **didn't go** to the supermarket yesterday.
Did you **see** Karen last night?

A: Has she ever been to Australia?
B: Yes, she has. She **studied** there last year.

Have you ever...?

Have you ever + verb in the past participle form

We use *have you ever + verb in the past participle form* to ask about life or personal experiences in the past.

Have you ever been to Scotland?
Have you ever eaten octopus?

Short Answers

Have you ever seen a dolphin?	Yes, I have. / No, I haven't.

Simple Past vs. Present Perfect

We use the Simple past to talk about complete or time-defined actions in the past.

We use the Present Perfect to talk about life or personal experiences in the past. We then give more details about the experience in the Simple Past.

A: Have you ever **been** to Australia?
B: Yes, I have. I **had** a lovely time! It was in 2016.
We **went** by plane. It **was** amazing.

Future with *will*

Affirmative
I will travel.
You will travel.
He / She / It will travel.
We will travel.
They will travel.

Interrogative
Will I travel?
Will you travel?
Will he / she / it travel?
Will we travel?
Will they travel?

Negative
I won't (will not) travel.
You won't travel.
He / She / It won't travel.
We won't travel.
They won't travel.

We use *will* to talk about:

1. a decision at the moment of speaking.

   ***I'll help** you, just a minute.*

2. a prediction based on an opinion.

   *Mark thinks it'**ll rain**.*

3. a future fact.

   *Winter **will come** sooner or later.*

4. promises, requests, and refusals in the future.

   ***Will** you **give** me a ride, please?*

The negative form of *will* is *won't* (*will not*). The short form of *will* is *'ll*.

*I'**ll go** to the movie theater. I won't get popcorn today.*

Short Answers

Will he come for lunch?	Yes, he will. / No, he won't.

Future with *going to*

Affirmative
I'm going to read.
You're going to read.
He / She / It is going to read.
We're going to read.
They're going to read.

Interrogative
Am I going to read?
Are you going to read?
Is he / She / It going to read?
Are we going to read?
Are they going to read?

Negative
I'm not going to read.
You aren't going to read.
He / She / It isn't going to read.
We aren't going to read.
They aren't going to read.

We use the future with *be going to* to talk about future plans and predictions based on an evidence.

*We'**re getting** married next June.*
*They'**re going** to win this game. They'**re playing** very well!*

Short Answers

Is Alice going to meet Lily at the mall?	Yes, she is. / No, she isn't.

Unit	Tracks	Page	Activities
Audio Tracks			
-	01	Introduction	
0	02	06	2
	03	10	4
1	04	12	2
	05	13	2
	06	16	4
2	07	18	1
	08	19	1
	09	22	4
3	10	24	2
	11	25	2
	12	25	3
	13	28	4
4	14	30	1
	15	34	4
5	16	35	1
	17	35	2
	18	38	3
	19	38	4
	20	40	4
6	21	42	1
	22	43	1
	23	43	2
	24	45	1
	25	46	4
7	26	47	1
	27	50	1
	28	52	4
8	29	54	1
	30	55	2
	31	55	3
	32	58	4

UNIT ZERO

Activity 2 02

I come from Denmark. I live in a city called Copenhagen. My school is modern, interesting, and fun. It's five minutes from my house. There are lots of students because it's a big school.

Activity 4 03

Hey, Kim. Thanks for your e-mail. I agree, boring classes are the worst! My English teacher is really good this semester. I like her a lot. We play games every lesson and do cool projects, too. I like to play games because I think I learn more. I think all my classes and teachers are nice. I guess I'm lucky. Why don't you ask your English teacher to play some games? I think he will listen to you. Anyway... Good luck with the classes. Bye.

UNIT ONE

Activity 2 04

I have a new project for school. We are learning about the environment and sustainability. I need to find some ideas on how to reuse water wisely in our community. I'm very happy with this project!

Activity 2 05

I really like to play video games with my friends online. I play almost every day. But first I do my homework and help my mom make dinner. I love cooking, but my mom doesn't like it. She loves to read and watch movies. My sister goes roller skating at the park after school. She's really good now. She also draws comics. My grandpa paints. He loves art. He sometimes takes a walk at the park to see my sister. He doesn't skate though!

Activity 4 06

Hey, I'm Awlad. I live in Bangladesh, near Dhaka. I have three brothers. I really like music. I listen to music after school every day. I usually exercise at the park with my brothers on Sundays or go shopping with my friends. Sometimes I do community service with my family on the weekends. I like it!

UNIT TWO

Activity 1 07

I live in Manchester, U.K. I don't like big supermarkets because I know there is a lot of food waste and they use a lot of plastic in the food containers. I like to shop at my local market. It's close to my house and they sell everything I need! Every Tuesday I go to the market and I buy fresh vegetables and fruit. I don't eat meat very often. But I usually buy that at the local store, too.

Activity 1 08

D: Diego L: Lily

D: Hi, Lily! How's your day?

L: Hiya, it's fine. I'm at the supermarket. What do you want for dinner?

D: What about a pizza?

L: Hmm, no, I want something healthy.

D: OK, maybe we can cook some chicken soup.

L: Yeah! That sounds good. Do we have chicken at home?

D: Yes, we do.

L: OK, what about milk?

D: No, no milk in the fridge.

L: Let me buy a milk carton, then.

D: Oh, we also need potatoes.

L: How many potatoes?

D: Maybe four. Oh! And rice!

L: How much rice?

D: A small bag is OK.

L: Great. Anything else?

D: No, that's all. See you soon!

L: Yes, bye!

Activity 4 09

Hi, Pedro. April wants to have dinner with us tonight. She is a vegetarian, so she doesn't eat meat. Please buy some cheese and she can eat pasta with vegetables and cheese, no ham! Also, buy a bottle of juice and a carton of eggs for breakfast tomorrow. Thanks, Bye!

UNIT THREE

Activity 2 10

Hi, Paul! Guess what? I have a new job as a designer. I'm very excited because it is my dream job. The office is near my house and the pay is great. I think there are lots of meetings every day, but that's OK!

Activities 2 and 3 11 and 12

H: Hans M: Mel

H: Hello?

M: Hi, Hans. How are you?

H: Oh, hi, Mel! I'm OK... But I'm having a busy day today.

M: Oh, no. Are you still at the hospital?

H: Yes, I am, but I'm not at the nursery looking after babies now.

M: What are you doing, then?

H: I'm visiting some patients with the doctor. What about you?

M: I'm having my lunch, and then I have a meeting.

H: OK, enjoy your food. I'd better go, a patient is calling.

M: Sure, talk to you soon!

H: Bye.

Activity 4 13
I work as a lawyer at a big law firm. Every day I start working at 8.30 a.m. We usually have a group meeting, and then I meet with clients. Sometimes I work on the weekends when there is a big case. But that's OK. I love my job because it is exciting, and I meet a lot of different people. The bad parts are the long hours and the stressful meetings.

UNIT FOUR

Activity 1 14
Hello, everyone. I want to remind you that this Saturday there is a special fundraising event at Fortis Secondary School. The event is to raise money to buy a new athletics wheelchair for Mateo, one of our students. There will be lots of games and fun on Saturday, so please come and spend some money!

Activity 4 15
Hi, Kaleb. I'm happy to hear you are enjoying the training camp. We miss you here! Your sister is sad without you. Now, love, you know you need to believe in yourself. You are the best: the fastest, the smartest, the kindest, and definitely the most handsome kid over there! But also remember you are playing on a team so the most important thing is to work together. OK, I have to go. Your sister is crying. Speak soon. Lots of love and a big kiss.

UNIT FIVE

Activities 1 and 2 16 and 17
Hey, Adam! I'm at my new school now. It's an international school. And it's great. The teachers are friendly and nice, and they help me a lot with my French. There are kids from different places in the world. One girl is from Finland, and another one is from Japan. There is a boy from Peru and another one from Cameroon. We are all in the same class. The school has a media room with computers and tablets, and a sofa. There is a good library with lots of books, too. But hey, what about you? What type of school do you go to now? Do you like it?

Activities 3 and 4 18 and 19

N: Nicole L: Leo

N: So, tell me about the language club. Do you like it?
L: It's great! I'm learning a lot of new things in Spanish.
N: I think your Spanish is much better!
L: Thanks! I have more confidence now.
N: I want to improve my French. Can you give me some advice?
L: Sure! You should join the language club. We speak French, too.
N: OK. Sure.
L: You should also check out our channel. There are lots of good videos there.
N: Great idea!
L: And the most important thing...You must practice every day!
N: Every day? Wow, that's a lot!
L: Let's practice together.
N: Of course!

Activity 4 20
Hi, sis! I really love the Spanish club. It's lots of fun. The people are nice, and they speak Spanish very well. We must speak only in Spanish, so we can practice a lot. I feel more confident now. I should practice my grammar because it is still difficult for me. Rob said I should download an app for help. Rob assigns homework every week. We don't have to do it, but I think I should because it can help me improve.

UNIT SIX

Activity 1 21
We meet at the park every Sunday morning. There are about 14 people in this class, but only two people compete at a time. I love my uniform. It is white and I have a yellow belt because I just started. My teacher has a black belt! He is amazing at judo.

Activities 1 and 2 22 and 23
On Saturday I visited grandma. We talked a lot about school and cooked chicken for lunch. Then I played baseball with my friends in the park. On Sunday I was tired, so I stayed home. I finished my math homework. My sister and step-mom weren't at home, so my dad and I watched a movie and ordered pizza. It was a lovely weekend.

Activity 1 24
It was a marvelous day. My sister was in a white dress. Her husband was in a gray suit. The ceremony was at the local registry office. There were about ten family members and friends there. After the event, we all were ready to celebrate their love with a big party. We headed to a local restaurant and ordered lots of different dishes to share. We danced and shared our happiness with them. I was very happy for my sister!

Activity 4 25
Congratulations! I am so happy for you. I wasn't surprised. You played really well. I wanted to congratulate you after the game, but I didn't see you. Did you celebrate? I noticed Nusrat didn't play. Was she OK? See you on Monday!

UNIT SEVEN

Activity 1 26

1. youth hostel
2. hotel
3. tent
4. vacation rental
5. room
6. house

Activity 1 27

1. go on a bus tour
2. book a hotel room
3. visit a museum
4. travel by plane
5. issue a passport
6. check in at the reception
7. reduce our carbon footprint
8. take pictures of historical buildings

Activity 4 28

Hi, Dan. I had such a good time at the eco-campsite. The staff were really friendly. They all believed in sustainable tourism, which was great. There were no plastic dishes. They grow food there so we all cooked and ate together. In the evening, we sat around a fire and I played the guitar. It was awesome. I need to go back there on my next vacation!

UNIT EIGHT

Activity 1 29

Welcome to Our Plant podcast. Today we are speaking to marine biologist Mauricio Lopez. He researches gray whale migration. He will talk to us about a research trip he's going to take to the Pacific Ocean, off the coast of Baja California.

Activities 2 and 3 30 and 31

I: Interviewer D: Dr. Lopez

I: Hello, Dr. Lopez. Welcome and thank you very much for joining us today!

D: Hello! It's great to be here.

I: So, you're going to spend three months with the gray whales.

D: Yes, I am. I'm very excited. I'm going to travel with the whales on their migration route up to the Arctic. I'm going to tag the baby whales – we call them calves. A tag is a tracking device so we know where the whales are.

I: Oh, OK. And why do you do that?

D: Well, the gray whales will be extinct very soon if we don't do anything to help. So we need to count how many gray whales there are. We are going to learn how many calves survive their migration.

I: That sounds very interesting and useful.

D: Yes, I hope it will tell us more about these beautiful animals.

Activity 4 32

Hi, Caleb! Thanks for inviting me to the beach, but I don't think I can come with you. I'm going to visit the aquarium with my sister. She has a school project, and I said I would help. Maybe I will come later and meet you at the beach. I'm going to get to the aquarium at 10 a.m. so we are going to be finished by about 1 p.m. I'll see what happens! Bye.

PICTURE CREDITS

Front cover (A) s_oleg/Shutterstock/Shutterstock / (B) Sebestyen Balint/ Shutterstock/Shutterstock / (C) 3dector/ Shutterstock/Shutterstock / (D) Doomu/ Shutterstock/Shutterstock / (E) Mix Tape/ Shutterstock/Shutterstock / (F) Oatawa/ Shutterstock/Shutterstock / (G) Natykach Nataliia/ Shutterstock/ Shutterstock; Page 6 (A) Marcel Conrad. 123rf.com/Asset Library / (B) Dennis Mortensen/shutterstock/Shutterstock / (C) Joerg Boethling / Alamy Stock Photo/ Alamy; Page 11 LightField Studios/Shutterstock/Shutterstock; Page 12 (A) Jordan Tan/Shutterstock/Asset Library / (B) LightField Studios/Shutterstock/Asset Library / (C) Studio 72/Shutterstock/Asset Library / (D) lmeleca (Leonid Meleca)/Shutterstock/Asset Library; Page 14 jackhollingsworth.com/Shutterstock/ Asset Library; Page 16 AJR_photo/Shutterstock/Asset Library; Page 17 (A) DONOT6_STUDIO/Shutterstock/Asset Library / (B) Greentellect Studio/Shutterstock/ Asset Library / (C) Billion Photos/Shutterstock/Asset Library / (D) Wavebreak Media Ltd /123rf/Asset Library; Page 18 (A) Y Photo Studio/Shutterstock/Asset Library / (B) Arisara Tongdonnoi/123rf/Asset Library / (C) turtix/Shutterstock/Asset Library; Page 19 Andrey_Popov/Shutterstock/Asset Library; Page 20 (A) Natthapon Ngamnithiporn/123rf/Asset Library / (B) glowonconcept/123rf/Asset Library / (C) Peter Vanco/Shutterstock/Asset Library; Page 22 Ivonne Wierink/ Shutterstock/Asset Library; Page 23 (A) Africa Studio/Shutterstock/Asset Library / (B) cubephoto/Shutterstock/Asset Library / (C) sz-shan Kwok/Pearson Education Asia Ltd/Asset Library; Page 24 (A) auremar/Shutterstock/Asset Library / (B) Rawpixel.com/Shutterstock/Asset Library / (C) Ian Allenden/123rf. com/Asset Library / (D) Olena Yakobchuk/Shutterstock/Asset Library; Page 25 (A) wavebreakmedia/Shutterstock/Asset Library / (B) Dmitry Kalinovsky/ Shutterstock/Asset Library / (C) wavebreakmedia ltd/Shutterstock/Asset Library / (D) michaeljung/Shutterstock/Asset Library; Page 26 (A) Goal_4_CMYK_ TARGET 1.1.eps / (B) Goal_4_CMYK_TARGET 1.1.eps / (C) Goal_4_CMYK_TARGET 1.1.eps / (D) Goal_4_CMYK_TARGET 1.1.eps / (E) Goal_4_CMYK_TARGET 1.1.eps / (F) Goal_4_CMYK_TARGET 1.1.eps; Page 27 dglimages/123rf.com/Asset Library; Page Jacob Lund/shutterstock/Shutterstock; Page 30 ACHPF/ shutterstock/Shutterstock; Page 32 Billion Photos/Shutterstock/Asset Library; Page 33 (A) Ihor Biliavskyi. Shutterstock/Asset Library / (B) Cathy Yeulet. 123rf.com/Asset Library; Page 36 (A) Wavebreak Media Ltd. 123rf.com/Asset Library / (B) Ian Allenden. 123rf.com/Asset Library / (C) YanLev. Shutterstock/ Asset Library / (D) Alexandre Rotenberg. Shutterstock/Asset Library; Page 37 (A) Cathy Yeulet. 123rf.com/Asset Library / (B) Hannamariah. Shutterstock/Asset Library; Page 40 (A) Siberian Photographer. Shutterstock/Asset Library / (B) mirvam. 123rf.com/Asset Library / (C) JONGSUK. Shutterstock/Asset Library / (D) owen1978. Shutterstock/Asset Library / (E) Shutterstock/Asset Library; Page 41 iconspro/Shutterstock/Asset Library/Asset Library; Page 42 fotoinfot/ Shutterstock/Asset Library; Page 43 (A) Thaiview/Shutterstock/Asset Library / (B) AlenaNex/Shutterstock/Asset Library / (C) Jules Selmes. Pearson Education Ltd/Asset Library; Page 45sondoggie/Shutterstock/Asset Library; Page 47 Ikonoklast Fotografie/Shutterstock/Asset Library / (B) Ema L/Shutterstock/Asset Library / (C) Adas Vasiliauskas/Shutterstock/Asset Library / (D) Cindy Goff/Shutterstock/Asset Library / (E) Jens Ottoson/Shutterstock/Asset Library / (F) romakoma/Shutterstock/Asset Library; Page 48 (A) Alexander Chaikin/Shutterstock/Asset Library / (B) Thanawach Nilnarong/Shutterstock/Asset Library / (C) Alexander Sviridov/Shutterstock/Asset Library; Page 50 M R Fakhrurrozi/123rf/123RF; Page 51 SpicyTruffel/Shutterstock/Asset Library; Page 53 (A) Frank Wasserfuehrer/Shutterstock/Asset Library / (B) wrangel/123rf/Asset Library / (C) Anna Ivanova/123rf/Asset Library; Page 54 Mogens Trolle/Shutterstock/ Asset Library; Page 55Justin Berken / Shutterstock/Asset Library; Page 56 (A) Chinnapong / Shutterstock/Asset Library/ / (B) TihyIrina/Shutterstock/Asset Library; Page 57 (A) Sergio Gutierrez Getino/Shutterstock/Asset Library / (B) schlyx/Shutterstock/Asset Library / (C) Victor Saul/Shutterstock/Asset Library / (D) NinaMalyna/Shutterstock/Asset Library / (E) jatmika/123rf/123RF / (F) iQoncept/Shutterstock/Asset Library; Page 60 (A) Shutterstock/Asset Library / (B) 1491896/Shutterstock/Asset Library / (C) Shutterstock/Asset Library / (D) AnaLysiSStudiO/Shutterstock/Asset Library; Page 62 (A) oliveromg/Shutterstock/ Asset Library / (B) xalanx/123rf/Asset Library / (C) MANDY GODBEHEAR/Shutterstock/Asset Library / (D) LightField Studios/shutterstock/Shutterstock; Page 64 beats1/Shutterstock/Shutterstock; Page 65 MikroKon/Shutterstock/Shutterstock; Page 66 (A) sanjagrujic/Shutterstock/Asset Library / (B) Proxima Studio/Shutterstock/Asset Library / (C) Studio 8/ Pearson Education Ltd/Asset Library / (D) PaO_STUDIO/Shutterstock / (E) Ekkasit Keatsirikul/ 123rf/Asset Library; Page 67Visual Generation/Shutterstock/Shutterstock; Page 68 (A) Kent Weakley/Shutterstock / (B) Oleksandr Zamuruiev/Shutterstock/Asset Library; Page 70 Tudor Photography/ Pearson Education Ltd/Asset Library; Page 72 (A) Sundali/Shutterstock/Shutterstock / (B) Allan Swart/123rf/Asset Library; Page 75 petrmalinak/Shutterstock/Shutterstock; Page 76 (A) Rich Carey/Shutterstock/Asset Library / (B) Rich Carey/Shutterstock/Asset Library / (C) Bernhard Staehli/Shutterstock/Asset Library / (D) nEwyyy/Shutterstock/Asset Library; Page 79 (A) Karen Keczmerski/123rf/Asset Library / (B) Handan Erek/ Pearson Education Ltd/Asset Library / (C) Cathy Yeulet/123rf/Asset Library / (D) famveldman/123rf/Asset Library; Page 80 (A) belchonock/123rf/Asset Library / (B) Andrey Shadrin/Shutterstock/Asset Library; Page 81 Evgeniya Pushai/Shutterstock/Asset Library; Page 82 (A) zhu difeng/Shutterstock/Asset Library / (B) kzenon/123rf/Asset Library; Page 83 (A) Leah-Anne Thompson/Shutterstock/Asset Library / (B) CREATISTA/Shutterstock/Asset Library; Page 84 (A) Zurijeta/ Shutterstock/Asset Library / (B) Rawpixel.com/Shutterstock/Asset Library; Page 85 Pushnova / Shutterstock/Asset Library; Page 86 (A) Maridav/Shutterstock/ Asset Library / (B) Sean Pavone/Shutterstock/Asset Library / (C) Lefteris Papaulakis/123rf/Asset Library; Page 87 (A) Andrey_Kuzmin/Shutterstock/Asset Library / (B) Ruslan Suseynov/Shutterstock/Asset Library; Page 89 Christos Georghiou/Shutterstock/Asset Library; Page 91 TAROKICHI/Shutterstock/ Asset Library; Page 99 (A) Iryna Inshyna/Shutterstock/Shutterstock / (B) MANDY GODBEHEAR/Shutterstock/Shutterstock / (C) wanshutter/Shutterstock/ Shutterstock; Page 101SrideeStudio/Shutterstock/Shutterstock; Page 102 (A) Romolo Tavani/Shutterstock/Asset Library / (B) thebigland/Shutterstock/ Shutterstock; Page 103 (A) Monkey Business Images/Shutterstock/Shutterstock / (B) MIA Studio/Shutterstock/Shutterstock; Page 104 Destinytum/ Shutterstock/Shutterstock; Page 105 BERMIX STUDIO/Shutterstock/Shutterstock

MÔNICA FIÃES **BICALHO**

HASHTAG ENGLISH 2

STUDENT'S BOOK
and e-book

with **Online Practice**

Pearson

MISTO
Papel | Apoiando o manejo florestal responsável
FSC® C103535

Catalogue Publication Data

Hashtag English 2 Elementary Student's Book and e-book with Online Practice

Authors: Mônica Fiães Bicalho

Pearson Educación de México, S.A. de C.V., 2023

ISBN: 978-607-32-5682-7

Area: Schools

Format: 20,5 × 24,7 cm Page count: 168

Product Vice President: Marianne Lewis ■ **ELT Director:** Marjorie Robles ■ **Product Managers:** Anita Heald, Priscila Marconi ■ **Product Developers:** Renata S. C. Victor, Carolina Andrade ■ **Editor:** Elaine Mendonça ■ **Art and Design Coordinator:** Anderson Ferreira ■ **Art and Design Editors:** Andréia A. Santa Rosa, Patricia Santos, Luiz Rubio ■ **Layout:** MRS Editorial ■ **Cover & Interior Design:** Apis Design ■ **Cover Photo:** Shutterstock ■ **Digital Development Supervisor:** Isabel Silva ■ **Digital Content and Development Editors:** Rafaela de Mendonça, Fernanda Patucci, Lara Tasso, Mirella Armentano ■ **Digital Content Authors:** 2014 Solucões Editoriais, Ohana Editorial, Bella Szyszkowska ■ **Audiovisual Coordinator:** Lucas Domingues ■ **Audiovisual Editor:** Lucas Motta ■ **R&P Coordinator:** Maiti Salla ■ **R&P team:** Maricy Queiroz, Cristiane Gameiro ■ **Content Support:** 2014 Soluções Editoriais (Editors: Carla Maurício Coelho da Silva Vianna, Joyce Rocha Gomes, Juliana Maria Franco Tavares, Marcos Carvalho Mendonça, Rebeca Pasqua de Andrade. Assistants: Cristine Zanela Monte, Elani Souza Gomes, Juliana Aga, Pedro Zanela) ■ **Proofreading:** 2014 Soluções Editoriais, Silva Serviços de Educação ■ **Picture Credits:** Pearson Asset Library, Shutterstock, 123RF, Alamy Stock Photo

Contact: soporte@pearson.com

First published, 2023

ISBN PRINT BOOK: 978-607-32-5682-7

Printed in Brazil by Reproset RPSZ 221221

1 2 3 4 5 6 7 8 9 0 - 25 24 23 22

Avenida Antonio Dovalí Jaime #70
Torre B, Piso 6, Colonia Zedec Ed. Plaza Santa Fe
Delegación Álvaro Obregón, México, Ciudad de México, C. P. 01210

www.PearsonELT.com

Pearson

Pearson Hispanoamérica

Argentina ■ Belice ■ Bolivia ■ Chile ■ Colombia ■ Costa Rica ■ Cuba ■ República Dominicana ■ Ecuador ■ El Salvador ■ Guatemala ■ Honduras ■ México ■ Nicaragua ■ Panamá ■ Paraguay ■ Perú ■ Uruguay ■ Venezuela

STUDENT'S BOOK INDEX

#TABLE OF CONTENTS

UNIT		VIDEO	GRAMMAR	LISTENING	READING
U0	**Our School is Great** #4 Quality Education	About My School	*like / don't like / think* *Why* and *Because* Giving Directions	School Subjects	About Students from Other Countries and Different Schools
U1	**A Wonderful Time** #6 Clean Water and Sanitation	My Friends and How We Spend Our Time	Simple Present *Yes / No* questions and *Wh-questions* *How often* and Adverbs of Frequency	Someone Talking About His / Her Weekend Routine	About Teenagers Who Care About the Environment
U2	**Food for Thought** #2 Zero Hunger	Breakfast at Home	Countable and Uncountable Nouns Definite and Indefinite Articles	Someone Talking About His / Her Favorite Food	About Food Markets Around the World
U3	**Love What You Do** #5 Gender Equality	Career Day	Present Continuous Simple Present and Present Continuous Prepositions with Time Expressions	Talking About Jobs	About People's Jobs and Work
U4	**Better Together** #10 Reduced Inequalities	A Friendly, Tall Classmate	Comparatives Superlatives Comparatives and Superlatives	About What Clothes to Wear to Important Events	About Other People's Realities and Preferences
U5	**Why Is Education Powerful?** #4 Quality Education	The New Media Room	*Must / Mustn't* *Should / Shouldn't* Making Requests with *Can* and *Could* *Have to / Don't have to*	Talking About School Rules	About Different Educational Models
U6	**A Healthy Mind in a Healthy Body** #3 Good Health and Well-being	Last Night's Game	Simple Past: *Was / Were* Simple Past: Regular Verbs, Affirmative, Interrogative, and Negative Forms	Talking About a Sequence of Events in the Past	About Teenagers and Their Lucky Days
U7	**Passport to the World** #15 Life on Land	Traveling	Simple Past: Irregular Verbs Present Perfect for Personal Experiences	About Tourism and Transportations	About People's Trips Around the World
U8	**The World is Ours** #14 Life below Water	It's a Beautiful World	Future with *Will* Future with *Be Going to*	About Helping the Environment and Animals Underwater	About Nature

SPEAKING	WRITING	PRONUNCIATION	VOCABULARY	USE OF ENGLISH	PROJECT
Interviewing a Classmate About His / Her Favorite Subject	Writing an Instant Message to a Classmate	Sound /θ/	School Subjects Adjectives	Giving directions	Instant Messaging App Profile for the School
Talking About What You Do to Protect the Environment	Answering an E-mail About a Sustainability Project	Sounds /s/, /tʃ/, /k/	Free-time Activities Collocations with *Have*, *Go*, and *Play* Prepositions	Talking About Weekend Routines and Using Adverbs of Frequency	A Travel Brochure
Talking About Someone's Menu	Making a Menu	Sounds /i/ and /iː/	Food Items and Food Adjectives	Making Arrangements for a Meal with Your Classmates	A Slide Presentation
Explaining Picture Captions	Creating Picture Captions	Silent Letters	Jobs Prepositions Related to Work *Teach* and *Learn*	Talking About Your Dream Job	An Online Board
Presenting a Classmate's Blog Profile Post	Writing a Blog Profile Post	Stressed Syllables: Numbers	Adjectives of Appearance and Personality Adjective Order	Talking About Clothes and Comparing Them	A Blog Post
Asking About Rules for Schoolwork	Writing an E-mail Requesting Information	Sounds /ð/ and /θ/	Types of Schools Collocations with *Exam / Test*	Asking for and Giving Advice	An Online Poster
Interviewing a Classmate About His / Her Day Yesterday	Writing About an Event in the Past	Sounds /æ/, /aː/, /ei/, /ə/ and *ed*- Endings	Sports *Play a Sport* vs. *Practice a Sport* Collocations with *Go*, *Do*, and *Play*	Talking About Teenagers in the Past	A Graphic Organizer
Interviewing a Classmate About His / Her Last Vacation Trip	Writing an E-mail of Complaint	Sounds /oʊ/, /ɑː/, and /ɔː/	Vacation Activities Types of Accommodations	Talking About Sustainability in My City	A Travel Brochure
Interviewing a Classmate About Plans for the Future	Writing a Social Media Stories Sequence	Sounds /aʊ/, /aɪ/, and /ɔɪ/	Geographical Features Underwater Animals	Having a Conversation About Plans and Predictions for the Future	An Online Program

WELCOME TO HASHTAG ENGLISH!

Hashtag English is a six-level course for lower- and upper-secondary students. You are going to interact with technology to learn English through task-based learning activities, working with UNESCO's Sustainable Development Goals (SDG), Bloom's Taxonomy, and 21st century skills. *Hashtag English* aims at providing thought-provoking content that recognizes your ability to observe and make a difference to the world around you, while still retaining a light-hearted and fun approach that is age appropriate.

OPENER

Each unit starts with a picture to arouse your curiosity about the theme and to introduce the focus on the SDG.

In this unit you will learn how to:
This shows the learning outcomes of the unit.

Say what you know:
This activates your prior knowledge of the language goals of the unit.

UNESCO'S Sustainable Development Goal

DISCOVER

The first page of this double-page section is based on a video in which two characters discuss the unit topic and the language is introduced in context. The second page introduces the vocabulary of the unit.

VIDEO **AUDIO** **FLASHCARDS**

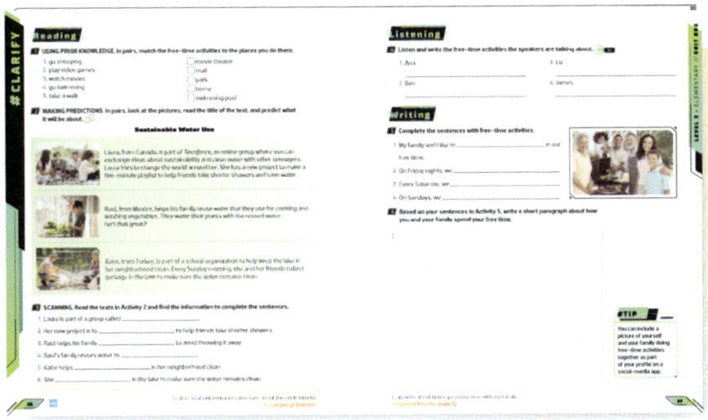

CLARIFY

This double-page section includes one or more texts that develop the SDG and work on a reading skill, a listening text, and a writing task on the topic of the text.

UNDERSTAND

This double-page section develops the grammar focus of the unit in an inductive manner. Grammar is presented in context and you are encouraged to work out the form for yourself.

EXAM PRACTICE

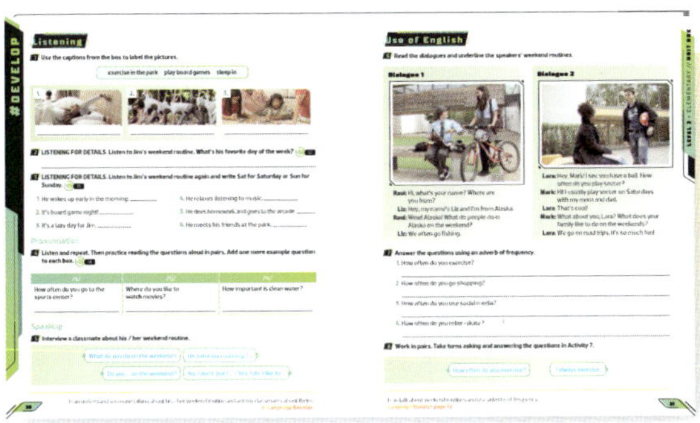

DEVELOP

The first page of this double-page section contains a listening text that develops a listening skill and sometimes a second vocabulary topic. The second page is where you develop speaking skills in natural, communicative contexts that use the grammar focus of the unit.

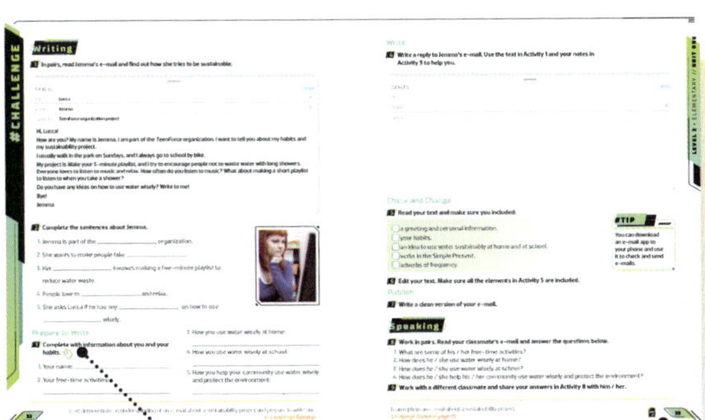

CHALLENGE

This double-page section develops your writing skills through a step-by-step writing task that puts into practice everything you have learned in the unit. The section culminates in a speaking task.

21ST CENTURY SKILL

EXAM PRACTICE

21ST CENTURY SKILL

UNESCO'S SUSTAINABLE DEVELOPMENT GOAL

CREATE

In this section, you work collaboratively on a project to identify, critically analyze, and present a problem or potential solution related to the SDG of the unit.

SELF-ASSESSMENT

This end-of-unit section presents a list of *can-do* statements related to the unit content that help you identify your progress and opportunities for improvement.

UNIT TEST

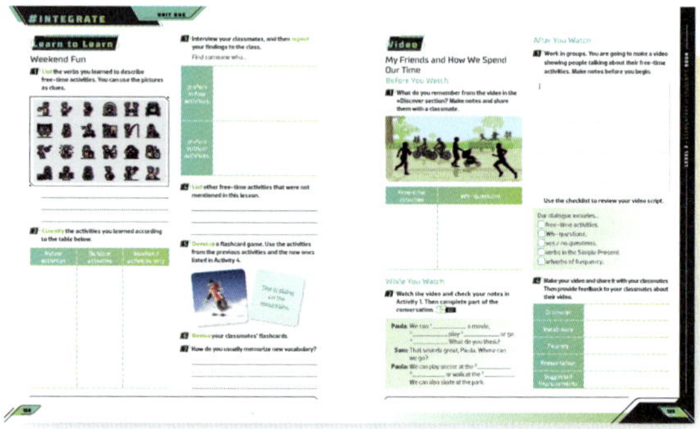

INTEGRATE

The first page of this section at the end of the book is called Learn to Learn. It aims at developing your learning skills using Bloom's Taxonomy. The second page contains new activities based on the video from the Discover section and proposes the recording of a new video to review the unit content.

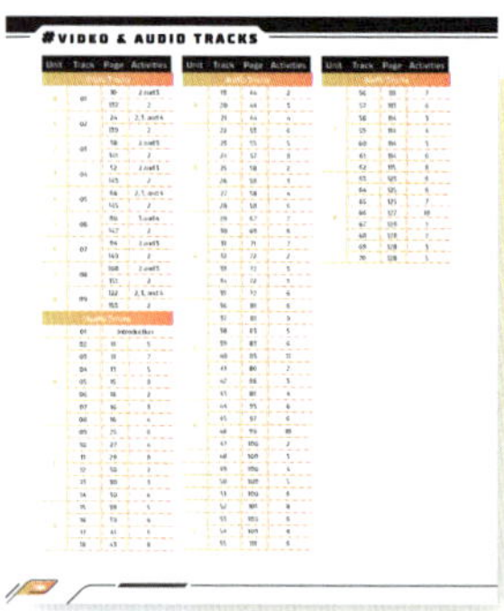

VIDEO & AUDIO TRACKS

This section at the end of the book lists the video and audio tracks from all the units.

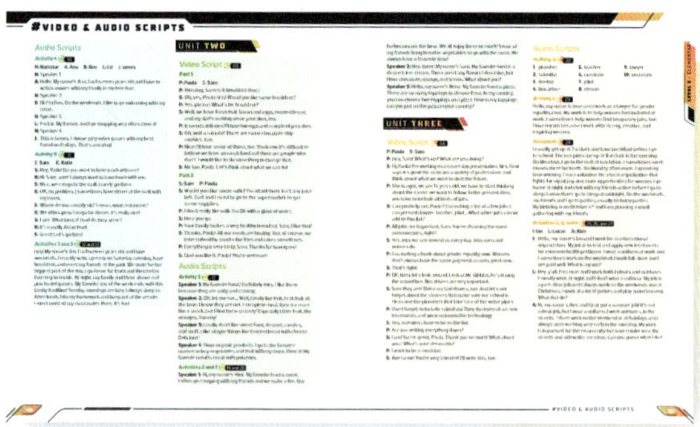

VIDEO & AUDIO SCRIPTS

This section at the end of the book contains the video and audio scripts from all the units.

OUR SCHOOL IS GREAT

In this unit, you will learn how to:

- Talk about school subjects you like and don't like.
- Write an instant message to a classmate.
- Create an instant messaging profile.

Say what you know:

- Reasons why you like or dislike something.
- One or two directions.
- Your favorite and least favorite school subjects.

#4 QUALITY EDUCATION

Video

About My School

Before You Watch

1 **Read the list below and check (✓) the school subjects.**

1. ☐ literature
2. ☐ science
3. ☐ artist
4. ☐ history
5. ☐ athlete

While You Watch

2 **Watch the video and check (✓) the correct sentences.** ▷ 01

1. ☐ Sam is curious about the science teacher.
2. ☐ Paula thinks science is fun.
3. ☐ Paula loves history.
4. ☐ Sam thinks science is hard.
5. ☐ Paula and Sam have to go to class.

3 **Watch the video again and mark the sentences T (True) or F (False).** ▷ 01

1. ☐ Sam and Paula are at school.
2. ☐ Paula knows the science teacher.
3. ☐ Paula likes history, too.
4. ☐ Sam thinks science is boring.
5. ☐ Paula invites Sam to go to the museum.

After You Watch

4 **Complete the dialogue with the words from the box. Then practice it with a classmate.**

fun	hi	interesting	science	subject	think

Paula: Hi, Sam! How are you?

Sam: [1] ______________, Paula! I'm good, and you?

Paula: I'm fine. I can't wait to find out who our [2] ______________ teacher is this year.
Sam: Why are you so curious about it?

Paula: Because I like science, I think it's [3] ______________.

Sam: I [4] ______________ science is hard, but I love history. It's my favorite [5] ______________.

Paula: History is [6] ______________, too. We can go to that Ancient Maya Exhibition.
Sam: Cool! Where is the exhibition?
Paula: Here! Just go straight on and turn left at the supermarket.
Sam: That's great! We can go after class. Let's go in...

I can demonstrate an understanding of a conversation between two classmates.

Vocabulary

School Subjects

5 **Listen and repeat. Then match the school subjects to their corresponding pictures.** 02

1. math
2. P.E.
3. science
4. history
5. literature
6. music
7. English
8. geography

a. 

b. 

c. 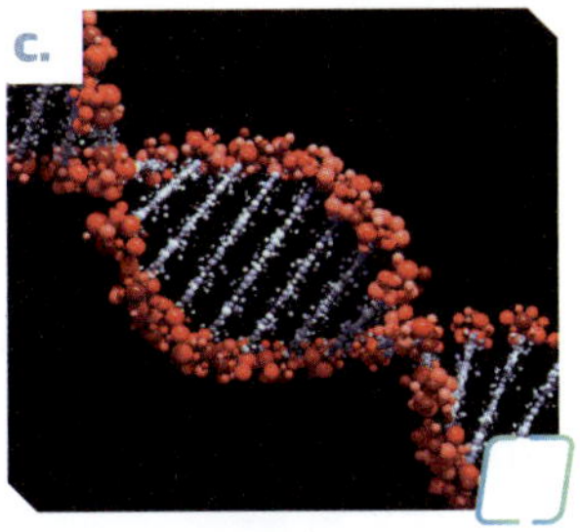

d. 

e. 

f. 

g. 

h. 

6 **Work in pairs to complete the sentences with school subjects.**

1. ______________ is all about numbers.
2. ______________ teaches us about countries.
3. In ______________ classes we learn how to play different sports.
4. ______________ is fascinating.
5. ______________ is my favorite subject.

Adjectives

7 **Listen and complete the sentences.** 03

Amy: Hello! What's your name?
Raúl: My name's Raúl. And yours?
Amy: My name's Amy. Is this the [1] ______________ class?
Raúl: I [2] ______________ so. Do you like history? I think it's [3] ______________.
Amy: I [4] ______________ history! But I don't like [5] ______________. It's very [6] ______________.
Raúl: You're right. Math and [7] ______________ are not [8] ______________.
Amy: What's your favorite subject, Raúl?
Raúl: My favorite subject is [9] ______________
Amy: Oh, really? I prefer [10] ______________!

8 **Read the dialogue in Activity 7 again and complete the sentences below with the words *easy*, *hard*, and *boring*.**

1. Raúl finds history ______________.
2. Math is ______________ for Amy.
3. Raúl says geography is not ______________.

9 **Work in pairs. Choose a school subject and describe it to your classmate. Can he / she guess the subject?**

This school subject is easy. We play instruments in this class.

I can talk about my favorite school subjects and ask my classmates about theirs.
Language Booster page 5

Reading

1 **USING PRIOR KNOWLEDGE. In pairs, look at the pictures and answer the questions.**

1. When do you go to school? ______________________________
2. What kind of school is the one in the picture? ______________________________

Time	Monday	Tuesday	Wednesday	Thursday	Friday
	literature	P.E.	P.E.	P.E.	P.E.
	science	English	English	English	English
	music	music	literature	literature	literature
	math	math	science	science	science
	history	history	history	music	music
	geography	geography	geography	math	math
				history	history
				geography	geography

2 **Read the title of the text and write down a question you would like to ask about this topic.**

What is quality education?

____

Quality Education

Hello, my name is Katie. I'm British, and I study in the U.K. My favorite subject is geography. It's so interesting! I take my pencil and my notebook and draw maps. The teacher plays a lot of videos in class. I like learning about other cities and countries.

Hi, my name is Lucy. I'm from the United States. I love my school. We use interactive boards with Internet, and our teachers are very kind. Students are the center of the classroom. We learn and create, we think and reflect. It's awesome!

Hey, there! I'm Sam. I live and study in Finland. Equality is the most important word in Finnish education. Teachers help us when it's necessary. We read a lot and love math. I think cooperation is more important than competition. I love my school!

3 **Read the texts in Activity 2 again and circle the best option to complete the sentences.**

1. Katie is **British** / **American**.
2. She likes **history** / **geography**.
3. Lucy's school has **a playground** / **interactive whiteboards**.
4. The most important word in education in Finland is **equality** / **testing**.
5. **Competition** / **Cooperation** is important in Sam's opinion.

4 **MAKING CONNECTIONS. Work in pairs. Think of two examples of quality education in your school and make notes.**

____

Listening

5 Listen and write the speakers' favorite subjects. 04

1. ______________________________
2. ______________________________
3. ______________________________
4. ______________________________
5. ______________________________

Writing

6 Complete with information about you.

My favorite subject is

______________________________.

I also like ______________________ and

______________________________.

______________________________ is very hard.

My school is special because

______________________________.

7 Write a short paragraph with the information in Activity 6.

____

____

____

____

____

____

____

____

#TIP

You can use this piece of information to introduce yourself to your classmates through you social media app. Include a picture of you studying your favorite subject!

I can write about my favorite school subject.

Language Booster page 6

Grammar

like / don't like / think

1 Check (✓) the sentences that are true. Then reread the texts on page 12 to check your answers.

1. ☐ Katie likes geography.
2. ☐ Katie doesn't like to draw places.
3. ☐ Lucy likes her school.
4. ☐ Sam doesn't like to study math.
5. ☐ Sam thinks cooperation is important.

2 Read the sentences in Activity 1 and circle the correct options to complete the statements below.

1. We can use the Simple Present to talk about **likes and dislikes / something happening now**.
2. We can also use the Simple Present to express **opinions / plans**.

3 Look at the pictures and complete the sentences with *like / don't like* in the correct form.

1.

They ____________ P.E.

2.

The boy ____________ music.

3.

She ____________ math.

Why and *Because*

4 Complete the sentences with why or because.

1. Katie doesn't like literature ____________ it's boring.
2. ____________ do you think music is fun?
3. Sam loves school ____________ it's a place to learn new things.
4. Lucy understands ____________ students are the center of the classroom.
5. ____________ do you find history interesting?
6. I like to study math ____________ I like numbers.
7. ____________ do they like history? It's so boring!

5 In pairs, read the sentences in Activity 4 again, compare them to the statements below, and check (✓) the correct ones.

1. ☐ We can use *why* to ask a question.
2. ☐ We can use *because* to talk about the reason why we do something.
3. ☐ In a question, after *why* we use an auxiliary verb (such as *do* and *be*) and a subject (*you*, *he*, etc.).
4. ☐ *Why* in the middle of the sentence is the same as *the reason why*.

6 In pairs, take turns practicing the dialogue.

I like history.

Why do you like history?

I like history because it's interesting.

I can talk about likes and dislikes, explain something, and ask why.

Giving Directions

7 **Match the sentences to the pictures.**

1. turn left
2. turn right
3. go straight on

a.  [ ]

b.  [ ]

c.  [ ]

8 **Circle the directions in the following sentences.**

1. At the traffic light, turn left.
2. When you see the school, go straight on.
3. Turn right after the hospital.

9 **Listen and complete the sentences.** 05

1. After the supermarket, ________________.
2. To get to the school, ________________ after the traffic lights.
3. ________________ and you will see the sports center.

10 **Look at the picture and complete the sentences with the directions from the box.**

go straight on turn left turn right

1. When you ________________ on Second Street, go past the supermarket and you will find the drugstore.
2. The drugstore is on Second Street when you ________________.
3. ________________ Fourth Street for the bakery.

11 **Work in pairs. Look at the picture in Activity 10 and practice giving directions to different places. You are number 1.**

How can I get to the bakery?

To get to the bakery, go straight on, and turn right on Fourth Street. It's next to the drugstore.

12 **Give directions to your classmates on how to get to your house from school.**

I can recognize and use directions.

Language Booster page 7

Listening

1 Label the pictures with the names of the school subjects they relate to.

geography music science

1.

____

2.

____

3.

____

2 LISTENING FOR DETAILS. Listen to Amy's interview for an exchange program. What's her favorite subject at school? 06

____

3 LISTENING FOR DETAILS. Work in pairs to complete the sentences about Amy. Then listen again and check. 07

1. Amy is going on an exchange program in ______________.
2. Amy ______________ to study.
3. She wants to study the ______________ in their natural habitats.
4. Amy doesn't like ______________ and ______________.
5. She thinks music is ______________.

Pronunciation

4 Listen and repeat. Then, in pairs, practice reading the sentences aloud. Add one more example sentence. 08

/θ/	I **th**ink music is fun.	Ma**th** is easy.

Speaking

5 Interview a classmate about his / her favorite subject. Ask him / her what he / she thinks about other subjects.

A: ______________________________

B: ______________________________

C: ______________________________

D: ______________________________

I can demonstrate an understanding of an interview about a student's favorite subjects.

e-Language Booster

Use of English

6 **Read the dialogues and underline the directions.**

1.

Tourist: Excuse me, can you help me? I want to go to the drugstore on Fifth Street.
Man: Oh, hello. Yes, sure, it's easy. Go straight on, and then turn left. The drugstore is next to the restaurant.

2.

Katie: Good morning! Can I ask you a question? Where is the National Bank?
Woman: Hmm... I think it's on Second Street. Turn right and you'll see it on the corner.

3.

Liz: Hi, my name's Liz. I'm new in this school. Can you tell me where the science lab is, please?
Ben: Hey! Nice to meet you, Liz! I'm Ben. Sure, let me walk with you. We'll turn right after the auditorium. The science lab is next to the school cafeteria.

7 **Look at the map and complete the dialogue. Use *turn right*, *go straight on*, and *turn left*.**

Jessy: Excuse me. How can I get to the mall?
Susan: Just [1] ____________________ and turn left. The mall is on your right.
Jessy: And how can I get to the park?
Susan: Oh, it's not far from the mall. Go straight on, but don't [2] ____________________ this time. [3] ____________________ and walk half a block. The park is on your left.
Jessy: Cool! Thanks.

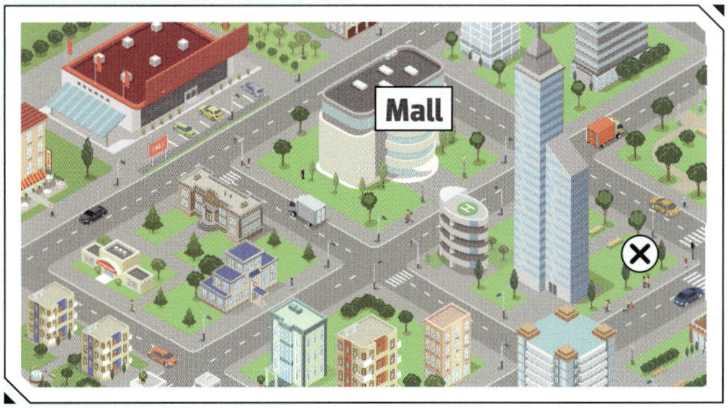

8 **Work in pairs. Practice the dialogue in Activity 7 choosing other places.**

I can practice giving directions.
Language Booster page 8

Writing

1 **Work in pairs. Read Bela's text and identify the genre. Circle the right answer below.**

1. e-mail
2. instant message
3. letter

Liz

Today

Hey, Liz! How are you? I'm at school, where are you?

Everything OK? Why aren't you in history class today?

Next class is science, and I need your help because I think science is hard. You know I don't really like it. My favorite subject is math, remember?

Are you coming? Don't forget to turn right at the entrance hall because our class is in the lab today!

What about our music class? Don't miss the fun!

2 **Answer the questions about Bela's text.**

1. Where is Bela? ______________________
2. What subject is she studying now?
____
3. What's her next class? ______________________
4. Who is she texting? ______________________
5. Why is she texting her? ______________________
____

Prepare to Write

3 **Look at the school subjects in your schedule for today, write a sentence for each using *like / don't like*, and explain why.**

geography	history	math
music	P.E.	

____
____
____
____
____
____
____
____
____
____
____
____
____
____

I can understand an instant message and prepare to write one.

Write

4 **Based on the instant message in Activity 1, write a similar one to a classmate.**

____

____

____

____

Check and Change

5 **Read your instant message and make sure you included:**

- [ ] school subjects.
- [ ] adjectives to describe school subjects.
- [ ] *like / don't like.*
- [ ] *why* and *because.*
- [ ] directions.

6 **Edit your message. Make sure all the elements in Activity 5 are included.**

Publish

7 **Write a clean version of your instant message.**

#TIP

You can create a free instant message account using your cell phone number.

Speaking

8 **Read your classmate's instant message and complete the sentences with information about him / her.**

1. His / Her favorite subject is ______________________.
2. He thinks ______________________ is ______________________.
3. He / She doesn't like ______________________ because ____.
4. He / She likes ______________________.

9 **Work in groups. Choose a classmate's message and present it to the group.**

Ben's favorite subject is..., but he doesn't like... because it's...

I can write an instant message to a classmate.

Language Booster page 9

Project: Instant Messaging App Profile for the School

#DIGITAL LITERACY

1. Choose a profile picture that shows the best part of your school.
2. Write a clear, short profile description.

Step 1 Think

1 Work in groups.

1. Discuss: How important is school for you?
2. Read the text: Is your school similar?

Strömberg school is one of the most modern and innovative schools, offering classes in subjects such as math, languages, and art, and workshops for music, drama, and environmental education, among others. Our school is located in Helsinki, Finland, and it also has a gym and a library. Find out more about Strömberg school.

Step 2 Plan

2 In groups, complete the sentences about your school.

The best profile picture for the school account is

______________________________.

The profile should include ______________________________

because ______________________________.

Step 3 Research

3 Research other school accounts on instant messaging apps. Compare and make notes.

____

____

____

____

Step 4 Design

4 In groups, create your school's instant messaging profile.

- Check the picture.
- Check the text.
- Check the spelling.

#TIP STEP 4
Choose a template that resembles instant messaging apps you are familiar with.

STEP 5 Present and Publish

5 In groups, present your instant messaging profile to the class.

#TIP STEP 5
Explain the choice of photo and information.

STEP 6 Evaluate

6 Complete the evaluation table.

★☆☆ More to learn ★★☆ Good ★★★ Excellent

Criteria	My Evaluation	Group Evaluation	Teacher Evaluation
Teamwork	★★★	★★★	★★★
Language	★★★	★★★	★★★
Design	★★★	★★★	★★★

I can create an instant messaging app profile for my school and present it to the class.

#SELF-ASSESSMENT

1 Mark the learning objectives according to the key.

★☆☆ I don't understand.	★★☆ I understand, but I need help.	★★★ I can do it!

Learning Objectives	Rating
To demonstrate an understanding of a conversation between two classmates.	☆☆☆
To talk about my favorite school subjects and ask my classmates about theirs.	☆☆☆
To read about students from other countries and different schools.	☆☆☆
To write about my favorite subject.	☆☆☆
To talk about likes and dislikes, explain something, and ask why.	☆☆☆
To recognize and use directions.	☆☆☆
To demonstrate an understanding of an interview about a student's favorite subjects and ask my classmates about theirs.	☆☆☆
To practice giving directions.	☆☆☆
To understand an instant message and prepare to write one.	☆☆☆
To write an instant message to a classmate.	☆☆☆
To plan an instant messaging app profile for my school.	☆☆☆
To create an instant messaging app profile for my school and present it to the class.	☆☆☆

2 Work in pairs. Discuss the questions.

1. What did I find most interesting to learn? Why?
2. How did I learn it?
3. How can I use it in real life?

UT Language Booster page 10

UNIT ONE 1

A WONDERFUL TIME

#6 CLEAN WATER AND SANITATION

In this unit, you will learn how to:

- Talk about your weekend routines and free-time activities.
- Write an e-mail.
- Create an online brochure.

Say what you know:

- Weekend routine activities.
- Free-time activities.
- Actions for sustainable water use.

#DISCOVER

Video

My Friends and How We Spend Our Time

Before You Watch

1 **In pairs, make a list of things you like to do in your free time.**

While You Watch

2 **Watch the video and circle YES or NO.** ▷ 02

1. Paula calls Sam. YES NO
2. They plan to hang out on Saturday. YES NO
3. Paula and Sam are brother and sister. YES NO

3 **Watch the video a second time and check (✓) the activities they mention.** ▷ 02

1. ☐ go shopping
2. ☐ go swimming
3. ☐ play soccer
4. ☐ go roller skating
5. ☐ do gymnastics
6. ☐ go for a walk
7. ☐ play basketball
8. ☐ have dinner
9. ☐ have lunch
10. ☐ watch a movie

4 **Watch the video again and mark the sentences T (True) or (F) False.** ▷ 02

1. ☐ Paula invites Sam to go out.
2. ☐ Paula suggests they play soccer or take a walk in the park.
3. ☐ Sam doesn't want to go out with Paula.
4. ☐ Paula wants to go swimming.
5. ☐ Sam goes to the new restaurant at the mall very often.

After You Watch

5 **Complete the sentences about you and your friends. Use words / expressions from the video and from Activities 3 and 4.**

1. I always go ______________.
2. We ______________ go swimming.
3. My friends and I ______________ play soccer.
4. We ______________ play video games.
5. I ______________ movies on Saturday nights.

I can demonstrate an understanding of a conversation about free-time activities.

e-Language Booster

Vocabulary

Free-time Activities

6 **Listen and repeat.** 09

1. 
do community service

2. 
do gymnastics

3. 
go shopping

4. 
go swimming

5. 
play video games

6. 
take a walk

7. 
use social media

8. 
watch a movie

7 **Work in pairs. Complete the sentences with free-time activities.**

1. We always ____________ in the swimming pool.
2. The boys ____________ at Sam's house.
3. Nina and her friends sometimes ____________ in the park.
4. My mom ____________ at the mall on Mondays.
5. Dad and I often ____________ at the movie theater on Fridays.

Collocations with *Have*, *Go*, and *Play*

8 **Complete the sentences with *have*, *go*, or *play*.**

1. We usually ____________ dinner at nine o'clock.
2. They don't like to ____________ video games on weeknights.
3. Sara and Lila ____________ shopping every month.
4. Sam and his friends ____________ breakfast at school every morning.
5. My friends and I ____________ swimming in the lake every day in the summer.
6. Do you ____________ basketball at the sports center?

Prepositions

9 **Circle the correct preposition to complete the sentences.**

1. We go swimming **in** / **on** the lake.
2. Sam takes a walk in the park **in** / **on** Luthor Avenue on the weekends.
3. There's a new restaurant **on** / **at** the mall.
4. Sam and Paula don't have breakfast **at** / **to** school every day.
5. I want to swim **on** / **in** the swimming pool.

10 **Work in groups. Make a list of the activities you do in your free time and write where you do them.**

I have lunch at a restaurant on Sundays.

I can talk about free-time activities.

Language Booster page 11

Reading

1 USING PRIOR KNOWLEDGE. In pairs, match the free-time activities to the places you do them.

1. go shopping
2. play video games
3. watch movies
4. go swimming
5. take a walk

- ☐ movie theater
- ☐ mall
- ☐ park
- ☐ home
- ☐ swimming pool

2 MAKING PREDICTIONS. In pairs, look at the pictures, read the title of the text, and predict what it will be about.

Sustainable Water Use

Laura, from Canada, is part of *Teenforce*, an online group where you can exchange ideas about sustainability and clean water with other teenagers. Laura tries to change the world around her. She has a new project to make a five-minute playlist to help friends take shorter showers and save water.

Raul, from Mexico, helps his family reuse water that they use for cooking and washing vegetables. They water their plants with the reused water. Isn't that great?

Katie, from Turkey, is part of a school organization to help keep the lake in her neighborhood clean. Every Sunday morning, she and her friends collect garbage in the lake to make sure the water remains clean.

3 SCANNING. Read the texts in Activity 2 and find the information to complete the sentences.

1. Laura is part of a group called ______________________.
2. Her new project is to ______________________ to help friends take shorter showers.
3. Raul helps his family ______________________ to avoid throwing it away.
4. Raul's family reuses water to ______________________.
5. Katie helps ______________________ in her neighborhood clean.
6. She ______________________ in the lake to make sure the water remains clean.

I can read about teenagers who care about the environment.

e-Language Booster

Listening

4 Listen and write the free-time activities the speakers are talking about. 10

1. Ana ______________________
2. Ben ______________________
3. Liz ______________________
4. James ______________________

Writing

5 Complete the sentences with free-time activities.

1. My family and I like to ______________________ in our free time.
2. On Friday nights, we ______________________.
3. Every Saturday, we ______________________.
4. On Sundays, we ______________________.

6 Based on your sentences in Activity 5, write a short paragraph about how you and your family spend your free time.

#TIP

You can include a picture of yourself and your family doing free-time activities together as part of your profile on a social-media app.

I can write about how I spend my time with my family.

Language Booster page 12

#UNDERSTAND

Grammar

Simple Present

1 **Read the sentences, pay attention to the parts in bold, and check (✓) the correct statements about the Simple Present.**

- **Does** Katie **collect** garbage? Yes, she **does**. She **collects** garbage in the lake.
- Where **do** Katie and her friends **collect** garbage? They **collect** garbage in the lake.
- Laura **has** a new project. She **tries** to change the world around her.
- Raul **doesn't like** to waste water.

1. ☐ We use *do* and *does* to form questions in the Simple Present.
2. ☐ We use *does* and *doesn't* with *he*, *she*, and *it*.
3. ☐ We use *does* and *doesn't* with plural nouns.
4. ☐ With *he*, *she*, and *it*, we add *-s* or *-es* to the main verb in the affirmative form.
5. ☐ We use *has* with *he*, *she*, and *it* in the affirmative form.
6. ☐ We use the Simple Present to talk about habits and routines.

2 **Complete the sentences with the verbs in parentheses in the Simple Present.**

1. They __________ to play with us. (not want)
2. Mom and dad really __________ to take a walk. (like)
3. Liz __________ the balls from the soccer field after practice. (collect)
4. Sam __________ movies a lot. He __________ to play video games. (not watch, prefer)
5. You __________ swimming every day, right? (not go)

Yes / No Questions and *Wh-* questions

3 **Underline the correct option to complete the questions.**

1. **Where** / **What** do you like to go on the weekends?
2. **Which** / **What time** does your friend watch movies?
3. **When** / **Does** your teacher go shopping on Fridays?
4. **Why** / **Whose** do your classmates like video games?
5. **What** / **Do** you have breakfast at home?

4 **Now read the sentences in Activity 3 again and complete the statements below with Yes / No questions or Wh- *questions*.**

1. In __________, we use question words (e.g. who, what, where, when) to get specific information.
2. In __________, we expect either a positive (Yes) or a negative (No) answer.

5 **Answer the Yes / No questions below.**

1. Do Mary and Liz want to go out for lunch?
   Yes, __________.
2. Does the sports center open on Saturday?
   No, __________.
3. Does Raul go to the movies very often?
   Yes, __________.
4. Do you and your friends reuse cooking water?
   ____
5. Do you take long showers?
   ____

6 **In pairs, ask and answer the questions in Activity 3.**

Where do you like to go on the weekends?

I like to go to the park.

I can talk about habits and routines.

How often and Adverbs of Frequency

7 **Match the sentences to the pictures.**

1. They usually take a walk in the morning.
2. He sometimes reads at breakfast.
3. They always watch a movie on Saturday night.

a.

b.

c.

8 **How often do you do the free-time activities in the chart? Check (✓) the right adverb.**

	always	usually	often	sometimes	rarely	never
go shopping						
play video games						
take a walk						
play soccer						
watch a movie						

9 **Listen to Sam talk to a friend and mark the sentences T (True) or F (False).** 11

1. ☐ Katie never wants to have lunch with Sam.
2. ☐ Sam never goes to the mall.
3. ☐ Katie always has dinner with her mom at the mall.
4. ☐ Katie and her mom often go to Kaboo.
5. ☐ Congo usually serves Asian food.

10 **Rewrite the false statements in Activity 9 making them true.**

____

____

____

____

____

11 **Work in pairs. Ask questions with *How often ...?* and answer them using adverbs of frequency. Record your conversation and save a copy.**

How often do you go to the mall?

I never go to the mall.

I can use *how often* and adverbs of frequency to talk about free-time activities.

Language Booster page 13

Listening

1 **Use the captions from the box to label the pictures.**

exercise in the park	play board games	sleep in

1. 
____

2. 
____

3. 
____

2 **LISTENING FOR DETAILS. Listen to Jim's weekend routine. What's his favorite day of the week?** 12

____

3 **LISTENING FOR DETAILS. Listen to Jim's weekend routine again and write *Sat* for Saturday or *Sun* for Sunday.** 13

1. He wakes up early in the morning. __________
2. It's board game night! __________
3. It's a lazy day for Jim. __________
4. He relaxes listening to music. __________
5. He does homework and goes to the arcade. __________
6. He meets his friends at the park. __________

Pronunciation

4 **Listen and repeat. Then practice reading the questions aloud in pairs. Add one more example question to each box.** 14

/s/	/tʃ/	/k/
How often do you go to the **s**port**s** **c**enter?	Where do you like to wat**ch** movies?	How important is **c**lean water?
_______________	_______________	_______________

Speaking

5 **Interview a classmate about his / her weekend routine.**

What do you do on the weekend?

On Saturday morning, I ...

Do you ... on the weekend?

No, I don't, but I ... / Yes, I do. I like to ...

I can understand someone talking about his / her weekend routine and ask my classmates about theirs.

Use of English

6 **Read the dialogues and underline the speakers' weekend routines.**

Dialogue 1

Raul: Hi, what's your name? Where are you from?

Liz: Hey, my name's Liz and I'm from Alaska.

Raul: Wow! Alaska! What do people do in Alaska on the weekend?

Liz: We often go fishing.

Dialogue 2

Lara: Hey, Mark! I see you have a ball. How often do you play soccer?

Mark: Hi! I usually play soccer on Saturdays with my mom and dad.

Lara: That's cool!

Mark: What about you, Lara? What does your family like to do on the weekends?

Lara: We go on road trips. It's so much fun!

7 **Answer the questions using an adverb of frequency.**

1. How often do you exercise?

   ____

2. How often do you go shopping?

   ____

3. How often do you use social media?

   ____

4. How often do you roller-skate?

   ____

8 **Work in pairs. Take turns asking and answering the questions in Activity 7.**

How often do you exercise?

I always exercise.

I can talk about weekend routines and use adverbs of frequency.

Language Booster page 14

#CHALLENGE

Writing

1 **In pairs, read Jemma's e-mail and find out how she tries to be sustainable.**

CANCEL SEND

TO Lucca

FROM Jemma

SUBJECT TeenForce organization project

Hi, Lucca!

How are you? My name is Jemma. I am part of the *TeenForce* organization. I want to tell you about my habits and my sustainability project.

I usually walk in the park on Sundays, and I always go to school by bike.

My project is *Make your 5-minute playlist*, and I try to encourage people not to waste water with long showers. Everyone loves to listen to music and relax. How often do you listen to music? What about making a short playlist to listen to when you take a shower?

Do you have any ideas on how to use water wisely? Write to me!

Bye!

Jemma

2 **Complete the sentences about Jemma.**

1. Jemma is part of the ____________ organization.
2. She wants to make people take ____________.
3. Her ____________ involves making a five-minute playlist to reduce water waste.
4. People love to ____________ and relax.
5. She asks Lucca if he has any ____________ on how to use ____________ wisely.

Prepare to Write

3 **Complete with information about you and your habits.**

1. Your name: ____________
2. Your free-time activities: ____________
3. How you use water wisely at home: ____________
4. How you use water wisely at school: ____________
5. How you help your community use water wisely and protect the environment: ____________

I can demonstrate an understanding of an e-mail about a sustainability project and prepare to write one.

Write

4 **Write a reply to Jemma's e-mail. Use the text in Activity 1 and your notes in Activity 3 to help you.**

CANCEL SEND

TO

FROM

SUBJECT

Check and Change

5 **Read your text and make sure you included:**

- ☐ a greeting and personal information.
- ☐ your habits.
- ☐ an idea to use water sustainably at home and at school.
- ☐ verbs in the Simple Present.
- ☐ adverbs of frequency.

#TIP

You can download an e-mail app to your phone and use it to check and send e-mails.

6 **Edit your text. Make sure all the elements in Activity 5 are included.**

Publish

7 **Write a clean version of your e-mail.**

Speaking

8 **Work in pairs. Read your classmate's e-mail and answer the questions below.**

1. What are some of his / her free-time activities?
2. How does he / she use water wisely at home?
3. How does he / she use water wisely at school?
4. How does he / she help his / her community use water wisely and protect the environment?

9 **Work with a different classmate and share your answers in Activity 8 with him / her.**

I can reply to an e-mail about a sustainability project.

Language Booster page 15

Project: A Travel Brochure

#DIGITAL LITERACY

1. Include an attractive heading.
2. Be clear and brief.
3. Add images to illustrate the destination.

Step 1 Think

1 Work in groups.

1. Discuss: Are free-time activities the same in every country?
2. Read the travel brochure below. Is your country similar?

Welcome to Hong Kong!

Check out our most popular weekend activities. In Hong Kong, we like to be outdoors. We spend part of our weekend at parks. We go for walks and play board games in our green areas. Weekend activities also include calligraphy classes, kite-flying, and table tennis. Sounds interesting? Book a trip now!

Step 2 Plan

2 In groups, choose an interesting travel destination and add ideas about what you can do there on the weekend.

I can recognize the features of a travel brochure and plan to create one.

Step 3 Research

3 In groups, research what people do in their free time in the travel destination you have chosen. Choose some images to add. Make notes.

____

____

____

Step 4 Design

4 In groups, create your travel brochure.

- Check the text.
- Check the images.
- Check the organization.

#TIP STEP 4

Focus on free-time activities that are not common in your country. Choose images that represent them.

Step 5 Present and Publish

5 In groups, show your travel brochure to the class and publish it.

#TIP STEP 5

Explain the free-time activities and show any accessories that are necessary.

Step 6 Evaluate

6 Complete the evaluation table.

★☆☆ More to learn ★★☆ Good ★★★ Excellent

Criteria	My Evaluation	Group Evaluation	Teacher Evaluation
Teamwork	☆☆☆	☆☆☆	☆☆☆
Language	☆☆☆	☆☆☆	☆☆☆
Design	☆☆☆	☆☆☆	☆☆☆

I can create a travel brochure and present it to the class.

#SELF-ASSESSMENT

1 **Mark the learning objectives according to the key.**

★☆☆ I don't understand.	★★☆ I understand, but I need help.	★★★ I can do it!

Learning Objectives	Rating
To demonstrate an understanding of a conversation about free-time activities.	☆☆☆
To talk about free-time activities.	☆☆☆
To read about teenagers who care about the environment.	☆☆☆
To write about how I spend my time with my family.	☆☆☆
To talk about habits and routines.	☆☆☆
To use *how often* and adverbs of frequency to talk about free-time activities.	☆☆☆
To understand someone talking about his / her weekend routine and ask my classmates about theirs.	☆☆☆
To talk about weekend routines and use adverbs of frequency.	☆☆☆
To understand an e-mail about a sustainability project and prepare to write one.	☆☆☆
To answer an e-mail about a sustainability project.	☆☆☆
To recognize the features of a travel brochure and plan to create one.	☆☆☆
To create a travel brochure and present it to the class.	☆☆☆

2 **Work in pairs. Discuss the questions.**

1. What did I find most interesting to learn? Why?
2. How did I learn it?
3. How can I use it in real life?

UT Language Booster page 20

FOOD FOR THOUGHT

#2 ZERO HUNGER

In this unit, you will learn how to:

- Talk about food.
- Write about the food you like and don't like.
- Create a menu.

Say what you know:

- Your favorite food.
- Food adjectives.
- Food markets and festivals.

#DISCOVER

Video

Breakfast at Home

Before You Watch

1 **In pairs, check (✓) the food items.**

1. ☐ tomato
2. ☐ spoon
3. ☐ bacon
4. ☐ plate
5. ☐ frying pan
6. ☐ pancake

While You Watch

2 **Watch Part 1 of the video and complete the script with the words from the box.** 03

breakfast	cookies	delicious
pancakes	What's for	

Paula: Morning, Sam! Is it [1] ________________ time?

Sam: Oh, yes, Paula! It is! Would you like some breakfast?

Paula: Yes, please. [2] ________________ breakfast?

Sam: Well, we have bacon and eggs, toasted bread, and my dad's making some [3] ________________.

Paula: It sounds [4] ________________! I'll have two eggs and a couple of pancakes.

Sam: Oh, wait a minute! There are some chocolate chip [5] ________________, too.

Paula: Nice! I'll have some of those, too. You know, it's difficult to believe we have so much food and there are people who don't. I would like to do something to change that.

Sam: Me too, Paula. Let's think about what we can do!

3 **Now watch Part 2 of the video and answer the following questions.** 03

1. Is there any juice?

____

2. Does Paula like milk?

____

3. Who needs to go to the supermarket?

____

4. What is Paula having to drink?

____

5. Does Sam's family have a healthy diet?

____

6. How often does Sam have unhealthy snacks?

____

After You Watch

4 **Complete the sentences about you and your family.**

1. My family **always** / **never** / **often** has breakfast at home.
2. I like to have ________________ for breakfast.
3. I don't like ________________ because ________________.
4. I think ________________ is delicious.
5. I **sometimes** / **always** / **never** have unhealthy snacks.

I can demonstrate an understanding of a conversation about breakfast.

e-Language Booster

Vocabulary

Food Items and Food Adjectives

5 Listen and repeat. 15

eggs

bread

cake

meat

cheese

carrots

beans

rice

6 **Listen and complete the texts below with the words from the box.** 16

> beans bread cake carrots cheese
> coffee fish fruit omelet pie
> potatoes soup sugar vegetables

Dimitri, 14 years old, Russia

Breakfast: I have some cereal, and 1 ____________ and butter. I always have some tea or 2 ____________ in the morning.

Lunch: I usually have lunch at school. The school canteen doesn't offer many options. There's always 3 ____________, meat, and potatoes. On Fridays they serve fries, too!

Dinner: I have dinner with my family around 8:00 p.m. We watch TV during dinner to see the news. We eat 4 ____________ or red meat and 5 ____________. After dinner we drink tea with 6 ____________ or jam.

Nena, 15 years old, Greece

Breakfast: I usually have 7 ____________ for breakfast. Salty pies are the best, they can have cheese or meat in them.

Lunch: I have a bowl of 8 ____________ with meat and bread. There's always some salad, too. Greek food is very tasty! I have a piece of bitter chocolate for dessert!

Dinner: Dinner is almost always light. A spicy 9 ____________ for a healthy and balanced diet.

Vini, 14 years old, Brazil

Breakfast: I have a cup of coffee with milk and eat some 10 ____________. I know it's kind of unhealthy, but I try to make up for it with the other meals of the day.

Lunch: Lunch is my favorite meal! My mom makes rice, 11 ____________, meat, and different kinds of vegetables like 12 ____________, broccoli, and beets. We always have dessert on Sundays.

Dinner: First, I have bread, 13 ____________, and ham. Sometimes I have a snack before I go to sleep, usually some 14 ____________.

7 **Work in pairs. Copy the chart in your notebook and complete it with the words from the box. Then add a new word to each category.**

> beans cake cheese chocolate
> coffee sugar fries lemon meat rice

Bitter	Sweet	Savory

8 **Work in groups. Talk about what you often have for breakfast, lunch, and dinner.**

I often have bread and butter and a cup of milk for breakfast. Sometimes I have pie, too.

I can talk about food and how it tastes.

Language Booster page 17

#CLARIFY

Reading

1 USING PRIOR KNOWLEDGE. Check (✓) the places where we can buy food.

1. ◯ supermarket
2. ◯ bank
3. ◯ farmers' market
4. ◯ grocery store
5. ◯ post office
6. ◯ fire station

2 MAKING PREDICTIONS. In pairs, read the title of the text, look at the pictures, and predict which markets the text is about.

Food Markets Around the World

Food markets are helping end hunger around the world by donating the products they don't sell. They are also becoming zero food waste markets with compostable or recyclable packaging for their products.

Ferry Plaza

The Ferry Plaza Farmers Market in San Francisco, U.S.A., is a very famous farmers' market and open three days a week: Tuesdays, Thursdays, and Saturdays. The Ferry Plaza sells local organic products produced sustainably. We find fresh fruit, jam, artisan chocolate, and warm bread there, among other things.

Mercado Central

The Central Market of Santiago, Chile, is for fish lovers. It's an amazing fish market where you can find everything for a perfect dish with fish. Don't buy your fish in a can, buy it fresh!

Grand Bazaar

The Grand Bazaar, in Istanbul, Turkey, has over 5,000 stores selling jewelry, lamps, slippers, spices, and sweets. There you can have Turkish delight (lokum). It is a sweet treat and has different flavors such as rosewater, pistachio, and orange. New flavors include chocolate and coffee.

3 SCANNING. Read the text in Activity 2 and mark the sentences T (True) or F (False).

1. ◯ Farmers' markets are becoming sustainable.
2. ◯ You can buy bread and jam at the Ferry Plaza.
3. ◯ There isn't fresh fish at the Central Market of Santiago.
4. ◯ Mercado Central is a farmers' market.
5. ◯ Lokum is a typical sweet candy from Turkey.

4 In pairs, match the markets to the products they sell.

1. Ferry Plaza Market
2. Grand Bazaar
3. Mercado Central

◯ fresh fish
◯ fruit, bread, chocolate
◯ jewelry, lamps

I can read about food markets around the world.

Listening

5 **Listen and write Speaker 1, 2, 3, or 4 next to each sentence.** 17

1. He likes simple things, like bread and cheese.
______
2. Her favorite food is fries.
______
3. She really likes fruit.
______
4. She loves to go to the farmers' market.
______

Writing

6 **Complete with information about you.**

1. I ______ to the farmers' market.
2. My favorite food is ______.
3. I don't like to eat ______.
4. I try to reduce my food waste by ______ ______.

7 **Write a short paragraph about the food you like and don't like to eat. Use the texts on the previous pages and the information in Activity 6.**

#TIP

You can look online to see if there's a farmers' market in your neighborhood and find out what they do with the products they don't sell.

I can write a paragraph about the food I like and don't like.
Language Booster page 18

Grammar

Countable and Uncountable Nouns

1 **Work in pairs. Read the conversation and decide if the underlined words are countable or uncountable. Then complete the chart.**

Lia: Bill, we really need to get some supplies from the supermarket.
Bill: OK! Let's make a list!
Lia: There are only two eggs, so we need to buy some. I'm making an omelet tonight. There aren't any tomatoes, let's get three! And an onion, too.
Bill: That's right. What else do we need? Is there any milk in the refrigerator?
Lia: Yes, there is. But we need something for dessert, of course.
Bill: How about some chocolate? Oh, that reminds me, how much sugar do we have? I think we need sugar to make the lemon juice.
Lia: That's true!

Countable	Uncountable

2 **Use the information in Activity 1 to complete the statements below.**

1. Nouns that I can count and have plural forms are ________________ nouns.
2. Liquids are ________________ nouns.
3. We use ________________ nouns with singular verbs and they usually don't have a plural form.

3 **Look at the food items in the picture and use the words from the box to complete the sentences.**

apples	bananas	carrots	cheese
eggs	meat	milk	oranges
pears	soda	tomatoes	water

1. I can count ____
____.
2. I can't count ____
____.

4 **In pairs, role play the conversation in Activity 1 replacing the underlined nouns for other countable and uncountable nouns.**

I can identify countable and uncountable nouns.

e-Language Booster

Denifite and Indefinite Articles

5 Match the sentences to the pictures.

1. I use **the** lemons to make juice.
2. I want **a** tomato, please.
3. He often has **an** omelet for dinner.
4. Can you get **the** milk from the refrigerator, please?

a. b. c. d.

6 Read the sentences in Activity 5 and pay attention to the words in bold. Then check (✓) the correct statements below.

1. ☐ We use the definite article (*the*) to indicate that we don't know the identity of the noun.
2. ☐ We use indefinite articles (*a*, *an*) to indicate that a noun is general or when we don't know its identity.
3. ☐ We use the indefinite article *an* before a vowel sound.
4. ☐ We use the indefinite article *a* after a consonant sound.
5. ☐ We use the definite article before a singular or a plural noun.
6. ☐ We don't use indefinite articles before plural nouns.
7. ☐ We use indefinite articles before uncountable nouns.

7 Circle the articles in the following sentences.

1. The sun shines in Florida every day.
2. Don't you have a classmate to help you with homework?
3. Can you buy a carton of milk, please?
4. What about some eggs? The omelet I make is fantastic!
5. Let's have an ice cream festival to celebrate the beginning of summer.
6. My favorite snack is the cereal bar from the organic supermarket.

8 Listen and complete the sentences. 18

1. ________ ice cream parlor is on Sixth Street. You can't miss it!
2. Good morning, I'd like to order ________ hamburger, please.
3. Sam, where's ________ chocolate? I need it to make a cake!
4. ________ cake is delicious! Well done, Lara!
5. My dad goes to ________ farmers' market every Saturday. He gets some vegetables for our lunch.
6. Raul meets ______ different friend at ______ mall every Sunday. Isn't that awesome?

9 Complete the sentences with a, an, or the.

1. All ________ omelets in this menu have vegetables.
2. ________ farmers' market is a place to buy fresh fruit and vegetables.
3. This stand donates all ________ products they don't sell to communities in ________ neighborhood.
4. Sam really likes sweets. Give him ________ rice pudding and he's over ________ moon.
5. In the farmers' market downtown, it's easy to find ________ salad you are talking about.

10 Work in pairs. Ask and answer questions about your readings and discussions in this unit using definite and indefinite articles.

*Do you think **a** healthy diet is important?*

*Yes, I do. **The** food we eat is very important.*

*What is **the** best food for you?*

*I love vegetables. **The** vegetables my grandma makes are awesome.*

I can use definite and indefinite articles in my conversations.

Language Booster page 19

#DEVELOP

Listening

1 Use the words from the box to label the pictures.

ice cream	meat	pizza

1.  ____________

2.  ____________

3.  ____________

2 LISTENING FOR GIST. Listen and match the speakers to the pictures. 19

1.  Speaker ________

2.  Speaker ________

3.  Speaker ________

3 LISTENING FOR DETAILS. Now listen again and mark the sentences T (True) or F (False). 20

1. ☐ Alex's favorite food is pasta.
2. ☐ Alex loves barbecues with his friends.
3. ☐ Alex's friends have vegetables and bread in their camping barbecues.
4. ☐ Sam's favorite food is meat.
5. ☐ Sam's favorite ice cream flavor is vanilla.
6. ☐ In Nena's country, you can put two toppings on the pizza.

Pronunciation

4 Listen and repeat the sentences. Then complete the second chart with the words from the box. 21

/i/	/iː/
My favorite food **i**s pasta.	I love to cook m**ea**t.

beans	cream	eat
fish	milk	tip

/i/	/iː/
is	m**ea**t
1 ____________	4 ____________
2 ____________	5 ____________
3 ____________	6 ____________

Speaking

5 Interview a classmate about his / her favorite food.

I can interpret someone talking about his / her favorite food and ask my classmates about theirs.

e-Language Booster

Use of English

6 Read the text and complete it with the sentences from the box.

Great, let's have pizza, then.
How about having lunch together today?
Is it lunchtime already?
OK. See you there. Bye.
The meat is delicious.
What about pizza?

You (Tim), Sam, Raul

Today

You: Hello! Is everyone up yet?
1 ____________________

Sam: I'm up. Sure, lunch, that's great. What's the idea? Italian? Brazilian? Greek? Japanese?

Raul: Morning, I'm still in bed.
2 ____________________

You: No, not yet! So, let's think about the food. A good option is the vegetarian restaurant round the corner from my place. The vegetables there are always fresh, straight from the farmers' market.

Raul: Oh, Tim, I don't know. A portion of vegetables a day is healthy, but what about eating some meat, too? I don't like vegetables so much. The Brazilian restaurant at the mall is fantastic. The 3 ____________________.

Sam: I get it. You want different things. I have a solution. 4 ____________________ What do you think? This way everyone is happy. A pizza can have so many flavors!

Raul: 5 ____________________

You: OK. And then an ice cream at the parlor on Fifth Street.

Sam: Nice, the dessert is ice cream, then.

Raul: 6 ____________________

Sam: Bye.

7 Read the text in Activity 6 again, underline the definite articles, and circle the indefinite articles.

8 Are the nouns below countable or uncountable? Write C (countable) or U (uncountable).

1. ☐ bananas
2. ☐ potatoes
3. ☐ water
4. ☐ juice
5. ☐ paper bags

9 Work in groups. Based on the text in Activity 6, role play a conversation making arrangements for a meal. Make sure to discuss everybody's likes and dislikes before deciding where to go and what to order.

I can make arrangements for a meal with my classmates.

Language Booster page 20

#CHALLENGE

Writing

1 **In pairs, read the menu for the school Spring Dance and discuss what you like or don't like about it.**

SPRING DANCE MENU

Meals

Fish and fries

Meat with fresh vegetables and spicy potatoes

Meat with rice and beans

Pizza (vegetarian, pepperoni, margherita)

Desserts

Ice cream (chocolate, mango, lemon, vanilla)

Sweet rice pudding

Chocolate cake

Drinks

Water

Juice (orange, lemon)

Soda

2 **Complete the sentences about the Spring Dance menu.**

1. There are four options of ________________.
2. There are three different pizza ____________.
3. One of the dessert options is chocolate ______.
4. Students can choose to drink water, _______, or soda.
5. If you don't eat meat, you can have the ____________ or the ____________ pizza.

Prepare to Write

3 **Your school is organizing a party. Write your ideas for the menu.**

Meals

____

____

____

____

____

Desserts

____

____

____

____

____

Drinks

____

____

____

____

____

____

I can read a menu for a school party and prepare to write one.

e-Language Booster

Write

4 **Write a menu for the school party. Use the text in Activity 1 and your notes in Activity 3 to help you.**

_________________ MENU

Meals

Desserts

Drinks

Check and Change

5 **Read your menu and make sure you included:**

- [ ] 2–3 different options for each category.
- [ ] 1–2 adjectives to describe the food.
- [ ] an option for students who don't eat meat.
- [ ] 1–2 healthy options for each category.

6 **Edit your menu. Make sure all the elements in Activity 5 are included.**

Publish

7 **Write a clean version of your menu.**

#TIP

Go online to search for interesting menu templates. You can choose one that fits your school colors, for example.

Speaking

8 **Work in pairs. Read your classmate's menu and answer the questions below.**

1. How many options of meals are there?

____

2. Is there a vegetarian meal?

____

3. What are the healthy options in the menu?

____

9 **Work with a different classmate and share your answers in Activity 8 with him / her. Then listen to him / her talk about his / her classmate's menu. Is there anything in common between the two menus? Write.**

____

____

I can make a menu and ask and answer questions about my classmate's menu.

Language Booster page 21

Project: A Slide Presentation

#DIGITAL LITERACY

1. Include a heading to your presentation.
2. Use bullet points to present information clearly.
3. Add pictures to your presentation.

Step 1 Think

1 Work in groups.

1. Discuss: Do you like to go to food festivals? Why (not)?
2. Read the text. Is there a similar festival in your city?

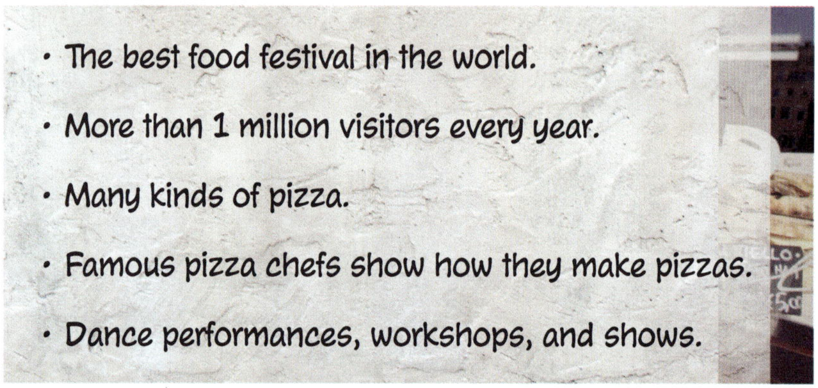

Step 2 Plan

2 In groups, discuss ideas for a food festival in your city. Make notes.

____

____

____

____

I can recognize the features of a slide presentation and plan to create one.

Step 3 Research

3 In groups, research food festivals in your country. If possible, focus on the ones that do charity work. Choose some pictures to add. Make notes.

____

____

____

Step 4 Design

4 In groups, create your slide presentation about an imaginary food festival in your city. Use the information from the previous activities. Remember to explain the festival's concern with providing everyone access to food.

- Check the text.
- Check the pictures.
- Check the organization.

#TIP STEP 4

Use high-quality pictures and graphics.

STEP 5 Present and Publish

5 In groups, show your slide presentation to the class.

#TIP STEP 5

Speak slowly and make eye contact with your audience.

STEP 6 Evaluate

6 Complete the evaluation table.

★☆☆ More to learn | ★★☆ Good | ★★★ Excellent

Criteria	My Evaluation	Group Evaluation	Teacher Evaluation
Teamwork	☆☆☆	☆☆☆	☆☆☆
Language	☆☆☆	☆☆☆	☆☆☆
Design	☆☆☆	☆☆☆	☆☆☆

I can create a slide presentation and present it to the class.

#SELF-ASSESSMENT

1 Mark the learning objectives according to the key.

★☆☆ I don't understand. | ★★☆ I understand, but I need help. | ★★★ I can do it!

Learning Objectives	Rating
To demonstrate an understanding of a conversation about breakfast.	☆☆☆
To talk about food and how it tastes.	☆☆☆
To read about food markets around the world.	☆☆☆
To write a paragraph about the food I like and don't like.	☆☆☆
To identify countable and uncountable nouns.	☆☆☆
To use definite and indefinite articles in my conversations.	☆☆☆
To interpret someone talking about his / her favorite food and ask my classmates about theirs.	☆☆☆
To make arrangements for a meal with my classmates.	☆☆☆
To read a menu for a school party and prepare to write one.	☆☆☆
To make a menu and ask and answer questions about my classmate's menu.	☆☆☆
To recognize the features of a slide presentation and plan to create one.	☆☆☆
To create a slide presentation and present it to the class.	☆☆☆

2 Work in pairs. Discuss the questions.

1. What did I find most interesting to learn? Why?
2. How did I learn it?
3. How can I use it in real life?

UT Language Booster page 22

LOVE WHAT YOU DO

#5 GENDER EQUALITY

In this unit, you will learn how to:

- Talk about jobs.
- Write picture captions.
- Create an online board.

Say what you know:

- Jobs and what they involve.
- Activities going on and routines.
- Names of inspirational women.

Video

Career Day

Before You Watch

1 **In pairs, label the pictures with the words from the box.**

cleaner	dentist	lawyer	musician
pilot	plumber	scientist	teacher

1.

2.

3.

4.
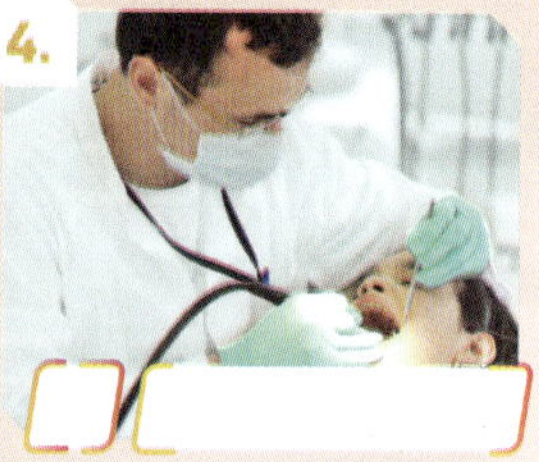

5.
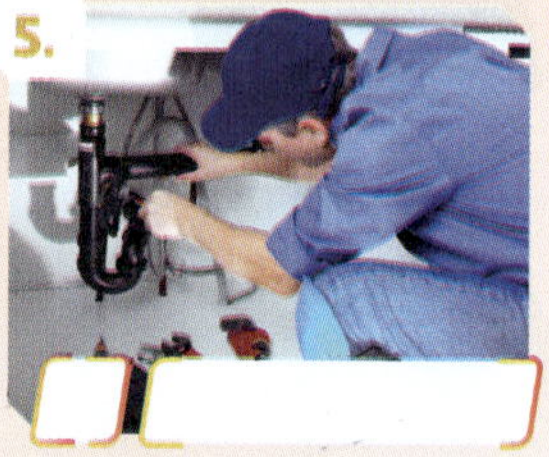

6.

7.
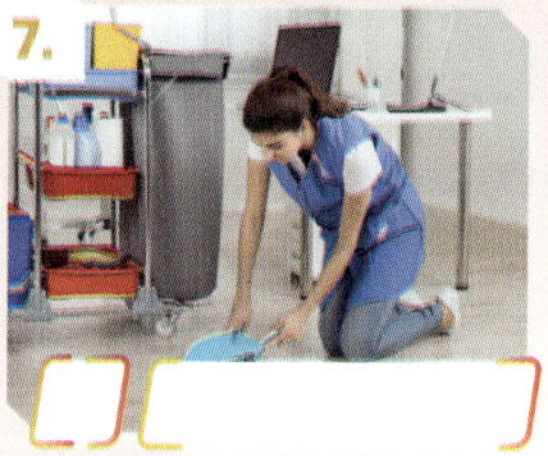

8.

While You Watch

2 **Watch the video. Check (✓) the jobs from Activity 1 Paula and Sam mention.** 04

3 **Watch the video again and underline the correct statements.** 04

1. Sam is organizing a Career Day presentation.
2. Paula thinks some jobs are more important than others.
3. Paula is reading a book on gender equality.
4. Sam wants to list jobs that are not so common.
5. Sam agrees that scientists must be on the list.
6. Paula wants to be a musician.

After You Watch

4 **Complete the following sentences about you and your family.**

1. I want to be a / an ____________________ because ____.
2. I don't want to be a / an ____________________ because ____.
3. My mom is a / an ____________________.
4. My dad is a / an ____________________.

5 **In pairs, make a short list of professions you think are important for a Career Day presentation in your school.**

I can demonstrate an understanding of a conversation about a Career Day.

Vocabulary

Jobs

6 **Look at the pictures and write the jobs you relate them to. Then listen, check, and repeat.** 22

1. 
2. 
3. 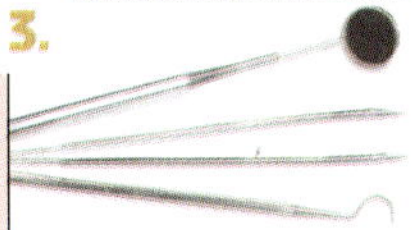
4. 
5. 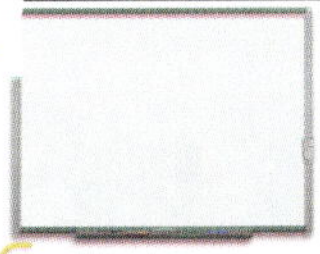
6. 
7. 
8. 
9. 
10. 

Prepositions Related to Work

7 **Circle the correct prepositions to complete the sentences. Then discuss when to use each preposition after the verb work.**

1. He is a bus driver. He works **as** / **for** the school district.
2. She is a lawyer. She works **in** / **as** international law.
3. My aunt is a teacher. She works **for** / **with** a middle school in Stockholm.
4. Before winning the competition, she worked **at** / **as** a musician **at** / **as** small parties.
5. My cousin works **in** / **for** finance. He's a financial advisor and works **as** / **at** a bank downtown.
6. My dad worked **as** / **in** an actor when he was young.

8 **Write sentences using *work as*, *work at*, *work in*, and *work for* using the jobs in Activity 6.**

A teacher works in education.

1. ____________________
2. ____________________
3. ____________________
4. ____________________
5. ____________________

Teach and *Learn*

9 **Complete the sayings with *teach* or *learn*.**

1. It's never too late to ____________.
2. You can't ____________ old dog new tricks.
3. We must ____________ to walk before we can run.
4. As we ____________, we learn.

10 **Work in pairs. Take turns asking and answering the questions below.**

1. Where does a lawyer work?
2. How often do you call ride-share drivers?
3. When do you call a plumber?
4. Who are the scientists you know? What field do they work in?
5. What do language teachers do?

I can recognize jobs and tell what some professionals do.

Language Booster page 23

Reading

Gender Equality

1 USING PRIOR KNOWLEDGE. In pairs, describe the pictures. Do you know what their jobs are?

No Gender Roles

Malala Yousufzai

Malala is a Pakistani activist for female education. In her country, many girls and women can't attend school, so she fights for the rights of girls and women. She helps them return to school and find a job. Her work is very important.

Ann Hernandez

Ann Hernandez is a software engineer. She works at a multinational company. She is a specialist in writing code, so she is now leading a team of ten software developers, mostly men. Ann says people believe it's a man's job, but she doesn't care because she loves it. And there's equal pay.

Jim Cook

Jim Cook is a teacher. He is teaching at a preschool in South Africa right now. He has a degree in education and a lot of experience, but he says it is very difficult to find a job as a male preschool teacher because teaching preschoolers is considered a woman's job.

2 SCANNING. Read the text and write *Malala*, *Ann*, or *Jim*.

1. __________ works for a multinational company.
2. __________ is an activist.
3. __________ fights for girl's rights.
4. __________ works as a preschool teacher.
5. People say __________ is doing a man's job.
6. __________ finds it difficult to find a job in his field because he is a man.

3 MONITORING COMPREHENSION. Read the text again and answer the questions.

1. What is Malala's mission?
____
2. Why is Malala's work important?
____
3. What does Ann do?
____
4. Does Ann get paid the same as men in her area?
____
5. According to Jim, why is it difficult to find a job as a male preschool teacher?
____
6. Where is Jim teaching right now?
____

4 Work in pairs. Which work do you find the most inspiring? Why?

I think Malala's work is the most inspiring because she fights for gender equality.

I can read about people's jobs and work.

Listening

5 Listen to Jose and underline the correct answers. 23

1. Jose is a **dentist** / **lawyer**.
2. He works at **genderequalityeverywhere.com** / **zerohungereverywhere.com**.
3. He helps women feel included at **home** / **work**.
4. He also helps women find **summer** / **temporary** jobs.
5. He loves his job because he works with inspiring **women** / **men**.

Writing

6 Choose a person you find inspiring and complete the sentences about him / her.

1. He / She works as a ____________________.
2. He / She works for ____________________.
3. He / She inspires me because ____________________.
4. He / She is now ____________________.

7 Write a short paragraph with the information in Activity 6. Use the texts on page 54 and the audio script on page 157 as models.

#TIP

You can prepare a digital presentation about the person that inspires you using slides. Make sure to use pictures to introduce him / her and his / her work.

I can write about a person that inspires me with his / her work.

Language Booster page 24

#UNDERSTAND

Grammar

Present Continuous

1 **Read the extracts from the video Career Day and pay attention to the parts in bold. Then use the information from the box to complete the statements about the Present Continuous.**

What **are** you **doing**?

I'm making a list of a few jobs I can present.

You're choosing some that are more common, right?

They are always **researching** new treatments and **working** on vaccines.

be + verb + ing	before
I'm making	now

1. We use the Present Continuous to talk about something that is happening ___________.
2. To form the Present Continuous we use ___________.
3. We form questions by putting the verb *be* ___________ the subject.
4. The negative form of ___________ is *I'm not making.*

2 **Complete the sentences using the verbs in parentheses in the Present Continuous.**

1. The woman in a yellow dress ___________ (push) a stroller.
2. The old man ___________ (wear) glasses.
3. Two women ___________ (use) their cellphones.
4. The woman in the wheelchair ___________ (carry) a bag.
5. Two women and one man ___________ (sit) on a bench.

3 **Order the words to make questions.**

1. for / are / rights / women / fighting /equal / ?

____

2. now / the /Malala / living / in / is / U.K. / ?

____

Simple Present and Present Continuous

4 **Underline the correct options to complete the sentences.**

1. **A: What do you do / What are you doing**?
   B: I'm a dentist.
2. **A: What does he do / What is he doing**?
   B: Mark's cooking our dinner.
3. Don't shout! The baby **is sleeping / sleeps**.
4. **A:** Good morning. Is Jim at home?
   B: No, he **is playing / plays** soccer with his brother now.
5. **A: Do you live / Are you living** in this area?
   B: No, I'm not from this town.

5 **Now read the sentences in Activity 4 and match the columns.**

1. We use the Simple Present
2. We use the Present Continuous

( ) to talk about an ongoing action or an action that is happening at the time of speaking.

( ) to talk about regular habits or routines and permanent situations.

I can use the Simple Present and the Present Continuous.
e-Language Booster

6 **Complete the sentences with the verbs from the box in the Simple Present or Present Continuous.**

do (2x)	have	love	pick up	play	tell	work

1. **A:** Hey, Sarah. What ________ you ________ here?
   B: I ________ some food for lunch.
2. **A:** What ________ your friend ________, Jim?
   B: Who, Mark? He ________ as a lawyer at a law firm downtown.
3. **A:** Listen! The children ________ soccer in their rooms again.
   B: I ________ them all the time that they can't do that.
4. **A:** Look! I can't believe The Johnson's ________ a party again.
   B: Yeah, our neighbors ________ parties.

Prepositions with Time Expressions

7 **Read the sentences, pay attention to the parts in bold, and complete the statements with the correct prepositions.**

On Mondays I leave home **at 8 o'clock** and only go back **at night**.

My flight to Spain is **on** May 24th.

We always travel **at** Christmas.

We can't help you with your presentation because we have classes **in** the morning.

1. We use ______ with times and festive dates.
2. We use ______ with days of the week and dates.
3. We use ______ with months of the year.
4. We use ______ with parts of the day such as *morning* and *afternoon*.
5. We use ______ with *night*.

8 **Circle the correct preposition to complete the sentences. Then listen to Amy and check your answers.** 24

1. Amy usually gets up **at** / **in** 7 o'clock and has breakfast.
2. She studies **at** / **in** the morning.
3. **In** / **On** Mondays, she goes to the mall **on** / **at** lunchtime.
4. **In** / **On** Monday afternoons, she works as a volunteer and goes back home **at** / **in** night.
5. She sometimes goes to sleep **at** / **on** midnight.
6. Her birthday is **in** / **on** October 24th.

9 **Complete the sentences with the correct prepositions.**

1. The company I work for has a break ______ Easter.
2. Mark starts a temporary job ______ April 13th.
3. She is a DJ, so she rarely works ______ the morning.
4. Lara works as a cook ______ lunchtime.
5. Remind me to write her an e-mail ______ July.

10 **In pairs, take turns asking and answering questions about your routine and activities going on now. Use the prepositions *at*, *in*, and *on* when possible.**

What do you do on Monday mornings?

I go to school.

What are you doing now?

I'm studying English.

I can use the prepositions *at*, *in*, and *on* with time expressions in the Simple Present.

Language Booster page 25

#DEVELOP

Listening

1 **Match the statements to the pictures.**

1. He's an engineer. He prefers to **work indoors**.
2. The rice farmer **works outdoors**.
3. He **wears a different uniform** when he's teaching.

a.

b.

c.

2 **INFERRING MEANING. Listen to three speakers talk about their jobs and guess what they do.** 25

1. Ian: ______________
2. Lucas: ______________
3. Alex: ______________

3 **LISTENING FOR DETAILS. Listen again and mark the sentences T (True) or F (False).** 26

1. ☐ Ian works at a laboratory.
2. ☐ He doesn't wear a uniform at work.
3. ☐ Lucas always works outdoors.
4. ☐ He has a part-time job.
5. ☐ Alex has a summer job.
6. ☐ She starts working at lunchtime.

4 **LISTENING FOR DETAILS. Mark the sentences A for Alex, L for Lucas, or *I* for Ian. Then listen again and check your answers.** 27

1. ☐ He / She tests and applies treatments.
2. ☐ He / She doesn't work indoors.
3. ☐ He / She doesn't wear a uniform.
4. ☐ His / Her job is full time.
5. ☐ He / She works at Christmas.

Pronunciation

5 **Listen and identify the silent letter in each word.** 28

1. climber
2. designer
3. government
4. lawyer
5. listen
6. plumber
7. writer

Speaking

6 **In pairs, think of a job and describe it. Ask your classmate to guess what job it is. Use the Simple Present to describe your routine as a professional.**

I don't wear a uniform. I don't work on the weekends. I work with teenagers.

Are you a teacher?

Yes, I'm a teacher!

Use of English

7 **Read the text about Sam's dream job and complete it with prepositions related to work and time.**

My Dream Job

People say you should love what you do, and I believe that. My dream job is to be a scientist. But I don't want to wear a uniform or work [1] ______ a laboratory. I want to be a scientist to work outdoors, with animals and plants. It is a difficult job that starts early [2] ______ the morning and continues [3] ______ night sometimes. Right now I'm studying a lot [4] ______ weekdays and weekends to make my dream come true. I'm focusing on biology and physics, two very important subjects for my work [5] ______ a scientist. My teachers are helping me with extra homework and I'm doing some online research, too. Working in nature is the best part of this job!

8 **Read the sentences about the text in Activity 7, pay attention to the parts in bold, and check (✓) the sentences that indicate actions happening at the time of speaking.**

1. ☐ Sam **is focusing** on biology and physics.
2. ☐ He **is doing** some online research.
3. ☐ He **doesn't want** to wear a uniform.
4. ☐ The job of a scientist **starts** early in the morning.

9 **Think about your dream job. Write sentences to describe it. Use the Present Continuous to say what you are doing now to get your dream job.**

10 **Work in pairs. Based on your notes in Activity 9, take turns describing your dream job to each other. Use the Simple Present, the Present Continuous, and expressions of agreement as in the dialogue below.**

*I **want** to be a musician because I **love** music. That's my dream job!*

You're right! We have to do what we love.

*I'm **attending** piano lessons and watching video lessons to learn how to play the violin, too. I need to learn to play a lot of instruments!*

I agree with you. If that's your passion, go for it!

I can talk about my dream job.

Language Booster page 26

#CHALLENGE

Writing

1 **In pairs, read the captions for pictures from online posts and write what you like or don't like about them.**

1.

adventurous1989
posted 3 hours ago

5 comments

adventurous1989 I just love weekend vibes!

2.

jo.wallen
posted 7 hours ago

5 comments

jo.wallen I'm dreaming big to reach for the stars!

2 **Match the explanations to the captions in Activity 1.**

- [ ] I want great accomplishments for my life.
- [ ] After a hard work week, I'm finally enjoying quality time with my friends.

Prepare to Write

3 **Use a search engine to look for four inspirational pictures for an online post. Save them.**

#TIP

Choose high-quality pictures to make your post more visually attractive.

I can talk about picture captions and prepare to write some.

Write

4 **Write inspirational captions for the pictures you chose in Activity 3. Make sure to use the Simple Present and the Present Continuous in your captions. Use the captions in Activity 1 and the explanations in Activity 2 as models.**

____

____

____

____

Every day is an exceptional day to learn a new lesson. I never **stop** learning! **I'm learning** right now!

Check and Change

5 **Read your captions and make sure you included:**

- [ ] an attractive picture.
- [ ] an inspiring message.
- [ ] a verb in the Simple Present.
- [ ] a verb in the Present Continuous.

#TIP

Browse the Internet for social media template ideas.

6 **Edit your captions. Make sure all the elements in Activity 5 are included.**

Publish

7 **Write a clean version of your captions.**

Speaking

8 **In pairs, take turns presenting your posts and explaining the captions of the pictures.**

9 **Answer the following questions about your classmate's captions.**

1. Are his / her captions related to the pictures he / she chose?

____

____

2. Is he / she using the right verb tenses?

____

____

3. Are his / her captions inspirational?

____

____

I can create and share picture captions.

Language Booster page 27

Project: An Online Board

#DIGITAL LITERACY

1. Choose a wallpaper that appeals to the reader.
2. Organize your information according to importance or chronologically.
3. Add pictures or drawings to your boards.

Step 1 Think

1 Work in groups.

1. What is gender equality?
2. How important are people like Malala for women around the world?
3. Take a look at the online board below. What do you know about those women? What do they have in common?

Malala Yousafzai
(1997 -)

Pakistani women's right activist

Greta Thunberg
(2003 -)

Swedish environmentalist fighting for climate action

Ada Lovelace
(1815 – 1852)

English mathematician known as the first computer programmer

Marie Curie
(1867 – 1934)

Polish-born French physicist famous for her work on radioactivity

Step 2 Plan

2 In groups, discuss ideas for an online board about women who inspire you either because they promote change and are outstanding in their fields or because they fight for gender equality. Make notes.

Step 3 Research

3 **In groups, research inspirational women. If possible, focus on the ones that work for gender equality. Choose some pictures to add. Make notes.**

____

____

____

____

Step 4 Design

4 **In groups, create your online board. Use the information from the previous activities.**

- Check the text.
- Check the pictures.
- Check the organization.

Step 5 Present and Publish

5 **In groups, show your online board to the class.**

Step 6 Evaluate

6 **Complete the evaluation table.**

★☆☆ More to learn | ★★☆ Good | ★★★ Excellent

Criteria	My Evaluation	Group Evaluation	Teacher Evaluation
Teamwork	☆☆☆	☆☆☆	☆☆☆
Language	☆☆☆	☆☆☆	☆☆☆
Design	☆☆☆	☆☆☆	☆☆☆

#TIP STEP 4

1. Work on your texts carefully and correct any mistakes.
2. Choose pictures that represent the inspirational women you are talking about.
3. Listen to everyone's suggestions and be polite and encouraging. Make sure everyone in the group feels included.

#TIP STEP 5

During your presentation, show passion just like the women you are talking about did for their causes.

I can create an online board and present it to the class.

#SELF-ASSESSMENT

1 Mark the learning objectives according to the key.

★☆☆ I don't understand.	★★☆ I understand, but I need help.	★★★ I can do it!

Learning Objectives	Rating
To demonstrate an understanding of a conversation about a Career Day.	☆☆☆
To recognize jobs and tell what some professionals do.	☆☆☆
To read about people's jobs and work.	☆☆☆
To write about a person that inspires me with his / her work.	☆☆☆
To use the Simple Present and the Present Continuous.	☆☆☆
To use the prepositions *at*, *in*, and *on* with time expressions in the Simple Present.	☆☆☆
To listen to people talk about their jobs.	☆☆☆
To talk about my dream job.	☆☆☆
To talk about picture captions and prepare to write some.	☆☆☆
To create and share picture captions.	☆☆☆
To plan to create an online board.	☆☆☆
To create an online board and present it to the class.	☆☆☆

2 Work in pairs. Discuss the questions.

1. What did I find most interesting to learn? Why?
2. How did I learn it?
3. How can I use it in real life?

UT Language Booster page 28

BETTER TOGETHER

In this unit, you will learn how to:

- Talk about people's appearances and personalities.
- Write about clothes and preferences.
- Create a blog post.

Say what you know:

- Adjectives to describe someone's appearance and personalities.
- Clothes you wear.
- Comparatives and superlatives.

#10 REDUCED INEQUALITIES

Video

A Friendly, Tall Classmate

Before You Watch

1 Read the adjectives below and check (✓) the ones that describe size.

1. ☐ beautiful
2. ☐ old
3. ☐ smart
4. ☐ short
5. ☐ small
6. ☐ tall

While You Watch

2 Watch the video and write P for Paula and S for Sam. 05

1. ☐ wants to talk to other classmates about financial problems in the community.
2. ☐ thinks many families are having financial difficulties.

3 Watch the video again and check (✓) the correct sentences. 05

1. ☐ Rick is tall and friendly.
2. ☐ Rick was very happy in the morning class.
3. ☐ Paula wants to post about a classmate.
4. ☐ Sam thinks people can try to be more generous.
5. ☐ Paula and Sam believe they can think together about how to help.

4 Watch the video once more and mark the sentences T (True) or F (False). 05

1. ☐ Sam and Paula are at school.
2. ☐ Paula is looking for information in a book.
3. ☐ Paula is worried about a classmate, Rick.
4. ☐ Sam knows what is going on with Rick.
5. ☐ Paula thinks many families are having financial difficulties.

After You Watch

5 Complete the sentences about the video using the words from the box.

classmates	community	financial	generous	help

1. Paula and Sam are ______________.
2. Paula thinks many families in their ______________ are having ______________ problems.
3. Paula and Sam think they can talk to their ______________ about the problem.
4. Sam thinks everybody can ______________.

6 Work in pairs. What can Paula and Sam do to help Rick and other families? Make notes.

We can all try to be more generous.

____

____

____

I can interpret a conversation between two classmates.

e-Language Booster

Vocabulary

Adjectives of Appearance and Personality

7 Match the words to the pictures. Then listen and repeat. 29

beautiful blond friendly lazy
old overweight serious short

1.

____

2.

____

3.

____

4.

____

5.

____

6.

____

7.

____

8.

____

8 Work in pairs. Complete the sentences with some adjectives from Activity 7.

1. Sam is very ________. He's always smiling.
2. Don't be ________. Tidy up your room, please.
3. I really like your ________ hair.
4. That parrot is so ________.
5. It's difficult for ________ people to find jobs. There's a lot of discrimination because of their age.

Adjective Order

9 Read the sentences and pay attention to the parts in bold. Then complete the statement about the order of adjectives with the words from the box.

- She has **short, blond** hair.
- She's a **happy, old** woman.
- It's a **smart, big** dog.
- He is a **beautiful, little** baby.

age color size

The order of the adjectives is: opinion, [1] ________, [2] ________, shape, and [3] ________.

10 Work in pairs. Complete the sentences with the adjectives in parentheses in the correct order.

1. My grandma is a ________, ________ woman. (old, serious)
2. Mark is a ________, ________ boy. He plays soccer a lot. (friendly, tall)
3. You are a ________ girl. (blond, beautiful)
4. Ana has pretty, ________ hair. (long, dark)

11 In groups, use pictures from social media pages to describe people to each other.

This is my friend Sean. He is tall. He has short, brown hair.

I can talk about people's appearances and personalities.

Language Booster page 29

#CLARIFY

Reading

1 **Work in pairs. Answer the following questions.**

1. Do you like music? What kind of music do you prefer?
2. What sports do you like practicing? Why?

2 **Read the title of the text. Do you agree with it? Why?**

____

3 **ESTABLISHING A PURPOSE FOR READING. Read the text once and complete the sentences with Jin and Sam's preferences.**

1. Jin prefers ______________________ to any other kind of music.
2. Sam prefers ________________ to basketball or running.

Life Is Not Always About Preferences

My name's Jin, and I'm Korean. My family lives in the U.K. now, and we started a new life here. I go to school every day, and English is the most interesting subject. I love English literature and listening to music. I prefer Korean pop music, K-pop. It's the most popular music in my school, and my classmates and I think it's better than any other kind of music. It also makes me more popular with kids my age. They all want to understand what the songs say, and they ask me to translate or sing them. It makes me feel welcome and included. K-pop helps me remember Korea, and it makes it easier to be far away from my country.

Hey, I'm Sam, and I love to play football. I think football is cooler than any other sport, but I live in a neighborhood where schools are very simple and there are no football teams. Unfortunately, my family does not have money to send me to a school that has a girl's football team. I know I can play other sports, like basketball or running, but football is the best sport to play. This week I applied for a football scholarship. This the easiest way to get into a better school with football practice. I'm so happy! My mom's helping me, and she's very kind. I'm very hard-working and will make her proud.

4 **SCANNING. Read the text again and circle the best options to complete the sentences.**

1. Jin is **Korean** / **Chinese**.
2. Jin **likes** / **does not like** K-pop music and English literature.
3. He prefers K-pop because it reminds him of his **friends** / **country**.
4. Sam's favorite sport is **tennis** / **football**.
5. Sam's family **has** / **doesn't have** money to pay for a school bus.
6. Sam is very **lazy** / **hard-working**.

5 **Work in pairs. Give two examples of things that are different and similar about your life and Jin's and Sam's lives.**

Jin lives in a different country, but I don't.

Sam likes football and I like football, too.

I can read about other people's realities and preferences.

e-Language Booster

Listening

6 **Listen and write the speakers' preferences.** 30

1. Paul prefers ______________________.
2. Niles prefers ______________________.
3. Keiko prefers to ______________________.
4. Muriel would rather practice ______________ than swimming.
5. Lilian prefers ______________________.

Writing

7 **Complete the sentences with information about you. Write about your preferences and give your opinion about music, sports, food, or free-time activities.**

1. I would rather listen to ______________ than ______________.
2. I'd rather play ______________ than ______________.
3. I'd rather ______________ than ______________.
4. I prefer ______________ to ______________.
5. I think ______________ is very ______________ and ______________.
6. In my opinion, ______________ is not very ______________.

8 **Write a short paragraph with the information in Activity 7.**

#TIP

You can use this information to introduce yourself to your classmates through your social media app. Include a picture of you listening to the music of your preference or playing the sport you prefer.

I can write about my preferences.

Language Booster page 30

#UNDERSTAND

Grammar

Comparatives

1 **Read the sentences and pay attention to the parts in bold. Then circle the correct words to complete the statements.**

Sam thinks football is **cooler than** any other sport.
Jin thinks K-pop makes him **more popular than** other students.
Schools with football practice are **more expensive**.
Sam is now **happier than** when she was in her old school.
Jin loves Korean food. He thinks it is **better than** English food.
Sam's old school is **worse than** her new school.

1. The sentences are **comparing** / **describing** people or things.
2. To make a comparison using adjectives with one or two syllables, we add **-er** / **more** to the end of the adjective.
3. To make a comparison between two things or people using adjectives with more than two syllables, we add **-er** / **more** before the adjective.
4. The comparative form of *good* is **better** / **worse**. The comparative form of *bad* is **better** / **worse**.
5. We use ***than*** / ***then*** after the adjective when comparing two things or people.

2 **Complete the sentences using the comparative forms of the adjectives in parentheses.**

1. Technology is ____________ (important) now than before.
2. Jin is ____________ (funny) than Sam.
3. Your hair is ____________ (dark) than mine.
4. The teacher asked us to be ____________ (generous) than the adults.
5. I think people were __________ (kind) in the past.

Superlatives

3 **Who said the sentences below? Write J for Jin or S for Sam. Read the text on page 68 again, if necessary.**

1. ☐ K-pop is **the most popular** music in my school.
2. ☐ This is **the easiest** way to get into a better school.
3. ☐ Football is **the best** sport to play.
4. ☐ English is **the most interesting** school subject.

4 **Look at the adjectives in bold in the sentences in Activity 3 and complete the rules with the words from the box.**

-est   superlative   the   the best   the most

1. The sentences have adjectives in the ____________ form.
2. To make superlatives using adjectives with one or two syllables, we add ____________ before the adjective and ____________ to the end of the word.
3. To make superlatives using adjectives with more than two syllables, we use ____________ before the adjective.
4. The superlative form of *good* is ____________.

5 **Complete the sentences with the superlative form of the adjectives in parentheses.**

1. Jim is ______________ (tall) boy in our class.
2. Ann is ______________ (funny) girl I know.
3. My mom is __________ (kind) person in my family.
4. My dog is ______________ (beautiful) dog in this competition.
5. Lara is __________________ (hard-working) student in this school.

I can use comparatives and superlatives.
e-Language Booster

6 Order the words to form questions.

1. biggest / room / in / house / your / What / is / the / ?

____

2. you / generous / Who / the / know / most / person / is / ?

____

3. best / the / What / food / the / is / world / in / ?

____

4. your / What / hottest / in / is / city / the / country / ?

____

5. in / is / the / worst / your / problem / What / city / social / ?

____

Comparatives and Superlatives

7 Listen and complete the sentences. 31

1. Mt. Everest _______________ Aconcagua.
2. Brazil is _______________ all South American countries.
3. Sam is _______________ kid in our class.
4. Lila's brother is _______________ person I know.

8 Put the adjectives in parentheses in the comparative or superlative form.

1. Social inequality is _______________ (big) problem people face in this country.
2. Local people have _______________ (good) opportunities _______________ immigrants.
3. My father is _______________ (old) mailman in this neighborhood.
4. Zimbabwe is _______________ (beautiful) African country.
5. My physics teacher is _______________ (friendly) my math teacher.

9 Answer the questions in Activity 6. Use comparatives and superlatives in your answers.

____

____

____

____

____

I can tell the difference between comparatives and superlatives.

Language Booster page 31

Listening

1 **Match the pictures to the words.**

1. pants
2. shirt
3. suit
4. shoes
5. dress
6. jacket
7. skirt
8. jeans

2 **LISTENING FOR GIST. Listen to Paula and Raul. What are they talking about? Check (✓) the correct alternative.** 🔊 32

1. ☐ School subjects and free-time activities.
2. ☐ Clothes and people's appearances and personalities.
3. ☐ Healthy eating, food and drink items.

3 **Order the words to form sentences from the audio. Then listen and check.** 🔊 33

1. dresses / skirts / prefer / I / shirts / to / and / .

   ____

2. dance / to / easier / it's / like / this / And / !

   ____

3. night / school / most / lives / important / of / It's / our / the / .

   ____

4 **Work in pairs. Complete the sentences about Paula's and Raúl's clothes.**

1. Paula prefers [1] ______________ to [2] ______________ and [3] ______________.
2. Raúl wanted to wear a [1] ______________, but [2] ______________ and a [3] ______________ were cheaper.

Pronunciation

5 **Listen and repeat the pairs of numbers. What's the difference? Underline the stressed syllable in each word.** 🔊 34

1. sixty – sixteen
2. thirteen – thirty
3. fifteen – fifty
4. seventy – seventeen
5. ninety – nineteen

6 **Listen and circle the words you hear.** 🔊 35

1. sixty / sixteen
2. thirteen / thirty
3. fifteen / fifty
4. seventy / seventeen
5. ninety / nineteen

Speaking

7 **Interview a classmate. Ask him / her what he / she likes to wear in the situations below.**

1. A beach wedding.
2. A baby's birthday party.
3. A rock concert.
4. A day trip to the mountains.

What do you like to wear to a beach wedding?

A short dress.

Use of English

8 Read the dialogue and underline the comparative and superlative forms of the adjectives.

Lily: Lara, come take a look! What do you think of this yellow shirt?

Lara: Is it a shirt? Not a dress? It looks like a dress. A short dress.

Lily: Nah, dresses are longer than this. Like those dresses behind you. They are the longest ones in the store.

Lara: These are beautiful dresses. Are you looking for a dress? Would you prefer to try on some of these? They are cheaper than the shirts, too.

Lily: Well, I don't know. I feel more comfortable in pants and shirts, I guess. But I can try them on.

Lara: You don't need to. Wear what you like. I love to wear jeans and a jacket. There are some shorter jackets that are very cool. I prefer darker jeans, of course. Darker than usual, I mean.

Lily: What about these shoes, Lara? Do they match my shirt?

Lara: Lily, those are the ugliest shoes ever!

Lily: Haha, really? I think they are nice, and I need new shoes.

Lara: Your old shoes are better than these.

Lily: OK, Lara, I think I am ready. Yellow shirt, black jeans, shoes, all set.

Lara: You look amazing, Lily! Your long dark hair matches your new shirt.

Lily: Thanks, Lara! Let's go then. Big day today! My birthday party is in a few hours!

9 Match the adjectives from the box to their opposites.

cheap dark long new ugly

1. short ______________
2. beautiful ______________
3. expensive ______________
4. light ______________
5. old ______________

10 Complete the sentences below using the opposite of the adjectives in bold in the comparative form.

1. I don't like **long** skirts. I prefer ____________ ones.
2. You need **new** shoes for your graduation party. Your shoes are ____________ than your sister 's.
3. My mom bought me a pair of **dark** jeans, but I prefer ____________ colors.
4. I'd rather buy ____________ clothes than spend my money at this **expensive** store.

11 Work in pairs. Practice reading the dialogue in Activity 8 replacing the clothes and adjectives.

I can talk about clothes and compare them.

Language Booster page 32

#CHALLENGE

Writing

1 **Work in pairs. Read Lin's blog profile post and list the information she includes.**

____

____

____

NEW TAB

www.site.com

My blog

lifestyle | fashion | video | about

LIN CHANG

Who am I?

Hey! My name's Lin, and my family comes from China. I'm fourteen years old, and I live in the United States with my family. My new country is very beautiful, the people are friendly and kind, and we love it here. My mom and dad are very hard-working, and they make sure we have everything. This is my blog! It's about fashion and clothes. I prefer colorful clothes and shoes. I think girls and boys look taller in bright colors. Enjoy!

2 **Complete the sentences with information about Lin.**

1. Lin is from ____________.
2. She now lives in ____________.
3. She is ____________ old.
4. She thinks her new country is ____________.
5. She finds the people ____________ and ____________.
6. Her mom and dad are very ____________.

Prepare to Write

3 **You are going to write your blog profile post. Complete the chart with the information you want to include in each section.**

Your name	
Your age	
Where you live	
Your opinion of people in your country	
Your opinion of your family	
Your preferences	
What your blog is about	

I can read a blog profile post and prepare to write one.

e-Language Booster

Write

4 Write your blog profile post. Use the information in Activity 3 and the text in Activity 1 as a model.

NEW TAB +

www.site.com

My blog

lifestyle fashion video about

____

____

____

____

____

____

____

Check and Change

5 Read your blog profile post and make sure you included:

- ☐ personal information.
- ☐ adjectives to describe people.
- ☐ at least one adjective in the comparative or superlative form.
- ☐ a preference you have.

6 Edit your blog profile post. Make sure all the items in Activity 5 are included. Then choose a picture for your profile.

Publish

7 Write a clean version of your blog profile post.

#TIP

You can create a free blog online and talk about you and your interests.

Speaking

8 Read your classmate's blog profile post and complete the sentences with information about him / her.

1. His / Her name is ______________.
2. He / She is ______________ years old.
3. He / She thinks people in his / her country are ______________ and ______________.
4. He / She thinks his / her family is ______________.
5. He / She prefers ______________ to ______________.

9 In groups, choose a classmate's blog profile post and present him / her to the group.

This is Lara. She is... She thinks...

I can write a blog profile post.

Language Booster page 33

SUSTAINABLE DEVELOPMENT GOALS

Project: A Blog Post

#DIGITAL LITERACY

1. Keep your word count low.
2. Share your blog content to your social media, too. It helps you get more followers.
3. Upload good quality pictures.

Step 1 Think

1 Work in groups.

1. Are social changes important in your community?
2. Read the blog post. What social problem is it about?
3. Is there a similar situation in your country?

NEW TAB

Education in Pakistan

- 82 percent of the richest attend school while only 50 percent of the poorest attend school.
- The 18 million richest consume 1,5 times more than the 72 million poorest.
- The number of children who don't attend school in Pakistan is the second highest in the world.

Step 2 Plan

2 In groups, talk about the social changes you want to see in your country and add ideas to the list below. Then choose one of them.

NEW TAB

The Changes My Country Needs

1. Better Education
2. Better job opportunities
3. More efficient health care
4. More gender equality
5. Safer cities
6. Social equality
7. ____________________
8. ____________________

I can recognize the features of a blog post and plan to write one.

Step 3 Research

3 In groups, do some research online about social problems your country is facing. Make notes.

____

____

____

____

Step 4 Design

4 In groups, create your blog post for a free online blog platform. Use the information from your research and the previous activities.

- Check the text.
- Check the purpose.
- Check the organization.

#TIP STEP 4

You can add a video to your blog post to make it more interesting.

Step 5 Present and Publish

5 Work in groups. Present your blog post to the class.

#TIP STEP 5

Allow some time for your audience to make comments or ask questions.

Step 6 Evaluate

6 Complete the evaluation table.

★☆☆ More to learn | ★★☆ Good | ★★★ Excellent

Criteria	My Evaluation	Group Evaluation	Teacher Evaluation
Teamwork	☆☆☆	☆☆☆	☆☆☆
Language	☆☆☆	☆☆☆	☆☆☆
Design	☆☆☆	☆☆☆	☆☆☆

I can create a blog post and present it to the class.

#SELF-ASSESSMENT

1 Mark the learning objectives according to the key.

★☆☆ I don't understand.	★★☆ I understand, but I need help.	★★★ I can do it!

Learning Objectives	Rating
To interpret a conversation between two classmates.	☆☆☆
To talk about people's appearances and personalities.	☆☆☆
To read about other people's realities and preferences.	☆☆☆
To write about my preferences.	☆☆☆
To use comparatives and superlatives.	☆☆☆
To tell the difference between comparatives and superlatives.	☆☆☆
To talk about what clothes to wear to important events.	☆☆☆
To talk about clothes and compare them.	☆☆☆
To read a blog profile post and prepare to write one.	☆☆☆
To write a blog profile post.	☆☆☆
To recognize the features of a blog post and plan to write one.	☆☆☆
To create a blog post and present it to the class.	☆☆☆

2 Work in pairs. Discuss the questions.

1. What did I find most interesting to learn? Why?
2. How did I learn it?
3. How can I use it in real life?

Language Booster page 34

WHY IS EDUCATION POWERFUL?

#4 QUALITY EDUCATION

In this unit, you will learn how to:
- Talk about schools.
- Write an e-mail requesting information.
- Create an online poster.

Say what you know:
- Types of school.
- School rules.
- Educational models.

#DISCOVER

Video

The New Media Room

Before You Watch

1 **Work in pairs. Which of the following items represent quality education for you? Check (✓) the ones you think are the most important.**

1. ☐ Technology in the classroom
2. ☐ Modern spaces
3. ☐ Good teachers
4. ☐ A variety of courses

2 **What would you like to have in your school to improve the quality of education?**

____

____

While You Watch

3 **Watch the video and mark the sentences T (True) of F (False).** ▷ 06

1. ☐ Paula and Sam are in the media room.
2. ☐ The media room is a simple classroom with computers.
3. ☐ Students must keep the media room clean.
4. ☐ There isn't free Wi-Fi in the media room.
5. ☐ Sam and Paula go to a public school.

4 **Watch the video again and complete the following sentences with the words from the box. There is one extra option.** ▷ 06

can	can't	must	must not	should	shouldn't

1. Governments __________ make sure kids are in school.
2. They __________ leave empty cups around.
3. Sam thinks they __________ always talk to the principal first.
4. Sam tells Paula they __________ do anything without permission.
5. Students __________ eat or drink near the computers.

After You Watch

5 **Complete the sentences using information about you and your school.**

1. Students must ______________________________.
2. Students can't ______________________________.
3. I think we should ______________________________.
4. We shouldn't ______________________________.

Vocabulary

Types of Schools

6 **Look at the different types of schools. Then listen and repeat.** 36

1. 
Private school

2. 
Boarding school

3. 
Public school

4. 
Home school

5. 
International school

7 **Use the words from Activity 6 to complete the sentences below.**

1. Students study and sleep in this school. It's a ________________.
2. It is a school paid by the government. It's a ________________.
3. It is a school that families pay for. It's a ________________.
4. It is a school that has students from different countries. It's an ________________.
5. A ________________ refers to the education of students at home.

Collocations with *Exam / Test*

8 **Read the sentences and complete them with the words from the box in the correct form.**

fail	pass	take

1. Carin is afraid to ________________ the test. She's very nervous.
2. He never ________________ an exam. He's an excellent student!
3. Sarah really needs to ________________ this exam. Her scholarship depends on it!

9 **Complete the paragraph with the correct verbs. Then listen and check your answers.** 37

My exams are coming up, and I don't want to [1] ________ them. In two days, we are [2] ________ a history exam. I hope we all [3] ________ our tests and have a good summer!

10 **Work in groups. Take turns describing the types of schools for your classmates to guess. Then talk about the types of schools you have in your country.**

Your parents don't need to pay for this school.

Public school!

I can describe types of schools.

Language Booster page 35

#CLARIFY

Reading

1 **Check (✓) some of the items we use at school.**

1. ☐ pencils
2. ☐ books
3. ☐ skateboards
4. ☐ dolls
5. ☐ computers
6. ☐ chairs
7. ☐ bikes
8. ☐ desks

2 **ESTABLISHING A PURPOSE FOR READING. Read the texts below and find one way these schools are similar to and different from your school.**

____

Different Educational Models

High school in Finland offers students two options: vocational education to prepare students for a specialist profession and general education to take students to university. Students have to choose one of the options. The Finnish system uses alternative methods of teaching. In Finland, students must solve community problems with school projects. This can help them be independent and think in a different way.

Homeschooling is legal in 50 states in the United States, and it became more popular after the COVID-19 pandemic. Parents have to keep a portfolio for the students. They should teach specific subjects. Students must take tests and pass them to get a diploma.

In South Korea, education is a very serious topic. There are many international schools in this country, and high school students have to study for many hours to enter a good university. When school is over, at 4:00 p.m., students go to the library and study until late at night. There are special high schools for students to study science, arts, or languages.

3 **SCANNING. Read the texts in Activity 2 again and find the information to complete the sentences.**

1. Students in Finland must choose between ______________ and ______________ education.
2. They use ______________ to solve community problems.
3. In homeschooling, parents have to ______________ for the students.
4. Homeschooled students must take ______________.
5. To enter a good university in South Korea, students must ______________.
6. ______________, arts, and ______________ are special high schools in South Korea.

4 **SCANNING. Work in pairs. Match the countries to a common aspect of their educational systems.**

1. Finland
2. The United States
3. South Korea

☐ Homeschooling is common.
☐ Students learn to be independent.
☐ Students have to study until late.

I can read about different educational models.

Listening

5 **Listen and write the countries the speakers refer to (The United States, Finland, or South Korea).** 38

1. ____________ 2. ____________ 3. ____________

6 **Listen again and answer the questions.** 39

1. What does Speaker 1 do when he / she finishes school at the end of the day?

____

2. How many subjects does Speaker 2 study a day?

____

3. Who is Speaker's 2 tutor?

____

4. What is Speaker 3 going to learn this year?

____

Writing

7 **Complete the sentences below about your school. Then compare your answers with a classmate.**

1. My school is ______________________.
2. We study ______________________ in my school.
3. We have to take exams every ______________________.
4. When we fail our exams, we have to ______________________.
5. After high school, most students ______________________.

8 **Write a paragraph about your school. Use your notes in Activity 7 and consult the script on page 159 for help. Then read your paragraph and audio record it.**

I can write about schools in my country.

Language Booster page 36

Grammar

Must / Mustn't

1 **Match the rules to the pictures.**

1. You **must** be quiet in the school library.
2. Students **must** wash their hands after P.E.
3. You **mustn't** eat or drink inside the classroom.
4. All students **must** wear a uniform.
5. Teachers **mustn't** listen to loud music in the staff room.

2 **Read the sentences in Activity 1 and pay attention to the words in bold. Write the numbers of the sentences according to their meanings.**

1. It's an obligation to do this. ____________________
2. It's against the rules to do this. ________________

Should / Shouldn't

3 **Read the problems and relate them to the correct piece of advice.**

1. A friend asked me to help him study math, but I don't have enough time.
2. Some classmates think it's OK to listen to music in the classroom.
3. Lila and Mark are planning to travel after the exams, but they don't want me to go with them.
4. My parents want me to study medicine after high school, but I want to study languages.
5. My girlfriend wants to study in another country, but I can't go with her. But I don't want to lose my girlfriend.

- ☐ You **should** tell them it's OK to listen to music during breaks only.
- ☐ You **should** explain to your parents that you would prefer to do something you really like.
- ☐ You **should** try and find the time to help your friend.
- ☐ You **shouldn't** worry about losing your girlfriend.
- ☐ You **should** talk to them and ask why they don't want you to come.

4 **Based on the sentences in Activity 3, underline the correct options to complete the rules.**

1. We use *should* / *shouldn't* to **give advice** / **talk about obligations**.
2. We use *should* to advise a person **what not to do** / **what to do**.
3. We use *shouldn't* to advise a person **what not to do** / **what to do**.

5 **Use *must*, *mustn't*, *should*, or *shouldn't* to complete the sentences.**

1. I was so happy to hear the news. You ____________ definitely go to college in the United States!
2. The teacher said we ____________ hand in our papers by Friday. She won't grade them if we hand them in after that.
3. It's difficult to explain what happened at school today. You ____________ talk to the principal about it.
4. We ____________ keep the media room organized. It's one of the school rules.
5. Students ____________ postpone doing homework. It's not advisable to do all tasks on the weekend.

Making Requests with *Can* and *Could*

6 **Look at the dialogue below and underline the requests with can / could. There's also one suggestion. Can you identify it?**

____

____

A: Hey Mom, can I ask you something?
B: Sure, how can I help you?
A: Could I go to Mandy's for a sleepover tonight?
B: A sleepover? We can certainly think about it. Can I have her mom's phone number, please? Where do you know Mandy from?
A: We see each other at school every day, Mom. We have lab classes together.
B: Oh, yes. I know her family. You could tell her mom to call me sometime. She's really nice.
A: So... Please...
B: OK then, of course, have fun!
A: Thanks, Mom!

7 **Use the information from the box to complete the statements below.**

certainly	could	make a request

1. We use *can* and *could* to ______________ .
2. Some of the ways to answer a request are *Sure*, *Of course*, ______________, and *I'm not sure.*
3. We can also use ______________ to make suggestions.

8 **Work in pairs. Read the dialogue in Activity 6 again and practice making requests and giving suggestions. Try to replace the requests and the suggestion from the dialogue with some of your own.**

Have to / Don't have to

9 **Match the sentences to the pictures.**

1. You **don't have to** pay to watch this movie.
2. You **have to** log in to play the game.
3. You **don't have to** go to school on Sundays.

a. 

b. 

c. 

10 **Now check (✓) the option that best explains each sentence.**

1. You don't have to pay to watch this movie.
   a. ☐ It isn't necessary to pay to get into the exhibition.
   b. ☐ You can pay after the exhibition.
2. You have to log in to play the game.
   a. ☐ It isn't necessary to log in to play this game.
   b. ☐ It is mandatory to log in to play this game.
3. You don't have to go to school on Sundays.
   a. ☐ You can't go to school on Sundays.
   b. ☐ There are no classes at school on Sundays.

11 **Listen to Paul talk to a friend and mark the sentences T (True) or F (False).** 40

1. ☐ Paul has to visit Germany next year.
2. ☐ Paul doesn't have to take a language exam.
3. ☐ June has to take an Italian language exam.
4. ☐ Paul and June have to take a science test.
5. ☐ Paul has to take a sports test.

12 **Work in groups. Talk about the things you must do in the classroom. Then give some advice using *should / shouldn't*.**

We must all listen to the teacher.
We should ask our classmates to be quiet and respect the teacher.
Students shouldn't talk when the teacher is explaining.

I can use can, could, have to, and don't have to.
Language Booster page 37

Listening

1 **Look at the pictures, read their captions, and complete the descriptions.**

Preschool

Elementary School

Middle School

High school

1. In this school, students need to study very hard to get into university.

____

2. This is the first school we go to as kids, from two to five years old.

____

3. In this school, students continue to develop their skills before going to high school.

____

4. In this school, students explore the basics of reading, writing, math, science, etc.

____

2 **LISTENING FOR GIST. Listen and check (✓) the topic of the audio.** 41

1. ☐ The advantages of homeschooling.
2. ☐ The four levels of education in the United States.
3. ☐ The educational system around the world.

3 **LISTENING FOR DETAILS. Listen again and identify the school levels listed in Activity 1.** 42

1. In this level of education, the only rule is to have fun. ______________________
2. This is the level when you learn more about science. ______________________
3. Students study the basics and don't have to take tests. ______________________
4. At this level, students have to study hard to enter university. ______________________

Pronunciation

4 **Work in pairs. Listen to the words and write them in the correct column.** 43

math the their these third through

/ð/ **this**	/θ/ **think**

Speaking

5 **Interview a classmate about the rules his / her parents have for schoolwork. Then give advice.**

What rules for schoolwork do you have at home?

I must do my homework before dinner.

You should start doing homework earlier, then.

I can talk about school rules.

e-Language Booster

Use of English

6 **Circle the correct options to complete the teen advice column texts.**

1. A question about tests

Mark: Hi, Dr. Who, so I'm fourteen, and I am taking an online exam soon. My classmates tell me it's OK to use my book while I'm doing the test, but I don't know. Is it the right thing to do?

Mark, November 11

Dr. Who: Hello, Mark. I'm very happy you are thinking about this. I think you **shouldn't use / don't have to use** your book and just show what you know.

Dr. Who

2. To go or not to go?

Lin: Hi, Dr. Who! I'm in Junior High, and my classmates invited me to go to a high school party. My mom says I shouldn't go. All of my friends are going. What **should I do / must I do?**

Lin, November 13

Dr. Who: Hello, Miss Lin. You could explain to your mom that your friends are going. I think she will understand that. You shouldn't go without her permission.

Dr. Who

3. The Media Room

Liz: Hey, I'm Liz. Our teacher told us today that we can't use the media room at all. The media room is the place I meet my friends and relax when we're at school. I think we **must speak / should speak** to the principal, what do you think?

Liz, November 29

Dr. Who: Hmm, Liz. I think you should speak to your teacher first. **Should you do this? / Can you do this?** Your teacher shouldn't stop you from using the media room. Students just **could follow / have to follow** the rules to access these areas.

Dr. Who

7 **Dr. Who is making a suggestion to one of the teenagers. Find it and write it down.**

____

____

8 **Write to Dr. Who asking for advice about a problem at school.**

____

____

____

9 **Work in groups. Write five pieces of advice you can give to some of your classmates to have a better school life. Use your notebook.**

Leo, I think you should study harder for the tests.
Marina, I think you shouldn't talk to the teacher like that.

WHAT DO YOU THINK

I can ask for and give some advice.
Language Booster page 38

#CHALLENGE

Writing

1 Read Allie's e-mail. What does she need help with?

____

TO Mrs. Harrison (harrison.courses@hashtaghigh.com) SEND

FROM Allie Thompson (alliet@hotmail.com)

SUBJECT Advanced Coding Course

Mrs. Harrison,

I am writing to request some information about the Advanced Coding course at Hashtag High School. Could you send me information about the dates and prices of the course? I took an intermediate coding course at my high school last year, but it doesn't offer an advanced course. What topics does the course cover? Do I need to take a test before the course? What happens if I fail the test? Do I need a laptop?

I always get good grades in technology classes, and I hope to study Computer Science in college in the future. This course will help me reach that goal.

Best wishes,
Allie

2 Complete the sentences with information about Allie's e-mail.

1. Allie is writing to ______________________.
2. She's interested in an ______________________ program.
3. She wants information about the ______________________ and ______________________ of the course.
4. She wants to study ______________________ in the future.
5. She wants to know if she needs a ______________________ for any of the courses.

Prepare to Write

3 You are going to write an e-mail asking for information about a course. Make notes about the information you want to include in your text.

1. Explain why you are writing.
2. Ask about the dates and prices of the course.
3. Ask for more information on the subjects you will study.
4. Ask about any extra devices you might need.
5. State why you want to take this course.

I can plan to write an e-mail requesting information.

e-Language Booster

Write

4 **Write an e-mail requesting information about a course you are interested in using your ideas from Activity 4. You can use Allie's e-mail as a model.**

TO SEND

FROM

SUBJECT

Check and Change

5 **Read your e-mail and make sure you included:**

- [ ] your purpose for writing.
- [ ] the name of the course you are interested in.
- [ ] *can / could* for requests.
- [ ] collocations related to exams and tests.
- [ ] questions about the information on the school website.

6 **Edit your e-mail. Make sure all the elements in Activity 5 are included.**

Publish

7 **Write a clean version of your e-mail.**

#TIP

Do not use emojis in your e-mail and revise it before you send it.

Speaking

8 **Work in pairs. Read your classmate's e-mail and give advice to each other.**

You should ask about the bus service, too.

You should check if there is an exam at the end of the year.

I can write an e-mail requesting information.

Language Booster page 39

#DIGITAL LITERACY

1. Choose an attractive template.
2. Use pictures to illustrate your poster.
3. Make your poster easy to read.
4. Increase the size of fonts or pictures for emphasis.
5. Make creative use of colors.

Project: An Online Poster

Step 1 Think

1 Discuss in groups.

1. What do you think a good school must have? Why?

____

2. Read the poster below and reflect on its features. Is the design attractive? Is the message objective? Are there any pictures? Is the poster convincing?

____

____

My School

My school has the best teachers in the world. In a good school, teachers support us and help us learn. Our schools should give students access to Wi-Fi, laptops, tablets, and modern technology to provide us with quality education. My school is an example of a good school. Our schools must provide supportive learning environments for us. I think they should also have more arts and sports, too. My school has all that!

Step 2 Plan

2 Work in groups. You are going to create an online poster about your school. Make a list of the key points (what a good school must have, what it should offer, etc) and the images you would like to use.

____

____

____

Step 3 Research

3 Work in groups. Go online and research into quality education, school infrastructure, and teaching. Make notes in your notebook, if necessary. Choose a picture to add to your poster.

quality education

Step 4 Design

4 Work in groups. Use online tools to create your poster.

- Check the text.
- Check the pictures.
- Check the organization.

#TIP STEP 4
Create a small version of your poster for a social media post. Don't forget to have fun!

Step 5 Present and Publish

5 Work in groups. Present your poster to the class.

#TIP STEP 5
When you present in public, make sure to make eye contact with your audience.

Step 6 Evaluate

6 Complete the evaluation table.

★☆☆ More to learn ★★☆ Good ★★★ Excellent

Criteria	My Evaluation	Group Evaluation	Teacher Evaluation
Teamwork	☆☆☆	☆☆☆	☆☆☆
Language	☆☆☆	☆☆☆	☆☆☆
Design	☆☆☆	☆☆☆	☆☆☆

#SELF-ASSESSMENT

1 Mark the learning objectives according to the key.

★☆☆ I don't understand.	★★☆ I understand, but I need help.	★★★ I can do it!

Learning Objectives	Rating
To talk about my classroom rules.	☆☆☆
To describe types of schools.	☆☆☆
To read about different educational models.	☆☆☆
To write about schools in my country.	☆☆☆
To use *must* and *should*.	☆☆☆
To use *can, could, have to,* and *don't have to.*	☆☆☆
To talk about school rules.	☆☆☆
To ask for and give some advice.	☆☆☆
To plan to write an e-mail requesting information.	☆☆☆
To write an e-mail requesting information.	☆☆☆
To identify the features of a poster and plan to create one.	☆☆☆
To create an online poster and present it to the class.	☆☆☆

2 Work in pairs. Discuss the questions.

1. What did I find most interesting to learn? Why?
2. How did I learn it?
3. How can I use it in real life?

Language Booster page 40

A HEALTHY MIND IN A HEALTHY BODY

In this unit, you will learn how to:

- Talk about sports.
- Write about an event in the past.
- Create a graphic organizer.

Say what you know:

- Sports.
- Things you did in the past.
- Ways to promote health and well-being.

Video

Last Night's Game

Before You watch

1 In pairs, check (✓) the words that are related to sports.

1. ☐ ball
2. ☐ bike
3. ☐ coach
4. ☐ exercise
5. ☐ player
6. ☐ uniform

While You Watch

2 Watch the video and check (✓) the statements that are true about it. ▷ 07

1. ☐ Paula and Sam watched a soccer game last night.
2. ☐ The game wasn't interesting.
3. ☐ Paula and her friends don't exercise.
4. ☐ Sam believes we should find pleasure in the sports we play.
5. ☐ There isn't a girls' volleyball team at Paula and Sam's school.
6. ☐ Sam tells Paula to talk to the coach about the girls' soccer team.

3 Watch the video again and answer the questions. ▷ 07

1. Where does Sam and Paula's conversation take place?

____

2. How does Sam describe the game they watched last night?

____

3. What does Paula want to start this year?

____

4. Can boys that play for the basketball team play for the soccer team, too?

____

5. What does Sam say about a healthy mind?

____

After You Watch

4 Use words or expressions from the video to complete the sentences.

1. I like to play ______________________.
2. My friends like to play ______________________.
3. I think exercising is ______________________.
4. The best sports at my school are ______________________.
5. I want to learn how to play ______________________.

5 Work in pairs. Compare your sentences in Activity 4 to your classmate's. Are they similar?

I can interpret a conversation about sports.
e-Language Booster

Vocabulary

Sports

6 **Listen and complete the texts below with the words from the box. Why do you think these people play sports?** 44

aerobics	basketball	cricket	golf
gymnastics	judo	swimming	tennis	volleyball

My friends and I played [1] __________ on the beach that day. It was great! We love to play sports. Sometimes we go [2] __________ or play [3] __________, too.

My sister practices [4] __________ for many hours because she takes part in competitions. My other sister does [5] __________. In this picture, it was the first day I tried to play tennis. What an amazing feeling! Tennis is a sport people love to watch. I prefer to do [6] __________ in my free time. It's an individual sport, not a team sport.

I remember this picture, I was so nervous! It was the end of the [7] __________ season, and everything we did or didn't do was important. Everything could change the game. I remember I tried an [8] __________ class to relax, but it didn't really work out. Now, when I want to relax, I play [9] __________.

Play a Sport vs. Practice a Sport

7 **Read the excerpts from the texts in Activity 6 and circle the correct options.**

My friends and I **played** cricket on the beach that day.

My sister **practices** tennis for many hours because she takes part in competitions.

1. **Playing / Practicing** a sport is often linked to enjoyment and involves a sport you already know how to play.
2. **Playing / Practicing** a sport involves training to get a new skill, improve a skill, or keep a skill.

8 **Complete the sentences below with play or *practice*.**

1. We __________ soccer so well! I think we should try to join a professional team.
2. I don't want to __________ basketball anymore; my dunk isn't any better. I quit!

Collocations with *Go*, *Do*, and *Play*

9 **Read the table and complete the statements about collocations with *go*, *do*, and *play*.**

Go	cycling, dancing, running, swimming
Do	ballet, gymnastics, judo, yoga
Play	baseball, basketball, soccer, volleyball

1. We use __________ with sports in which we don't use a ball and with recreational activities.
2. We use __________ sports that we don't need any equipment to do.
3. We use __________ with team sports and sports in which we use a ball or a similar object.

10 **Add other sports or activities to the table in Activity 9.**

I can talk about sports.

Language Booster page 41

Reading

1 USING PRIOR KNOWLEDGE. In pairs, check the habits that are healthy.

1. ☐ doing sports
2. ☐ eating a lot of candy
3. ☐ walking 30 minutes a day
4. ☐ drinking soda every day
5. ☐ sleeping well
6. ☐ playing video games all day long

2 MAKING AND CONFIRMING PREDICTIONS. Read the titles of the texts and relate them to the title of this unit: *A Healthy Mind in a Healthy Body*.

____

The Luckiest Day of My Life

Hi, I'm Ezekiel, and I'm from Mexico. I'm an e-athlete, and last year I played in the League of Legends. I worked very hard to compete and loved every minute! I traveled to Mexico city, and I received a medal at the end of the tournament. It was the luckiest day of my life! E-sports are very good for our mental health as they keep our brains active.

My Lucky Charm

Hey, this is Teresa and that's me in the picture! It's my favorite picture ever because on this day I danced in a gymnastics competition for the first time. I loved this experience, and nowadays I help other teenagers get into sports for their well-being. It's important to exercise and take care of yourself. The colored ribbon in the picture was my lucky charm in the competition.

I Was Lucky to Find My Best Friends

Hi! My name's Edith. When my friend Tracy and I were in high school, two boys at school started making fun of us. It wasn't nice of them, so we talked to our teacher. The teacher asked us to talk to the boys about our issues. Was it awkward? Yes, but in the end, we discovered we were just curious about our differences and needed to talk. We are friends now, best friends. We hang out together and we're all part of our college cheerleader group.

3 SCANNING. Read the sentences about the texts and mark them T (True) or F (False).

1. ☐ Ezekiel doesn't believe e-sports are good for our health.
2. ☐ Ezekiel participates in computer / video games competitions.
3. ☐ Teresa believes sports are important for our health.
4. ☐ Teresa's lucky charm is a hair clip.
5. ☐ Edith and Tracy are in high school.

4 Read the texts again and write Ezekiel, Teresa, or Edith to complete the sentences.

1. ____________ loved her experience of dancing in a gym competition for the first time.
2. ____________ worked hard to win the League of Legends.
3. ____________ and Tracy talked to their teacher.

5 When was the luckiest day of your life?

The luckiest day of my life was my first day at school.

Listening

6 Listen and write the number of the speaker that does each action. 45

Who...

- ☐ goes to practice every day and exercises for many hours?
- ☐ does a sport that doesn't require special equipment?
- ☐ does an e-sport?
- ☐ says his / her life changed because of sports?
- ☐ practices online?
- ☐ mentions that doing sports helped kids go to better schools?

Writing

7 Read an excerpt from the audio in Activity 6 and answer: Which sport changed the speaker's life?

____

I didn't want to go to school or leave the house. My parents were worried about me. Until one day, one of my friends asked me to go running with her. You don't need any special equipment, just a pair of sneakers and off you go. We talked so much! Running changed my life. I get up every morning to run, and I start my days happy. It's great for my mental and physical health.

8 Do you know anyone who changed his / her life through sports? Research and make notes. Who is he / she? Where is he / she from? What sport does he / she play?

____

____

9 Complete the sentences about yourself.

1. Sports make me feel ______________________.
2. I like / don't like to play sports because ______________________.
3. Sports are important for our body because ______________________.
4. Sports are important for our mind because ______________________.
5. In my opinion, sports ______________________.

I can talk about the importance of sports.

Language Booster page 42

#UNDERSTAND

Grammar

Simple Past: *Was / Were*

1 The sentences below were extracted from the texts on page 96. Read them, pay attention to the parts in bold, and underline the correct options in the following statements.

It **was** the luckiest day of my life!
The colored ribbon in the picture **was** my lucky charm in the competition.
When my friend Tracy and I **were** in high school...
It **wasn't** nice of them...
Was it awkward?

1. The sentences are about the **present** / **past**.
2. The verbal form *was* is **singular** / **plural**.
3. The negative contraction of *was* is **wasn't** / **was not**.
4. The verbal form *were* is **singular** / **plural**.
5. In the question, *was* comes **before** / **after** the subject.

2 Complete the table.

Verb *Be* (Simple Past)	
Affirmative	I / He / She / It **was**
Negative	I / He / She / It [1] ________ (was not)
Interrogative	[2] ____________ I / he / she / it?
Short Answers	Yes, I / he / she / it [3] ________.
	No, I / he / she / it [4] ________.

Verb *Be* (Simple Past)	
Affirmative	You / We / They **were**
Negative	You / We / They weren't ([5] ________)
Interrogative	[6] ____________ you / we / they?
Short Answers	Yes, you / we / they [7] ________.
	No, you / we / they [8] ________.

3 Use was or were in the affirmative, negative, or interrogative forms to complete the sentences.

1. I ____________ at school yesterday morning when you called me at home. I'm sorry I ____________ there for you.
2. ____________ Sam and Ally in the school kitchen? No, they ____________.

Simple Past: Regular Verbs — Affirmative Form

4 Read these sentences and circle the correct options to complete the statements.

Until one day, one of my friends **asked** me...
We **talked** so much!

1. The sentences are in the **present** / **past**.
2. The verbs in the example sentences above are **regular** / **irregular** and they form the past in the same way.
3. We form the Simple Past of regular verbs by adding **-ing** / **-ed** to the base form of the verb.
4. The verbs in the Simple Past **have the same form** / **have different forms** for all persons.

5 Complete the sentences with the verbs from the box in the Simple Past.

ask call dance talk

1. I ____________ to my teacher about the P.E. test last week.
2. Maria ____________ in an international competition two weeks ago.
3. My friends ____________ me to go to the sports center this weekend.
4. We ____________ our classmates to the laboratory after class yesterday.

6 In pairs, use two verbs from Activity 5 to write meaningful sentences in your notebook.

Simple Past: Regular Verbs — Interrogative and Negative Forms

7 **Read the text below. Is it an account about a day in the past or an arrangement for a day in the future?**

____

It was a beautiful day, and I invited my sister for a walk. I didn't imagine it would rain so much. We were in the street when the rain started. Of course, we didn't have an umbrella. Did we care? No, we didn't! We were just happy to be out and about.

8 **Read the text in Activity 7 again and underline the verbs in the Simple Past (affirmative, negative, and interrogative forms).**

9 **Now complete the statements about the Simple Past with the information from the box.**

answers	did	did not / didn't	-ed

1. We use ______________ to form negative sentences in the Simple Past.
2. We use ______________ to ask questions in the Simple Past.
3. In the negative and interrogative forms we remove the ______________ ending from the main verb.
4. *Yes, they did.* and *No, she didn't.* are examples of short ______________.

10 **Listen and complete the sentences.** 46

1. He ______________ me after the school games yesterday.
2. ______________ you ______________ for water for the runners?
3. ______________ the players ______________ at the competition on time?
4. The girls ______________ to dance at the spring ball.
5. ______________ you happy when you received that medal?
6. Steve ______________ lucky at sports.

11 **Unscramble the words to form sentences.**

1. World of Wars / time / the / night / on / for / didn't / last / arrive / We / .

____

____

2 Were / sport / curious / about / you / the / ?

____

____

3. didn't / organization / receive / support / the / Athletes / from / .

____

____

12 **In pairs, ask and answer questions using the Simple Past with regular verbs. Audio record the discussion.**

Did *you* ***go*** *to school yesterday?*

Yes, I ***did****. I* ***talked*** *to the teacher about the test.*

Listening

1 **Read the sentences and answer: Do you play any of these sports? Which ones? Talk in pairs.**

1. We **go** swimming every week.
2. I **play** tennis with my best friend.
3. Cecilia **does** yoga on Saturdays.

2 **INFERRING MEANING. Listen and number accordingly.** 47

3 **LISTENING FOR DETAILS. Listen again and mark the sentences T (True) or F (False).** 48

1. ☐ He played for a long time and lost track of time.
2. ☐ Lidia called him on Monday.
3. ☐ Lin's luck changed after some time.

4 **In pairs, complete the audio scripts with the words from the box. Then listen and read along to check your answers.** 49

first finally next (2x) then

1.

[1] ____________, my friend called me, and we talked about the tournament. [2] ____________, I turned on my PC and logged into the game. I asked if anyone needed help, and everyone was OK. [3] ____________ I started to play, and the time passed fast. I didn't realize it was already midnight when my mom called me to turn off the lights and go to sleep. The next day, I decided to go running with my dog and stay away from the computer.

2.

Lidia called very early on Sunday morning. It was the day we would go horse riding, and I was very excited. I didn't want to drive to the place, so I called a taxi. Before I arrived, I asked the trainer to prepare my horse. [4] ____________, I put on my boots and called my horse. He was so beautiful. [5] ____________. I headed home.

Pronunciation

5 **In pairs, practice reading the following words aloud. Then put them in the right column in the table below. Listen and check.** 50

ask celebrate family game
have make party start

/æ/	/a:/	/ei/	/a/
basketball	car	play	teacher

6 **Listen and pay attention to the *-ed* endings. Then write the verbs from the box in the corresponding columns.** 51

arrived asked closed
stopped texted waited

/d/	/t/	/id/
called	looked	wanted

Speaking

7 **Interview a classmate about his / her day yesterday. Make sure he / she uses the Simple Past and sequence words (*first*, *next*, *then*, *finally*) in his / her answers.**

What did you do yesterday?

Well, first I called my best friend. Next, I...

I can talk about a sequence of events in the past.
e-Language Booster

Use of English

8 **Listen to a podcast and check (✓) what it is about.** 52

1. ☐ Physical, mental, and emotional health in adulthood.
2. ☐ Physical, mental, and emotional health in childhood.
3. ☐ Physical, mental, and emotional health in teenage years.

9 **Complete this excerpt from the podcast with the verbs in parentheses in the Simple Past.**

A: How was our physical, mental, and emotional health in the past? [1] __________ (be) teenagers happier then?
Here's Dr. Alexander to answer all our questions.

B: Well, Linda, in the past, teenagers [2] __________ (need) to ask their parents for permission to watch certain TV programs, to go out with their friends, etc. They [3] __________ (dance) at school parties and [4] __________ (watch) movies at drive-through movie theaters. They [5] __________ (play) on the streets. [6] __________ (be) they happier? I don't know, but they [7] __________ (not be) afraid of violence, for example, and they [8] __________ (celebrate) even the smaller things.

10 **Use the verbs from the box in the Simple Past to complete another excerpt.**

arrange be (2x) call not be not need not stop

A: How did teenagers deal with sports in the past?

B: Some teens did sports. The most common sports [1] __________ soccer, volleyball, basketball, and tennis. But we [2] __________ to think about these things back then. We just [3] __________ our friends and [4] __________ to meet outside to play soccer, for example. There [5] __________ video games or streaming services. It [6] __________ fantastic to be a teenager back then. We [7] __________ to worry about the future. It was a good life!

11 **Work in groups. Research online and find out more about teenagers in the past. Then write a paragraph about how teenagers were and what they did and didn't do in the past.**

____

____

____

I can talk about teenagers in the past.

Language Booster page 44

Writing

1 Read the text and check (✓) the picture that best relates to it.

NEW TAB +

The 2019 Summer Festival in Florida was an amazing event! 20 DJs from all over the world in a tropical paradise.
The participants enjoyed different kinds of music, played games, and participated in other activities. The festival opened with an Instagram competition for the best picture of the crowd as young people waited for the DJs to start. There were people from everywhere around the world. Everyone enjoyed the festival very much. A young girl from Brazil was the winner of the online competition. This was the picture she took. Do you like it?

1.

2.

3.

4.

2 Complete the sentences about the text.

1. The 2019 Summer Festival was in ____________.
2. The DJs were from ________________.
3. The festival started with an Instagram ____________.
4. People really ____________ the festival.
5. The ____________ of the online competition was from ____________.

Prepare to Write

3 Answer the questions about an event you attended.

1. Where was it?
____
2. When was it?
____
3. Was it an international event?
____
4. Where were the people in the event from?
____
5. Was the music / food, etc. good?
____
6. Did you enjoy it?
____
7. What was the best moment in this event in your opinion?
____

4 You are going to write a description of an event you attended. Go online and choose a picture to illustrate your text.

#TIP

Select the words to use in your search according to the event you are going to describe.

Write

5 **Write your text. Use the information in Activity 3 and the text in Activity 1 as a model.**

Check and Change

6 **Read your text and make sure you included:**

- [ ] the type of event it was.
- [ ] when and where the event happened.
- [ ] the activities included in the event.
- [ ] regular verbs in the Simple Past.
- [ ] *was / were*.

7 **Edit your text and make sure all elements in Activity 6 are included.**

Publish

8 **Write a clean version of your text.**

#TIP

Use adjectives to describe the event and your feelings about it.

Speaking

9 **Work in pairs. Read your classmate's event description and answer the following questions about it.**

1. What was the name of the event? ______
2. What type of event was it? ______
3. When was the event? ______
4. Where was the event? ______
5. Did he / she like the event? ______
6. What was the best moment of the event in his / her opinion? ______

10 **Join another classmate and tell him / her about the event in Activity 9.**

My classmate Lucas participated in a street art event. The name of the event was...

I can write about an event in the past.
Language Booster page 45

Project: A Graphic Organizer

#DIGITAL LITERACY

There are free templates online that you can use for your graphic organizer.

#TIP STEP 1

Use graphic organizers as a learning tool, presenting information and ideas to make comprehension easier.

Step 1 Think

1 Discuss in groups.

1. Do you believe sports can improve our physical and mental health?
2. Read the text. Are there any similar opportunities in your school?

How Can Schools Ensure Students' Well-being?

- Mindfulness lessons: students take breaks from their schedules to focus on activities such as breathing, contemplating, and reflecting.
- Teacher training: teachers learn to read the first signs when something is going wrong with their students.
- Diversified events (such as chat sessions, clubs, mentor programs, yoga sessions, etc.) to grow bonds among students, teachers, and school staff.
- Sports sessions: help students develop and practice different skills (and also their emotional intelligence) through sports.

2 Complete the graphic organizer with key information from the text in Activity 1.

1.

2.

How can schools ensure students' well-being?

3.

4.

I can interpret a text about ways for schools to promote well-being.

Step 2 Plan

3 In groups, come up with ideas on how to improve and promote health and well-being in your school. Make notes.

____

____

Step 3 Research

4 In groups, research what schools around the world are doing to promote health and well-being to students. Add your notes to Activity 3.

Step 4 Design

5 In groups, create your graphic organizer to display the information from Activity 3 and from your research.

- Check the text.
- Check the images.
- Check the organization.

Step 5 Present and Publish

6 In groups, present your graphic organizer to the class.

Step 6 Evaluate

7 Complete the evaluation table.

★☆☆ More to learn ★★☆ Good ★★★ Excellent

Criteria	My Evaluation	Group Evaluation	Teacher Evaluation
Teamwork	☆☆☆	☆☆☆	☆☆☆
Language	☆☆☆	☆☆☆	☆☆☆
Design	☆☆☆	☆☆☆	☆☆☆

#TIP STEP 4

Research and choose the type of graphic organizer to match your purpose.

#TIP STEP 5

Show enthusiasm while presenting your graphic organizer.

I can create a graphic organizer and present it to the class.

#SELF-ASSESSMENT

1 Mark the learning objectives according to the key.

★☆☆ I don't understand.	★★☆ I understand, but I need help.	★★★ I can do it!

Learning Objectives	Rating
To interpret a conversation about sports.	☆☆☆
To talk about sports.	☆☆☆
To read about teenagers and their lucky days.	☆☆☆
To talk about the importance of sports.	☆☆☆
To use *was*, *were*, and regular verbs in the past.	☆☆☆
To ask and answer questions in the Simple Past.	☆☆☆
To talk about a sequence of events in the past.	☆☆☆
To talk about teenagers in the past.	☆☆☆
To read about an event in the past and prepare to write one.	☆☆☆
To write about an event in the past.	☆☆☆
To interpret a text about ways for schools to promote well-being.	☆☆☆
To create a graphic organizer and present it to the class.	☆☆☆

2 Work in pairs. Discuss the questions.

1. What did I find most interesting to learn? Why?
2. How did I learn it?
3. How can I use it in real life?

Language Booster page 46

PASSPORT TO THE WORLD

#15 LIFE ON LAND

In this unit, you will learn how to:

- Talk about tourism.
- Write an e-mail of complaint.
- Create a travel brochure.

Say what you know:

- Types of transportation.
- Types of accommodations.
- Vacation activities.

Video

Traveling

Before You Watch

1 In pairs, check (✓) the words that are related to traveling.

1. ☐ passport
2. ☐ take pictures
3. ☐ airplane
4. ☐ school
5. ☐ hotel
6. ☐ homework

While You Watch

2 Watch the video and underline the statements that are true about it. ▷ 08

1. Paula is going to Brazil.
2. Paula is going to an ecological reserve called Brasília.
3. Sam's parents bought tickets to Germany to visit his aunt.
4. Sam is going to stay at his uncle's house.
5. Paula is going to hike and go sightseeing.
6. Sam is excited about his trip.

3 Watch the video again and answer the questions. ▷ 08

1. Where does Sam and Paula's conversation take place?
____
____
2. How is Paula going to Bonito with her family?
____
____
3. Why did Paula's parents choose an ecological reserve?
____
____
4. What is Paula going to do in Bonito?
____
5. How does Sam feel about his vacation?
____
6. Why did Sam have to leave?
____
____

After You Watch

4 Complete the sentences about yourself. You can use information from the video or add new ideas.

1. My favorite vacation activity is ______________________________
______________________________.
2. The best means of transportation when I'm on vacation is ______________________________
______________________________.
3. My favorite vacation destination is ______________________________
______________________________.

5 Work in pairs. Compare your sentences in Activity 4 to your classmate's. Are they similar?

I can interpret a video about traveling.
e-Language Booster

Vocabulary

Vacation Activities

6 **Listen and repeat. Then label the pictures with the words from the box.** 53

board a plane	check in	go hiking
go sightseeing	read a book	sunbathe
take pictures	walk	

1. 
____

2. 
____

3. 
____

4. 

____

5. 
____

6. 
____

7. 
____

8. 
____

7 **Work in pairs. Take turns talking about your plans for your next vacation.**

On my next vacation, I want to go to the beach. I want to go hiking and sightseeing.

Types of Accommodations

8 **Listen and repeat. Then match the words to the pictures.** 54

1. hotel
2. house
3. room
4. tent
5. vacation rental
6. youth hostel

a.  ☐

b.  ☐

c.  ☐

d.  ☐

e.  ☐

f.  ☐

9 **Complete the sentences with the words from Activity 8.**

1. The ______________ was awesome!
2. Can't find a cheaper place? Why don't you look online on a ______________ app?
3. We're visiting a friend in Spain and staying at his ______________. He was very kind to let us stay with him.
4. Can you believe Mark forgot to take a ______________? He had nowhere to sleep!
5. Cintia and her family booked a ______________ at the Ritz Carlton for the first night.
6. My classmates and I went backpacking around Latin America last year. We stayed in ______________.

I can identify words related to traveling.

Language Booster page 47

Reading

1 USING PRIOR KNOWLEDGE. In pairs, describe the pictures below with as many details as possible.

A Boat Trip (Naya, Greece)

My family spent 80 days on a boat last year. We went from Athens to Venice and then to Lisbon, and finally Porto. We didn't need any tickets or passports. It was a great trip, and I learned a lot. Every city was different. In some places, it's easy to see the effects of tourism. The green areas have disappeared and there are enormous hotels in their place. I love to travel, but this makes me so sad!

A Backpacking Trip (Steven, the Netherlands)

My friends and I traveled around Europe last July, for 25 days. We decided to go backpacking around Europe by interrail. We left Amsterdam, arrived in Berlin, stayed there for a couple of days, and then moved on to Prague, Krakow, Budapest, and Vienna. We spent most of our nights traveling and sleeping on the train. Did you know that railroads help preserve the environment? They reduce gas emissions and highway pollution, and the view is amazing!

A Trip to Latin America (Nena, the United States)

Have you ever been to Machu Picchu? It was my dream to see this place. But I wanted to find a way to reduce my carbon footprint. Peru is so far away and the only way to get there would be by plane. So I decided to use trains and walk when I was in Peru. There are many places you can visit on foot. This way I could preserve the land and its life and enjoy nature in a responsible way.

2 SKIMMING. Read the texts in Activity 1 and write *Naya*, *Steven*, or *Nena*.

1. ________ didn't need a passport to travel.
2. ________ slept most nights on the train.
3. ________ wanted to reduce his / her carbon footprint.
4. ________ visited Poland.
5. ________ wanted to enjoy nature in a responsible way.
6. ________ was sad to see what tourism does to the green areas.

3 Read the texts again and answer the questions.

1. How did Naya travel?
____
2. What countries did she visit?
____
3. How many days did Steven's backpacking vacation last?
____
4. Which cities did he visit?
____
5. According to Steven, how do railroads preserve the environment?
____

4 What type of vacation around the world would you choose and why?

I would like to visit Japan, because I love Japanese food and I want to see Mount Fuji.

____

____

5 Work in groups. Take turns talking about the place you chose in Activity 4.

I can read about people's trips around the world.

e-Language Booster

Listening

6 **Listen to Sam describe his vacation to Malaysia. Circle the right options.** 55

1. Sam **went to** / **lived in** Malaysia with his family.
2. He went **sightseeing** / **hiking** in the jungle.
3. Sam was **a volunteer** / **a worker** on a project to preserve life on land.
4. The program helps to **preserve** / **create** the orangutan population.
5. Our carbon footprint is how our **sleep** / **life** affects the environment.
6. Green areas are **disappearing** / **growing**.

7 **Listen again and answer the questions.** 56

1. What was Sam surprised to see?
____
2. Where did Sam stay?
____
3. What was the project about?
____
4. How did Sam feel when he arrived home?
____

Writing

8 **How can you reduce your carbon footprint while traveling? Write your ideas.**

I can save water at the hotels.

1. _______________
2. _______________
3. _______________

9 **Write a short paragraph with the ideas you listed in Activity 8.**

____
____
____

#TIP

You can use a search engine to find more ways of minimizing your carbon footprint and add ideas to your paragraph.

10 **Work in groups. Take turns reading your paragraphs to each other. What new information did you find out about ways to reduce your carbon footprint while traveling?**

I can talk about preserving life on land.

Language Booster page 48

#UNDERSTAND

Grammar

Simple Past: Irregular Verbs

1 Read the sentences. Underline the verbs in the Simple Past.

1. Did you spend 80 days on a boat last year?
2. We didn't leave Amsterdam before Christmas.
3. My family chose an ecological reserve for our vacation in Brazil.
4. My parents bought tickets and made reservations at a hotel.

2 Check (✓) the correct alternative to complete each statement below.

1. The sentences in Activity 1 are in the ________.
   a. ☐ past
   b. ☐ present
2. The Simple Past forms of the verbs in Activity 1 are ________ their base forms.
   a. ☐ similar to
   b. ☐ different from
3. The verbs in the sentences in Activity 1 are called ________ verbs.
   a. ☐ regular
   b. ☐ irregular

3 Rewrite the sentences below in the interrogative (?) or negative (-) forms.

1. They went from Athens to Venice and then to Lisbon last week. (?)

____

____

2. We bought camping equipment yesterday morning. (-)

____

____

3. Her family chose an ecological reserve to visit on their next vacation. (?)

____

____

4. I made a reservation at that vegetarian restaurant. (-)

____

____

Present Perfect for Personal Experiences

4 Read the dialogues below and pay attention to the words in bold. Then answer the questions.

A: Have you **been** to Machu Picchu?
B: Yes, I **have**. Amazing place, right?

A: Have you **chosen** a new travel destination?
B: No, I **haven't**. But I want to use my new passport soon!

A: Have they **seen** the new museum?
B: No, they **haven't**. They decided to go hiking instead.

1. Do the parts in bold in the dialogues refer to the present or the past?

____

2. Are the questions in the dialogues about possibilities or personal experiences?

____

3. Which word in bold in the questions is the auxiliary verb?

____

4. What are the short answers to the questions in the dialogues?

____

I can use the Simple Past and the Present Perfect tenses.

5 **Match the sentences to the pictures.**

1. **Have** you **been** to Perito Moreno Glacier?
2. I **slept** late last night and now I'm tired.
3. Mark **didn't go** to the National Gallery when he **was** in London.

a. 

b. 

c. 

6 **Listen to Davi and Ross. Then mark the sentences T (True) or F (False).** 57

1. ☐ Davi hasn't been to a glacier before.
2. ☐ Ross has been to a glacier before.
3. ☐ Davi hasn't traveled to Salvador.
4. ☐ Ross has been to Argentina.
5. ☐ According to Ross, global warming isn't melting the glaciers.

7 **Read the dialogues and complete the statement that follows.**

1. **A:** Have you ever traveled abroad?
   B: Yes, I have.
2. **A:** Have they ever been to China?
   B: No, they haven't.
3. **A:** Has Ted ever driven a car?
   B: No, he hasn't.

We can use [1] ______________ for questions in the Present Perfect to ask about life (or personal) [2] ______________.

8 **Write short answers to the questions below.**

1. Have you ever eaten octopus?
   ____
2. Have you ever been to Italy?
   ____
3. Have you ever seen a dolphin?
   ____
4. Have you ever read an e-book?
   ____
5. Have you ever swum in the ocean?
   ____

9 **Write four questions with *Have you ever* and take turns asking and answering them in pairs.**

1. ____________________
2. ____________________
3. ____________________
4. ____________________

I can talk about personal experiences.
Language Booster page 49

#DEVELOP

Listening

1 **Match the sentences to the pictures.**

1. Lena went to the hotel **on foot**.
2. Did Lisa go from Greece to Serbia **by car** or **by bus**?
3. Has Luis ever traveled to Scotland **by train**? It's an awesome ride.

a.  b.  c. 

2 **Use the highlighted expressions in Activity 1 to write sentences about your personal experiences. Use the Present Perfect.**

I have traveled to another country by car.

1. ______
2. ______
3. ______

3 **Listen to three speakers talk about their vacations and write the means of transportation they used.** 58

1. ______
2. ______
3. ______

4 **Listen again and mark the sentences T (True) or F (False).** 59

Speaker 1

1. ☐ There was a long line to board her flight.
2. ☐ She was angry about waiting in line.

Speaker 2

3. ☐ He was in the Sherlock Holmes Museum in London.
4. ☐ He met his best friend after the boat ride.

Speaker 3

5. ☐ She didn't know they could go sightseeing on the River Thames.
6. ☐ She went under the bridge and took a lot of pictures.

5 **Identify who did the actions below. Complete the sentences with the numbers 1, 2, or 3 to refer to the speakers.** 60

☐ visited the Harry Potter platform.
☐ went sightseeing by boat.
☐ was very excited and called a friend to talk about what happened.
☐ traveled alone.
☐ took many pictures.

Pronunciation

6 **Listen and complete the table with the words from the box.** 61

before boat don't hotel stop

/oʊ/	/ɑː/	/ɔː/
go	want	always

Speaking

7 **Work in pairs. Think about a means of transportation to go on a trip. Give clues and have your classmate guess what it is.**

You need to go to a gate to board.

Use of English

8 **Listen to a radio report and check (✓) what it is about.** 62

1. ☐ Vacation activities in Ibiza.
2. ☐ Transportation in Ibiza.
3. ☐ Sustainability in Ibiza.

9 **Complete the script of the radio report with the verbs in parentheses in the Simple Past or the Present Perfect.**

Pablo: Welcome to **Ibiza's Sustainability Report**. Today, our guest is Mateo Sanchez responsible for environmental actions in Ibiza. Welcome, Mateo!

Mateo: Thank you, Pablo! [1] ________ you [2] ________ (be) to Ibiza? It is a very **touristy** Spanish island. More than four million people visit it every summer. The island is beautiful, but there are some problems, too. The sustainability report of Ibiza [3] ________ (show) low **forest cover**, which causes forest fires. Temperatures [4] ________ (increase) a lot, too, and we [5] ________ (lose) our **biodiversity**. Last year, a local school [6] ________ (do) an environmental project about what species mostly disappear when there are forest fires. Students and teachers [7] ________ (make) **water tanks** to store water in case there are forest fires and [8] ________ (invite) tourists to join in!

10 **Read the script again and write the words in bold next to their definitions.**

1. A description of how a place is protecting and preserving the environment.
____
2. A place full of tourists.
____
3. The amount of land that is covered by forest.
____
4. The variety of plants and animals.
____
5. Large containers for water.
____

11 **Are there interesting environmental initiatives in your city? Research and write a short paragraph to explain your findings. Use your notebook.**

12 **Work in pairs. Read your classmate's text from Activity 11 and discuss the environmental activities in your city. Use irregular verbs in the Simple Past for completed and time-defined actions in the past and the Present Perfect for experiences.**

I can talk about sustainability in my city.

Language Booster page 50

#CHALLENGE

Writing

1 **In pairs, read Dani's e-mail and write what it is about.**

____

____

____

____

CANCEL SEND

TO portofino_portofino_hotel@hashtagmail.com

SUBJECT A complaint

Dear Sir / Madam,

I am writing to complain about the unsatisfactory service my friends and I received at your hotel. We stayed at Portofino Hotel, in room 124 on the 12th floor, between September 20th and 27th.

When we arrived, the line was so long that it took two hours just to check in. Your website mentioned there was free Wi-Fi and breakfast, but that information is not true.

Your website also mentioned sightseeing tours. Suzan, the morning receptionist, said there was an extra fee. We had to pay for activities and for the transportation to go sightseeing, and it cost us a fortune!

At the end of our stay, we had to pay the full cost without discount for all the inconvenience. Therefore, we would like to ask you for a refund of our payment.

Please consider my complaint as an opportunity for improvement as you are a great hotel franchise.

Looking forward to your reply.

Kind regards,

Dani Hernandez

2 **Complete the sentences about Dani's e-mail.**

1. Dani and her friends ____________________ at Portofino Hotel.
2. They stayed on the 12th ____________________.
3. She complained about ____________________, long line for check-in, no free Wi-Fi or breakfast, no vacation activities or sightseeing tours.
4. Dani starts her e-mail formally using... ____________________.
5. She uses ____________________ language.
6. She ends her e-mail asking for action of the hotel by saying ____________________.

Prepare to Write

3 **You are going to write an e-mail of complaint. Think of a place you have visited on previous vacations. Was there anything you didn't like? Was there anything on the website that didn't match what you found? Create a graphic organizer to make notes about the information you want to include in your text.**

#TIP

Use graphic organizers as a learning tool, presenting information and ideas to make comprehension easier.

I can read an e-mail of complaint and prepare to write one.

Write

4 **Write an e-mail complaining about a place you have visited on previous vacations. Use your notes in Activity 3 and the text in Activity 1 to help you.**

CANCEL SEND

TO

SUBJECT

Check and Change

5 **Read your e-mail and make sure you included:**

- ☐ a sentence to explain why you are writing.
- ☐ irregular verbs in the Simple Past.
- ☐ Present Perfect for personal experiences.
- ☐ your complaints.
- ☐ a request.
- ☐ formal language.

6 **Edit your e-mail and make sure all the elements in Activity 5 are included.**

Publish

7 **Write a clean version of your text.**

#TIP

Use a search engine to find out about customers' rights. What can you request as a customer who had a bad experience?

Speaking

8 **In pairs, take turns reading your e-mail and explaining your complaints to each other.**

This is my email. I complained about the Portofino Hotel. My friends and I stayed there for seven days, and we had a terrible experience.

9 **In groups, answer the following questions about your classmate's e-mail.**

1. What place did he / she choose to complain about?
2. Have you ever visited that place? What was your experience like?
3. Did he / she complain about accommodation and transportation?
4. Did he / she complain about tourism in the area?

I can write an e-mail of complaint.

Language Booster page 51

Project: A Travel Brochure

#DIGITAL LITERACY

1. Search for an appealing template. There are very interesting free options online.
2. Use an attractive title and don't include too much information.
3. Search online for attractive pictures of the travel destination.

Step 1 Think

1 Discuss in groups.

1. Have you ever read a brochure about a tourist destination?
2. Was it online or paper?
3. Did it make you want to go to the place it was advertising?
4. How did it make the destination attractive?

2 Read the travel brochure below. Is it attractive?

Kalimera Ellada!

Welcome to Greece

Have you ever visited amazing Greece? Come to Greece to sunbathe on the beautiful beaches and enjoy its impressive destinations. You can come by train, plane, or boat!

Amazing Sunsets

Sunsets in this country are famous and very popular with tourists. You can see the most beautiful sunsets from the Greek islands.

Places to Visit

Very old but also very modern, Athens has everything. A long history, shopping malls, and tasty food. Visit the Acropolis and go sightseeing to see the ancient theaters and museums.

Greek Cuisine

The four secrets of Greek cuisine: simple, fresh, spicy, and with lots of Greek olive oil. The Greek diet is healthy, and the food is delicious.

Make a hotel reservation now!

I can read a travel brochure for a tourist destination.

Step 2 Plan

3 You are going to create a travel brochure about a destination you want to visit. In groups, brainstorm ideas you want to include in the brochure. Where is this place? What kind of transportation is there? What can a tourist do there? What about sightseeing? Use headlines to organize the information.

Step 3 Research

4 In groups, research the travel destination you chose and the places a tourist can visit there. Add more ideas to Step 2.

Step 4 Design

5 In groups, use the information from Steps 2 and 3 to create your brochure.

- Check the text.
- Check the pictures.
- Check the organization.

#TIP STEP 4
Be creative and avoid big words and long sentences.

Step 5 Present and Publish

6 In groups, present your brochure to the class.

#TIP STEP 5
Keep it simple and tell stories, don't just read your brochure while presenting.

Step 6 Evaluate

7 Complete the evaluation table.

★☆☆ More to learn · ★★☆ Good · ★★★ Excellent

Criteria	My Evaluation	Group Evaluation	Teacher Evaluation
Teamwork	★★★	★★★	★★★
Language	★★★	★★★	★★★
Design	★★★	★★★	★★★

I can create a travel brochure.

#SELF-ASSESSMENT

1 Mark the learning objectives according to the key.

★☆☆ I don't understand.	★★☆ I understand, but I need help.	★★★ I can do it!

Learning Objectives	Rating
To interpret a video about traveling.	☆☆☆
To identify vocabulary related to traveling.	☆☆☆
To read about people's trips around the world.	☆☆☆
To talk about preserving life on land.	☆☆☆
To use the Simple Past and the Present Perfect tenses.	☆☆☆
To talk about personal experiences.	☆☆☆
To talk about tourism and transportation.	☆☆☆
To talk about sustainability in my city.	☆☆☆
To read an e-mail of complaint and prepare to write one.	☆☆☆
To write an e-mail of complaint.	☆☆☆
To read a travel brochure for a tourist destination.	☆☆☆
To create a travel brochure.	☆☆☆

2 Work in pairs. Discuss the questions.

1. What did I find most interesting to learn? Why?
2. How did I learn it?
3. How can I use it in real life?

UT Language Booster page 52

THE WORLD IS OURS

In this unit, you will learn how to:

- Talk about the future.
- Write to express opinions and present arguments.
- Create an online calendar.

Say what you know:

- Environmental problems and solutions.
- Animals that live under water.
- Different types of weather.

#14 LIFE BELOW WATER

DISCOVER

Video

It's a Beautiful World

Before You Watch

1 **Read the words and circle the ones that are related to geography.**

1. volleyball
2. skirt
3. mountain
4. subway
5. river
6. lawyer

While You Watch

2 **Watch the video and match the parts.** 09

1. Paula
2. Sam

☐ suggests talking about the lake at the foot of the mountain.

☐ thinks we all are responsible for keeping the oceans clean and preserving life below water.

3 **Watch the video again and check (✓) the correct sentences about it.** 09

1. ☐ Sam is going to visit his friends in Bonito at Christmas.
2. ☐ Paula saw a lot of animals that live underwater on her vacation.
3. ☐ Paula is going to book a hotel for Christmas in Bonito.
4. ☐ Sam loves the water.
5. ☐ Sam thinks it will rain soon.

4 **Watch the video once more and mark the sentences T (True) or F (False).** 09

1. ☐ Sam is going to have a white Christmas.
2. ☐ There are no rivers in Bonito.
3. ☐ Many underwater animals live in the ecological reserve.
4. ☐ When Paula was on vacation, it rained a lot one day.
5. ☐ Sam doesn't like underwater animals.
6. ☐ Sam suggests talking about their vacation in the school meeting tomorrow.

After You Watch

5 **Complete the dialogue with the words from the box. Then practice the dialogue with a classmate. Use a dictionary to look up the words you don't know.**

lake	mountains	nature	river	weather

John: Hey Allie, where were you? I didn't see you at school yesterday.

Allie: Hey John, I was packing for my camping trip this weekend. My family and I are going to go to Yosemite National Park. It will be sunny and cool; it's the perfect [1] ________________ to stay close to [2] ________________.

John: How nice, Allie! What are you going to do in Yosemite?

Allie: Well, we are going to hike in the [3] ________________ and swim in the [4] ________________. My dad is going to fish in the [5] ________________, too.

John: That sounds so much fun, Allie. Have a great time!

I can interpret a conversation about nature.

e-Language Booster

Vocabulary

Geographical Features

6 **Match the words to the pictures. Then listen and repeat.** 63

1. continents 2. desert 3. island 4. lake 5. mountains 6. ocean 7. river 8. sea

7 **Work in pairs. Complete the sentences with some words from Activity 6.**

1. Santorini is a very famous Greek ____________.
2. The Yosemite National Park has beautiful green ____________.
3. The Sahara ____________ is in Africa.
4. There are seven ____________. Europe is one of them.
5. There is a ____________ going through the city of London. It's called the Thames.
6. The Mediterranean ____________ is very warm in the summer.

Underwater Animals

8 **Complete the sentences with the words from the box.**

animal fish legs sea

1. A whale is a huge animal that lives in the ____________ but is not a fish. It's a mammal.
2. An octopus has eight ____________.
3. A shark is a big sea ____________. It is dangerous to humans.
4. A squid is a sea ____________ with a long soft body and ten limbs around its mouth.

9 **List the underwater animals in the sentences in Activity 8.**

____

____

____

10 **Work in groups. Choose an underwater animal and write a short description in your own words.**

This sea animal has a long, grey, pointed nose.

____

____

____

____

I can talk about geographical features and underwater animals.

Language Booster page 53

#CLARIFY

Reading

1 **Work in pairs. Discuss the following questions.**

1. Why is it important to have many kinds of plants and animals on Earth?
2. "We must be the change we want to see in the world." What do you think this quote means?

2 **MAKING PREDICTIONS. Look at the pictures below. What do you think you are going to read about?**

A Natural Wonder: The Great Australian Coral Reef

The Great Barrier Reef in Australia is one of the wonders of nature, and it's so big it is visible from space. It's the only living thing that can be seen from space. Coral reefs are very important because they are home to many kinds of marine life, generate clean air, and protect the coast from storms. Whales, dolphins, and sea turtles live in the 3,000 reefs. Reefs take carbon from the atmosphere and clean it. This way they are helping us stop climate change.

Amazing Oceans: We Wouldn't Be Here Without Them

Oceans are complete ecosystems. They have everything, from microscopic life to the largest animals on Earth, from colorless to colorful animals, and from hot to freezing water. Oceans give us food, entertainment, and influence our weather. However, climate change is affecting the temperature of the oceans, and, because of that, marine life is having problems growing and reproducing. Also, our garbage is damaging the oceans, but we can help by keeping the oceans clean. When you are at the beach, remove some of the garbage that is around. The oceans thank you!

3 **MONITORING COMPREHENSION. Read the texts in Activity 2 and circle the correct options to complete the sentences below.**

1. The Great Barrier Reef can be seen from **China** / **space**.
2. The reef is a **living thing** / **group of rocks and stones**.
3. Reefs are important because many kinds of **marine life** / **birds** live there.
4. Oceans are amazing because they are **complete** / **small** ecosystems.
5. Climate change is **affecting** / **not affecting** the oceans and life in them.

4 **Write three reasons why oceans are important to us. Use your notebook.**

Oceans are an inspiration for art and movies.

5 **Work in groups. Share your sentences from Activity 4. Do you have similar opinions?**

I can read about nature.

e-Language Booster

Listening

6 **Listen and answer: Where do the speakers live? Complete.** 64

1. The speaker lives in front of an ______________.
2. The speaker lives close to a ______________.
3. The speaker lives close to a ______________.
4. The speaker lives close to a ______________.

7 **Listen again and mark the sentences T (True) or F (False).** 65

Speaker 1

1. ☐ Winters are easy and calm.
2. ☐ In winter, it is wet and noisy by the ocean.

Speaker 2

3. ☐ She doesn't like summer.
4. ☐ She likes to go hiking and camping.

Speaker 3

5. ☐ Ice skating is fun for kids.
6. ☐ The lake is not good for ice skating.

Speaker 4

7. ☐ On the weekends, she spends time with her friends.
8. ☐ She likes to live life like an adventure.

Writing

8 **Complete the sentences about yourself. Use the vocabulary you have learned so far in this unit.**

1. I live close to a / an ______________________.
2. I like to ______________________ on the weekend.
3. I prefer the ______________________ to the ______________________.
4. I help keep water ecosystems clean by ______________________.

9 **Write a short paragraph with your answers in Activity 8. Read the script on page 162 for help.**

____

____

____

10 **Work in groups. Take turns reading your paragraphs to each other. What new information did you find out about ways to help keep water ecosystems clean?**

#TIP

You can use this information to introduce yourself to your classmates through your social media app. Include a picture of a way to help keep water ecosystems clean.

I can talk about ways to keep water ecosystems clean.

Language Booster page 54

#UNDERSTAND

Grammar

Future with *Will*

1 **Read the sentences. Pay attention to the parts in bold. Do they refer to the past or to the future?**

____

Marine life **will** always have a home in coral reefs.

Sea animals **won't reproduce** if the ocean temperature changes.

Garbage **will damage** the oceans.

2 **Check (✓) the correct alternatives to complete the statements below.**

1. The sentences with *will* in Activity 1 talk about
   - **a.** ☐ predictions for (or facts about) the future.
   - **b.** ☐ plans for the future.
2. The affirmative form of the Simple Future is
   - **a.** ☐ *will* + infinitive without *to*.
   - **b.** ☐ *will* + verb in the *–ing* form.
3. For each subject, the form of *will* is
   - **a.** ☐ different.
   - **b.** ☐ the same.
4. The negative form of the Simple Future is
   - **a.** ☐ *won't* (*will not*) + infinitive without *to*.
   - **b.** ☐ *won't* (*will not*) + verb *be* + *ing*.

3 **Match the sentences to what they indicate.**

1. Don't worry. I'**ll help** you carry the groceries home.
2. The winter **will come** when fall ends.
3. **Will** you please **get** some milk from the supermarket for me?
4. It **won't rain**. We need a sunny day, and we'll have it!

☐ a decision made at the moment of speaking.
☐ a prediction based on an opinion.
☐ a fact about the future.
☐ a request for the future.

Future with *Be Going to*

4 **Match the sentences to the pictures.**

1. She **is going to rent** a raft for an adventure down the river.
2. **Are** they **going to book** the hotel rooms for the family?
3. The adults **aren't going to have fun** ice skating on the lake with the kids.

5 **Based on the sentences in Activity 4, complete the statements with the information from the box.**

before	future plans	infinitive	negative

1. We use *be going to* to talk about ____________ and predictions based on evidence.
2. After *be going to* we use the verb in the ____________ form.
3. We form questions by putting the verb *be* ____________ the subject.
4. We form ____________ sentences by adding *not* after the verb *be*.

6 **Think of answers to these questions about your plans.**

1. What are you going to do on your next vacation?
2. When are you going to buy new clothes?
3. How are you going to celebrate your next birthday?

7 **Work in pairs. Use the questions in Activity 6 to interview your classmate.**

I can use *will* and *be going to* to talk about the future.

e-Language Booster

8 **Use a verb from the box and the correct form of *going to* or *will* to complete the sentences.**

be	carry	close	go	help	play

1. There are dark clouds in the sky. I ____________ all the windows before we go to sleep.
2. Wait a minute, is that bag heavy? I' ____________ it to your car.
3. Sea turtles ____________ to the reef to reproduce, just like every year.
4. The river ____________ dangerous today. It rained a lot yesterday.
5. ______ you ____________ play tennis tonight? Can I come?
6. ______ you ____________ me plan my trip, Dad?

9 **Now read the sentences in Activity 8 and check (✓) what they indicate.**

1. ☐ a plan made before the moment of speaking
   ☐ a decision made at the moment of speaking
2. ☐ a plan made before the moment of speaking
   ☐ a decision made at the moment of speaking
3. ☐ a plan for the future
   ☐ a fact about the future
4. ☐ a prediction based on an evidence
   ☐ a prediction based on an opinion
5. ☐ a request for the future
   ☐ a plan for the future
6. ☐ a request for the future
   ☐ a plan for the future

10 **Listen and complete the sentences.** 66

1. An octopus ____________ ink when it is in danger.
2. ________ sharks and dolphins ____________ to colder water in the summer?
3. According to evidence, monk seals ____________ ____________ extinct in a few years.
4. Many teenagers ____________ ____________ projects to protect the land and water. There aren't any plans for those activities.

11 **Unscramble the words to make questions.**

1. Are / you / next / an / summer / going / visit / island / to / ?
   ____
2. in / Are / to / going / octopus / Greece / eat / you / ?
   ____
3. dolphins / the / with / in / us / play / sea / Will / the / ?
   ____
4. survive / sea star / Will / water / a / the / outside / ?
   ____
5. visible / barrier reef / be / Will / the / space / from / ?
   ____

12 **In groups of three, ask and answer the questions in Activity 11.**

Are you going to visit an island next summer?

Yes, I am. / No, I'm not.

I can ask and answer questions about the future.

Language Booster page 55

Listening

1 Look, listen, and repeat. 67

1. 
stormy

2. 
foggy

3. 
snowy

4. 
rainy

5. 
sunny and windy

6. 
cloudy

2 LISTENING FOR SPECIFIC INFORMATION. Listen to Andy talk about Christmas trees. Which Christmas tree is better for the environment? 68

____

3 LISTENING FOR DETAILS. Complete the sentences from the audio. Listen and check. 69

1. Real trees help fight ____________ change.
2. Real trees ____________ products made of wood.
3. For every real tree we buy, farmers ____________ three more!
4. When we buy a real tree, we are supporting the ____________ farmers.
5. ____________ forests fight climate change and extreme ____________.

4 Work in pairs. Complete the sentences about real and fake trees. Then read the script on page 162 and check.

1. Real trees are better for the environment than ____________.
2. Plastic trees are not ____________ and their production causes a lot of ____________ emission.
3. I know we aren't supposed to be ____________ trees.

Pronunciation

5 Listen and repeat the words. Then put them in the right column. 70

buy cloudy enjoy fight
hike house island noise
out point

/aʊ/	/aɪ/	/ɔɪ/
cloudy	hike	enjoy

Speaking

6 Interview a classmate about his / her plans for the future. How is he / she going to help the environment and the underwater animals? What are the most interesting animals for him / her?

What are you going to do to keep the oceans clean?

I am going to help collect garbage for recycling.

I can talk about helping the environment and underwater animals.

e-Language Booster

Use of English

7 **Read the dialogue and underline the verb forms that express future time.**

Ana: Hey, Tim! So good to see you. Are you going to do anything tonight?

Tim: Hi, Ana! Yes, I'm going to have dinner with my parents.

Ana: Ah, that's nice. I'm going to meet some classmates at school. Will you come after dinner? We're going to talk about a **campaign** to clean Lake Dale and make it a clean **home** for the aquatic life there.

Tim: That's awesome, Ana. There are a lot of fish and **turtles** living in that **lake**... Can I invite my brother, too? He really knows a lot about **ecosystems** and the environment. He'll love it.

Ana: Of course, you can! Great! We'll wait for you then. We have so much to talk about.

Tim: It's really cold and cloudy today; it's going to **rain** later. But I'll get an umbrella right now, and we'll join you at school after dinner.

Ana: OK, see you! Bye!

Tim: Bye!

8 **Read the dialogue again and match the words in bold to their definitions below.**

1. All the animals and plants in an area
   ____
2. Large area of water surrounded by land
   ____
3. A series of actions to achieve a result
   ____
4. The place where we live
   ____
5. A reptile that lives mainly in water
   ____
6. Water that falls from the clouds
   ____

9 **In pairs, write a dialogue similar to the one in Activity 8. Use *be going to* and *will* accordingly.**

10 **Practice the dialogue in Activity 9 with your classmate.**

I can have a conversation about plans and predictions for the future.

Language Booster page 56

Writing

1 **Work in pairs. Read Lin's social media stories sequence. Why should we protect the oceans to help stop climate change?**

____

____

2 **Match the words in bold from Lin's social media stories sequence to their definitions.**

1. storm
2. boiling hot
3. hurricane

- ☐ It is a storm with very fast winds over the oceans.
- ☐ It is a period of very bad weather with rain and strong winds.
- ☐ It is when temperatures are extremely high.

Prepare to Write

3 **You are going to work on a social media stories sequence about climate change or protecting the environment. Complete the chart below with information you want to include in your sequence.**

What I want to protect	
Why I want to protect it	
Argument 1	
Argument 2	
Argument 3	

I can write arguments to support my opinion.

Write

4 **Work on your social media stories sequence. Create three stories using the information from Activity 3. Do some research, if necessary.**

#TIP

Draw pictures to illustrate your stories.

#TIP

You can follow teen activists such as Greta Thunberg on social media and get to know the work they are doing to protect the environment.

Check and Change

5 **Read your social media stories sequence and make sure you included:**

- ☐ what you think needs protection.
- ☐ your opinions / explanations.
- ☐ arguments to support your opinion.
- ☐ predictions for the future.
- ☐ drawings, GIFS, or emojis to make your stories more attractive.
- ☐ correct spelling and grammar.

6 **Edit your social media stories sequence. Make sure all the elements in Activity 5 are included.**

Publish

7 **Prepare a clean version of your social media stories sequence.**

Speaking

8 **Work in pairs. Read your classmate's social media stories sequence and complete the sentences below.**

1. He / She chose to talk about ______________.
2. He / She thinks it is important to protect ______________.
3. He / She believes that ______________.

9 **Work in groups. Present your classmate's social media stories sequence.**

Lara chose to talk about marine life. She thinks it's important to protect sea turtles...

I can present my classmate's social media stories sequence.

Language Booster page 57

Project: An Online Program

#DIGITAL LITERACY

1. Use short sentences to describe the event of the day.
2. Divide the event into clear steps.
3. Share the program with everyone at school.

Step 1 Think

1 Work in groups. Look at the online program and discuss the questions.

1. Is your school going to have a Science Fair this year? What do you know about it? What activities are they going to offer?
2. Look at the Bloomberg Middle School program. Does your school have a similar one online?

Bloomberg Middle School | Science Fair Program	
Monday	Collection of food for the animals
Tuesday	Lake visitation to take pictures of the animals
Wednesday	Printing pictures and talking about the animals we saw
Thursday	Research into the most interesting animals
Friday	Observations about the weather at the lake and mountains
Saturday	Organization of the school fair and exhibition
Sunday	Science fair

Step 2 Plan

2 In groups, choose an event you want to organize at school and create a program in your notebook to add your ideas.

I can plan to create an online program for a school event.

Step 3 Research

3 In groups, do some research about the activities you want to include in your event. Make notes here and add new ideas to the program in Activity 2.

____

____

____

____

Step 4 Design

4 In groups, create your online program.

- Check the text.
- Check the steps
- Check the organization.

#TIP STEP 4

Search for free online templates that look appealing.

Step 5 Present and Publish

5 In groups, present your online program to the class.

#TIP STEP 5

Give some time for your audience to ask questions.

Step 6 Evaluate

Complete the evaluation table.

★★★ More to learn | ★★★ Good | ★★★ Excellent

Criteria	My Evaluation	Group Evaluation	Teacher Evaluation
Teamwork	★★★	★★★	★★★
Language	★★★	★★★	★★★
Design	★★★	★★★	★★★

I can create an online program and present it to the class.

#SELF-ASSESSMENT

1 **Mark the learning objectives according to the key.**

★☆☆ I don't understand.	★★☆ I understand, but I need help.	★★★ I can do it!

Learning Objectives	Rating
To interpret a conversation about nature.	☆☆☆
To talk about geographical features and underwater animals.	☆☆☆
To read about nature.	☆☆☆
To talk about ways to keep water ecosystems clean.	☆☆☆
To use *will* and *be going to* to talk about the future.	☆☆☆
To ask and answer questions about the future.	☆☆☆
To talk about helping the environment and underwater animals.	☆☆☆
To have a conversation about plans and predictions for the future.	☆☆☆
To write arguments to support my opinion.	☆☆☆
To present my classmate's social media stories sequence.	☆☆☆
To plan to create an online program about a school event.	☆☆☆
To create an online program and present it to the class.	☆☆☆

2 **Work in pairs. Discuss the questions.**

1. What did I find most interesting to learn? Why?
2. How did I learn it?
3. How can I use it in real life?

UT FT Language Booster page 58

INTEGRATE

Learn to Learn

Bloom's Taxonomy Revisited

1 **Can you remember the names of the sections in the units?**

2 **Go back to Unit 0 and identify the section names according to the verbs below.**

1. Remember #______________
2. Understand #______________
3. Apply #______________
4. Analyze #______________
5. Create #______________
6. Evaluate #______________

3 **Read the definitions. Relate them to the verbs from the pyramid in Activity 4.**

1. ____________: recall facts and basic concepts.
2. ____________: explain ideas and concepts.
3. ____________: use information in new situations.
4. ____________: make connections between ideas.
5. ____________: produce new or original work.
6. ____________: justify a decision.

4 **Match the verbs from the box to the ones in the pyramid that have the same function or purpose.**

build choose (x2) classify compare conclude (x2) contrast decide design develop examine explain extend identify infer invent justify match name organize recall select (x2)

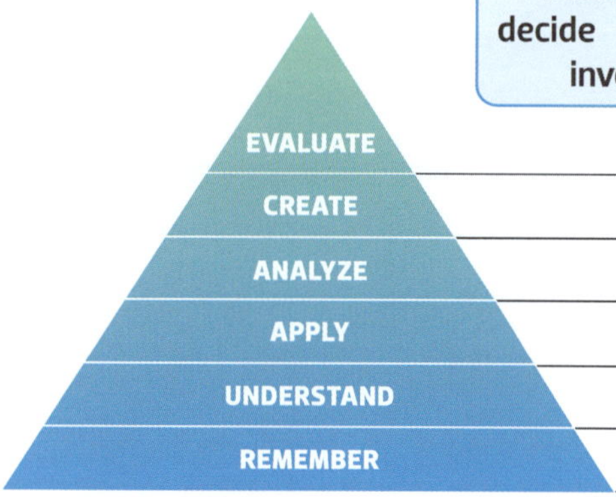

5 **Contrast the verbs in Activity 3 with the processes below.**

1. What fruit is this? ______________
2. How do bananas grow? ______________
3. How can you use them in healthy meals? ______________
4. Are there different kinds of bananas? ______________
5. Can you invent a new healthy recipe using bananas? ______________
6. Which recipe is the best? ______________

6 **How can you organize the verbs you learned in a mind map? Create one in your notebook and share it with your classmates.**

7 **Decide on the most efficient mind map in terms of organization.**

Video

About My School

Before You Watch

1 What do you remember from the video in the #Discover section? Make notes and share them with a classmate.

Sentences with *why* and *because*	Opinions and likes

While You Watch

2 Watch the video and check your notes in Activity 1. ▷ 01

After You Watch

3 Work in groups. You are going to make a video showing students talking about their school subjects. Make notes before you begin.

Use the checklist to review your video script.

Our dialogue includes...

- [ ] questions with *why* and answers with *because*.
- [ ] directions to a place in the school.
- [ ] school subjects and adjectives.
- [ ] expressions of *like* / *dislike*.

4 Make your video and share it with your classmates. Then provide feedback to your classmates about their video.

Grammar	
Vocabulary	
Fluency	
Presentation	
Suggested Improvements	

Learn to Learn

Weekend Fun

1 **List** the verbs you learned to describe free-time activities. You can use the pictures as clues.

___

___

___

2 **Classify** the activities you learned in the table below.

Indoor activities	Outdoor activities	Weekend activities only

3 Interview your classmates, and then **report** your findings to the class.

Find someone who...

prefers indoor activities.	
prefers outdoor activities.	

4 **List** other free-time activities that were not mentioned in this lesson.

___

___

___

5 **Develop** a flashcard game. Use the activities from the previous activities and the new ones listed in Activity 4.

6 **Review** your classmates' flashcards.

7 How do you usually memorize new vocabulary?

___

___

___

Video

My Friends and How We Spend Our Time

Before You Watch

1 What do you remember from the video in the #Discover section? Make notes and share them with a classmate.

Free-time activities	*Wh-* questions

While You Watch

2 Watch the video and check your notes in Activity 1. Then complete part of the conversation. ▷ 02

Paula: We can [1] ____________ a movie, [2] ____________, play [3] ____________, or go [4] ____________. What do you think?

Sam: That sounds great, Paula. Where can we go?

Paula: We can play soccer at the [5] ____________ [6] ____________ or walk in the [7] ____________. We can also skate at the park.

After You Watch

3 Work in groups. You are going to make a video showing people talking about their free-time activities. Make notes before you begin.

Use the checklist to review your video script.

Our dialogue includes...

- [ ] free-time activities.
- [ ] *Wh-* questions.
- [ ] *yes / no* questions.
- [ ] verbs in the Simple Present.
- [ ] adverbs of frequency.

4 Make your video and share it with your classmates. Then provide feedback to your classmates about their video.

Grammar	
Vocabulary	
Fluency	
Presentation	
Suggested Improvements	

Learn to Learn

Food Pyramid

1 What can you remember about the verbs in Bloom's Taxonomy pyramid? Why do you think the layers are presented like this?

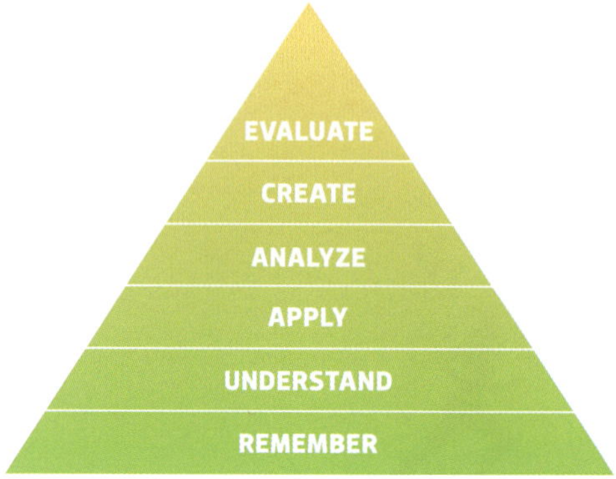

2 Now look at the food pyramid below. Why do you think the layers are distributed like this? Compare it to Bloom's pyramid above.

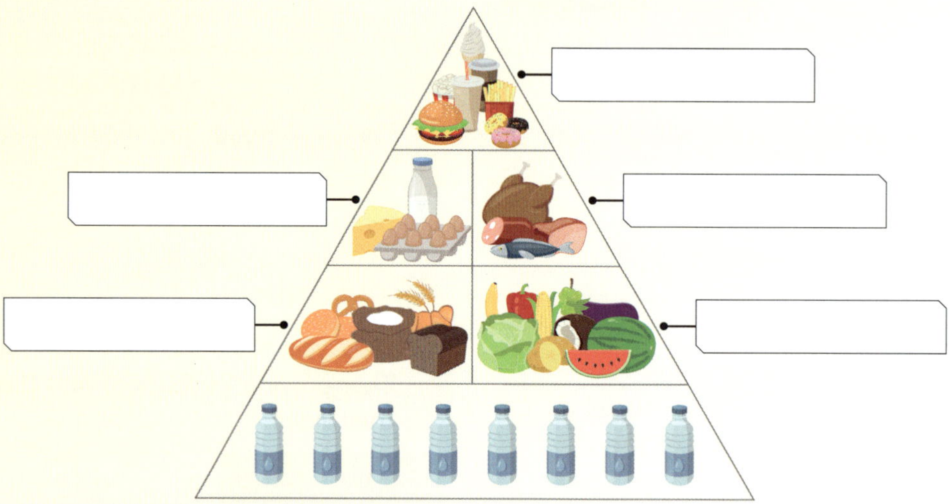

3 Complete the food pyramid in Activity 2 with food items you would include in your diet to have healthy eating habits.

4 Analyze your food pyramid with a classmate and find similarities and differences.

5 Create your healthy food pyramid. Include the information from Activity 3. Use your notebook.

6 Write a final version of your food pyramid. Evaluate your own eating habits.

7 Why is it important to organize information visually and hierarchically?

____

____

Video

Breakfast at Home

Before You Watch

1 What do you remember from the video in the #Discover section? Make notes and share them with a classmate.

Food	Drinks

While You Watch

2 Watch the video again and check your notes in Activity 1. Then read the statements and mark T (True) or F (False). ▷ 03

1. ▢ Paula doesn't want any breakfast.
2. ▢ Sam's mom is making some pancakes.
3. ▢ There isn't any water left in Sam's kitchen.
4. ▢ Sam's family makes a healthy breakfast.
5. ▢ Paula doesn't like milk.

After You Watch

3 Work in groups. You are going to make a video showing people talking about what they like to have for breakfast. Make notes before you begin.

Use the checklist to review your video script.

Our dialogue includes...

▢ questions to ask about likes and dislikes.
▢ food items and drinks.
▢ adjectives to describe food items and drinks.

4 Make your video and share it with your classmates. Then provide feedback to your classmates about their video.

Grammar	
Vocabulary	
Fluency	
Presentation	
Suggested Improvements	

Learn to Learn

New Occupations

1 **Name** the most popular occupations you know.

2 Read the names of some new occupations. **Summarize** what you think they are about.

1. Hotel hygienist: ____________________
2. NFT gamer: ____________________
3. Sports therapist: ____________________
4. Veterinary nurse: ____________________
5. App developer: ____________________
6. Guidance counselor: ____________________

3 **Identify** where the professionals from Activity 2 could work.

1.  ____________________

2.  ____________________

3.  ____________________

4.  ____________________

5.  ____________________

6.  ____________________

4 **Choose** one of the occupations you learned about. What skills and abilities do people need to be successful in it?

____

____

5 Now go back to the occupations you named in Activity 1. **Adapt** them to new occupations, as you saw in Activity 2.

____

____

____

6 **Evaluate** and **vote** on the best adaptations in class.

7 How do these new occupations match your skills and abilities?

____

____

____

____

____

____

Video

Career Day

Before You Watch

1 What do you remember from the video in the #Discover section? Make notes and share them with a classmate.

Jobs

While You Watch

2 Watch the video again and check your notes in Activity 1. Then answer the question. 04

What's Paula's dream job?

After You Watch

3 Work in groups. You are going to make a video preparing a Career Day presentation. Make notes before you begin.

Use the checklist to review your video script.

Our dialogue includes...

- [ ] common jobs.
- [ ] new jobs.
- [ ] dream jobs.

4 Make your video and share it with your classmates. Then provide feedback to your classmates about their video.

Grammar	
Vocabulary	
Fluency	
Presentation	
Suggested Improvements	

Learn to Learn

Video Game Character

1 Work in small groups and **tell** each other:

1. What video games you play.
2. What your favorite game character is.
3. What makes your favorite character special for you.
4. What characters you have heard about (in case you don't play video games).

2 **Compare** the characters you talked about in Activity 1.

1. What are their similarities?
2. What is the main difference among them?
3. How could these characters be blended to form a new one?

3 **List** the characteristics of a new character. Complete the table.

Physical characteristics	Personality traits	Special powers

4 **Plan** the creation of a set of three characters. Use the information from the table in Activity 3.

5 In your groups, **illustrate** the main characters of a video game.

6 **Evaluate** your classmates' illustrations from Activity 5.

7 What are the benefits of comparing information?

Video

A Friendly, Tall Classmate

Before You Watch

1 **What do you remember from the video in the #Discover section? Make notes and share them with a classmate.**

Appearance adjectives	Personality adjectives

While You Watch

2 **Watch the video again and check your notes in Activity 1. Then answer the questions.** 05

1. Where are Paula and Sam?

____

2. Who are they talking about?

____

3. What is the problem?

____

____

4. In Paula and Sam's opinion, what is the best way to help?

____

After You Watch

3 **Work in groups. You are going to make a video showing students talking about social changes they want to make. Make notes before you begin.**

Use the checklist to review your video script.

Our dialogue includes...

- ☐ adjectives to describe people.
- ☐ superlatives and comparatives.
- ☐ ideas to reduce inequalities.

4 **Make your video and share it with your classmates. Then provide feedback to your classmates about their video.**

Grammar	
Vocabulary	
Fluency	
Presentation	
Suggested Improvements	

Learn to Learn

Plan of Action

1 Select some of the problems you find at school and write them down.

____

____

____

2 Explain how these problems can affect you as a student.

3 How can you solve the problems you mentioned in Activity 1?

____

____

____

4 Categorize the problems you mentioned in Activity 1 in a mind map. You can create, for example, a tree mind map or a spider mind map.

5 Create a plan of action for one of the problems categorized in Activity 4. What can you do to solve it? Make some notes.

Problem	
Possible solution	
People involved	
Action needed	

6 Make an evaluation sheet. Include information about what worked and didn't work, what could be done differently next time, what other people could be involved, etc.

7 How does planning help us set and see a clear outcome?

____

____

____

____

Video

The New Media Room

Before You Watch

1 **What do you remember from the video in the #Discover section? Make notes and share them with a classmate.**

Rules and obligations	Advice

While You Watch

2 **Watch the video again and check your notes in Activity 1. Then complete the sentences.** ▷ 06

1. There are places for us to sit, there's ____________, and snacks… It's like a ____________.
2. This is a ____________, resources are limited, I know.
3. I know ____________ that don't have a ____________ like this one.
4. We're lucky to have ____________.

After You Watch

3 **Work in groups. You are going to make a video showing students talking about the quality of education at their school. Make notes before you begin.**

Use the checklist to review your video script.

Our dialogue includes…

- ☐ rules and obligations.
- ☐ advice and suggestions.
- ☐ basic items for quality education.

4 **Make your video and share it with your classmates. Then provide feedback to your classmates about their video.**

Grammar	
Vocabulary	
Fluency	
Presentation	
Suggested Improvements	

Learn to Learn

The Human Body

1 Identify the body parts below.

2 Demonstrate how these body parts work. How could you do the things you do without them?

3 Choose the body part that you think is the most essential. Draw it.

4 Examine how this body part connects to the rest of your body.

____

____

5 Create a new part of the body. Use the part you chose in Activity 3 and draw how the new version would look like.

6 Vote on the most interesting body part of the class.

7 How did the process of creating a new body part help you analyze its importance?

____

____

____

Video

Last Night's Game

Before You Watch

1 **What do you remember from the video in the #Discover section? Make notes and share them with a classmate.**

Sports

While You Watch

2 **Watch the video again and check your notes in Activity 1. Then mark the statements T (True) or F (False).** 07

1. ☐ Sam thinks last night's game was exciting.
2. ☐ Paula watched the game with her family.
3. ☐ Paula wants to make a soccer team for the girls.
4. ☐ Sam thinks sports are important.
5. ☐ Sam can't help Paula.

After You Watch

3 **Work in groups. You are going to make a video showing people talking about health and well-being with sports. Make notes before you begin.**

Use the checklist to review your video script.

Our dialogue includes...
- ☐ suggestions of sports to promote well-being.
- ☐ verbs used with sports.
- ☐ verbs in the Simple Past.

4 **Make your video and share it with your classmates. Then provide feedback to your classmates about their video.**

Grammar	
Vocabulary	
Fluency	
Presentation	
Suggested Improvements	

Learn to Learn

How to Create an App

1 **Select** some apps that are popular among teenagers. Write down five features that they have in common.

____

____

____

____

2 **Compare** the kind of information apps that are popular among teenagers have. Follow the steps below.

1. What does the initial page show?
2. Is there a main menu?
3. Does the app have a *profile* screen? If so, what kind of information is there?

3 **Contrast** the different designs of the apps. Which one draws your attention the most? Why?

4 **Analyze** the app that is more user-friendly. What are its features?

5 Work in groups. **Design** an app. Use the information you gathered in the previous activities and build the three main screens of the app.

6 **Present** the app to your classmates and **defend** it is the best option. Make notes before you start your presentation.

____

____

____

____

____

7 How would you test an app?

____

____

____

____

____

____

Video

Traveling

Before You Watch

1 What do you remember from the video in the #Discover section? Make notes and share them with a classmate.

Activities related to vacations

While You Watch

2 Watch the video and check your notes in Activity 1. Then mark the sentences T (True) or F (False). ▷ 08

1. ☐ Sam and Paula are traveling to the same tourist destination.
2. ☐ Paula is traveling by plane.
3. ☐ Paula and her family are going to Bonito by train.
4. ☐ Sam and his family rented a house in Germany.
5. ☐ Paula's family is worried about life on land.

After You Watch

3 Work in groups. You are going to make a video showing two classmates meeting at an airport, a bus station, or a train station. Make notes before you begin.

Use the checklist to review your video script.

Our dialogue includes...
- ☐ travel destinations.
- ☐ activities related to vacations.
- ☐ actions in the future.

4 Make your video and share it with your classmates. Then provide feedback to your classmates about their video.

Grammar	
Vocabulary	
Fluency	
Presentation	
Suggested Improvements	

Learn to Learn

Wrapping up

1 Name the layers of Bloom's Taxonomy pyramid that are missing.

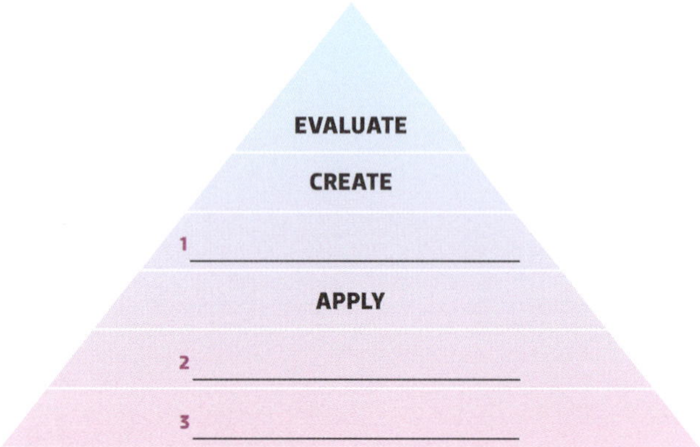

2 Work in small groups. Explain how the *remember* layer can be helpful when you are learning something new.

3 Reflect on what the *understand* layer means to you. Make notes.

____

____

____

____

____

____

4 When you make use of the taxonomy, how can your learning objectives be reached more easily?

5 Now that you know all the six categories of Bloom's Taxonomy, summarize what each one conveys.

6 Now that you know all the six categories of Bloom's Taxonomy, re-design Bloom's pyramid according to your own study routine.

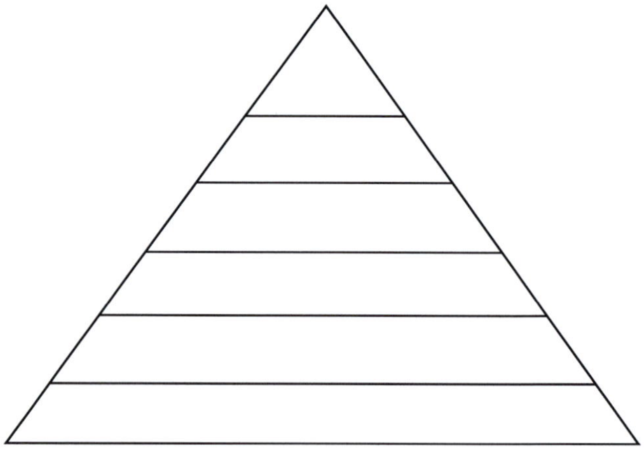

7 How can you improve your study routine using Bloom's Taxonomy?

____

____

____

____

Video

It's a Beautiful World

Before You Watch

1 **What do you remember from the video in the #Discover section? Make notes and share them with a classmate.**

Geographical features	Weather	Underwater animals

While You Watch

2 **Watch the video and check your notes in Activity 1. Then answer the questions.** 09

1. Where are Sam and Paula? ______________
2. What kind of animals did Paula see in the reserve? ______________
3. How was the weather in Bonito? ______________
4. When is Sam going to visit his uncle again? ______________
5. What is the school meeting going to be about? ______________

After You Watch

3 **Work in groups. You are going to make a video showing students talking about protecting the environment. Make notes before you begin.**

Use the checklist to review your video script.

Our dialogue includes...

- [ ] geographical features.
- [ ] weather.
- [ ] animals.
- [ ] *be going to* and *will* to talk about the future.

4 **Make your video and share it with your classmates. Then provide feedback to your classmates about their video.**

Grammar	
Vocabulary	
Fluency	
Presentation	
Suggested Improvements	

#VIDEO & AUDIO TRACKS

Unit	Track	Page	Activities
Video Tracks			
0	01	10	2 and 3
		137	2
1	02	24	2, 3, and 4
		139	2
2	03	38	2 and 3
		141	2
3	04	52	2 and 3
		143	2
4	05	66	2, 3, and 4
		145	2
5	06	80	3 and 4
		147	2
6	07	94	2 and 3
		149	2
7	08	108	2 and 3
		151	2
8	09	122	2, 3, and 4
		153	2
Audio Tracks			
-	01	Introduction	
0	02	11	5
	03	11	7
	04	13	5
	05	15	9
	06	16	2
	07	16	3
	08	16	4
1	09	25	6
	10	27	4
	11	29	9
	12	30	2
	13	30	3
	14	30	4
2	15	39	5
	16	39	6
	17	41	5
	18	43	8

Unit	Track	Page	Activities
Audio Tracks			
2	19	44	2
	20	44	3
	21	44	4
3	22	53	6
	23	55	5
	24	57	8
	25	58	2
	26	58	3
	27	58	4
	28	58	5
4	29	67	7
	30	69	6
	31	71	7
	32	72	2
	33	72	3
	34	72	5
	35	72	6
5	36	81	6
	37	81	9
	38	83	5
	39	83	6
	40	85	11
	41	86	2
	42	86	3
	43	86	4
6	44	95	6
	45	97	6
	46	99	10
	47	100	2
	48	100	3
	49	100	4
	50	100	5
	51	100	6
	52	101	8
7	53	109	6
	54	109	8
	55	111	6

Unit	Track	Page	Activities
Audio Tracks			
7	56	111	7
	57	113	6
	58	114	3
	59	114	4
	60	114	5
	61	114	6
	62	115	8
8	63	123	6
	64	125	6
	65	125	7
	66	127	10
	67	128	1
	68	128	2
	69	128	3
	70	128	5

UNIT ZERO

Video Script 01

P: Paula **S:** Sam

P: Hi, Sam! How are you?

S: Hey, Paula! I'm good, and you?

P: I'm fine. I can't wait to find out who our science teacher is this year.

S: Why are you so curious about it?

P: Because I like science, I think it's fun.

S: Well, I think science is hard, but I love history. It's my favorite subject.

P: History is interesting, too. We can go to that Ancient Maya Exhibiton.

S: Cool! Where is the exhibition?

P: Here! Just go straight on and turn left at the supermarket.

S: That's great! We can go after class. Let's go in...

Audio Scripts

Activity 5 04

1. We have science today, how boring! I prefer math.
2. My friend Lucy likes history, but my favorite subject is P.E.
3. My favorite subject? Hmm... I guess it's literature.
4. I don't really have a favorite subject, but I love music classes.
5. I like all subjects, but history is the best. My school is very interesting!

Activities 2 and 3 06 and 07

I: Interviewer **A:** Amy

I: Hello, how are you? My name's Sam, and I'm gonna ask you a few questions. This interview is part of the process for your exchange program, is that OK?

A: Sure! I'm ready. Go for it!

I: Great, Amy. I see you want to go on an exchange program in South Africa. Why did you choose South Africa?

A: Well, I really like to study. My favorite subject is science, by the way. I chose South Africa because I want to study the animals, their evolution, and their natural habitats.

I: That's very interesting, Amy. What other school subjects do you like?

A: I really like geography, I think that in South Africa I can learn a lot about the geography of the continent, too.

I: That's amazing, Amy! Are there any school subjects you don't like? I can make a note and inform your teachers in South Africa.

A: Umm... Well, I don't like history because it's boring and literature because it's hard. But, hmm... Music is fun! I like music classes.

I: OK, Amy, thank you very much! Have a great time in your exchange program.

A: Thanks! See you!

UNIT ONE

Video Script 02

P: Paula **S:** Sam

P: Hi, Sam! How are you?

S: Hi, Paula! I'm good, and you?

P: I'm OK, thanks. Do you want to do something on Sunday?

S: Yes, I do. What do you have in mind?

P: We can watch a movie, go for a walk, play soccer, or go skating. What do you think?

S: That sounds great, Paula. Where can we go?

P: We can play soccer at the sports center or walk at the park. We can also skate at the park.

S: What about swimming? The water in the lake is very clean and the weather is warm.

P: I don't know, I go swimming every Tuesday, I want to do something different on the weekend. Do you think we can have lunch later? There's a new restaurant at the mall.

S: Sure! Which restaurant is it?

P: It's called *Noboo* and my mom goes there for dinner.

S: Really? How often?

P: Sometimes she goes there with her friends after work.

S: Nice! What time do we meet?

P: Let's meet at 9:00 at the park?

S: Yeah, sure! See you there.

Audio Scripts

Activity 4 10

A: Ana **B:** Ben **L:** Liz **J:** James

A: Hello, My name's Ana. I'm fourteen years old, and I love to watch movies with my family in my free time.

B: Hi! I'm Ben. On the weekends, I like to go swimming with my sister.

L: I'm Liz. My friends and I go shopping very often. I love it!

J: This is James. I always play video games with my best friend on Fridays.

Activity 9 11

S: Sam **K:** Katie

S: Hey, Katie! Do you wanna have lunch with me?

K: Hi, Sam, sure! I always want to have lunch with you.

S: Nice, we can go to the mall. I rarely go there.

K: OK, no problem. I sometimes have dinner at the mall with my mom.

S: Where do you usually sit? I mean, what restaurant?

K: We often go to Congo for dinner. It's really nice!

S: I see. What kind of food do they serve?

K: It's usually Asian food.

S: Great! Let's go then!

Activities 2 and 3 12 and 13

Hey! My name's Jim. I'm 14 years old, and I love weekends. I usually wake up early on Saturday morning, have breakfast, and meet my friends at the park. I go home for lunch, and then I relax listening to music. At night, my family and I have dinner and play board games. My favorite day of the week ends with this family tradition! Sunday mornings are lazy, I always sleep in! After lunch, I do my homework and hang out at the arcade. I meet most of my classmates there. It's fun!

UNIT TWO

Video Script 03

Part 1

P: Paula S: Sam

P: Morning, Sam! Is it breakfast time?

S: Oh, yes, Paula! It is! Would you like some breakfast?

P: Yes, please! What's for breakfast?

S: Well, we have fresh fruit, bacon and eggs, toasted bread, and my dad's making some pancakes, too.

P: It sounds delicious! I'll have two eggs and a couple of pancakes.

S: Oh, wait a minute! There are some chocolate chip cookies, too.

P: Nice! I'll have some of those, too. You know, it's difficult to believe we have so much food and there are people who don't. I would like to do something to change that.

S: Me too, Paula. Let's think about what we can do!

Part 2

S: Sam P: Paula

S: Would you like some milk? I'm afraid there isn't any juice left. Dad and I need to go to the supermarket to get supplies.

P: I don't really like milk. I'm OK with a glass of water.

S: Oh, here you go.

P: Your family makes a very healthy breakfast, Sam, I like that!

S: Thanks, Paula! All our meals are healthy. But, of course, we have unhealthy snacks like fries and cakes sometimes.

P: Everything is very tasty, Sam. Thanks for having me!

S: Glad you like it, Paula! You're welcome!

Audio Scripts

Activity 5 17

1: My favorite food? Definitely fries. I like them because they are salty and crunchy.

2: Oh, let me see... Well, I really like fruit, I eat fruit all the time. I know they are not a complete meal, they are more like a snack, but I find them so tasty! Yummy!

3: I really don't like sweet food, dessert, candies, and stuff. I like simple things like toasted bread with cheese. Delicious!

4: I love organic products. I go to the farmers' market to buy vegetables and fruit with my mom. I love it! My favorite meal is meat with potatoes.

Activities 2 and 3 19 and 20

Speaker 1: Hi, my name's Alex. My favorite food is meat. I often go camping with my friends and we make a fire. Our barbecues are the best. We all enjoy them so much! Some of my friends bring bread or vegetables to go with the meat. We always have a fantastic time!

Speaker 2: Hey, there! My name's Sam. My favorite food is a dessert: ice cream. There aren't any flavors I don't like, but I love chocolate, mango, and lemon. What about you?

Speaker 3: Hello, my name's Nena. My favorite food is pizza. There are so many toppings to choose from. In my country, you can choose two toppings on a pizza. How many toppings can you put on the pizza in your country?

UNIT THREE

Video Script 04

P: Paula S: Sam

P: Hey, Sam! What's up? What are you doing?

S: Hi, Paula! I'm working on a career day presentation. Mrs. Kent says it's good for us to see a variety of professions and think about what we want to do in the future.

P: She is right, we are 14 years old, we have to start thinking about the career we want to follow. In the presentation, you have to include all kinds of jobs.

S: Can you help me, Paula? I'm making a list of a few jobs I can present: lawyer, teacher, pilot... What other important jobs can we add to this list?

P: All jobs are important, Sam. You're choosing the most common jobs, right?

S: Yes, jobs we see around us every day. Jobs men and women do.

P: I'm reading a book about gender equality now. Women don't always have the same payment as men, you know...

S: That's right!

P: OK, then, let's look around. Look at Mr. Gibbins, he's driving the school bus. Bus drivers are very important.

S: Sure they are! There are taxi drivers, too. And let's not forget about the cleaners that make sure our school is clean and the plumbers that take care of the water pipes.

P: Don't forget to include scientists! They do research on new treatments and work on innovative technology.

S: Yes, scientists have to be on the list.

P: Are you writing everything down?

S: I am! You're great, Paula. Thank you so much! What about you? What's your dream job?

P: I want to be a musician.

S: Awesome! You're very talented! I'll write this down, too.

Audio Scripts

Activity 5 23

Hello, my name is Jose, and I work as a lawyer for gender equality.com. My work is to help women feel included at work. I sometimes help women find temporary jobs, too. I love my job because I work with strong, creative, and inspiring women.

Activity 8 24

I usually get up at 7 o'clock and have breakfast before I go to school. The bus picks me up at 8 o'clock in the morning. On Mondays, I go to the mall at lunchtime. I sometimes meet friends there for lunch. On Monday afternoons, I spend my time working. I am a volunteer for a local organization that fights for equal pay and more opportunities for women. I go home at night and chat with my friends online before I go to sleep. I sometimes go to sleep at midnight. On the weekends, my friends and I go to parties, usually birthday parties. My birthday is on October 4th, and I am planning a small gathering with my friends.

Activities 2, 3, and 4 25, 26, and 27

I: Ian **L:** Lucas **A:** Alex

I: Hello, my name's Ian and I work for an international organization. My job is to test and apply new treatments for common health problems. I wear a uniform at work, and I sometimes work on the weekend. I work full-time, and I get paid well. What is my job?

L: Hey, y'all. I'm Lucas and I work both indoors and outdoors. I mostly work at night, and I don't wear a uniform. My job is a part-time job, and I always work on the weekends and at Christmas. I work at a lot of parties and play an instrument. What do I do?

A: Hi, my name's Alex, and I just got a summer job! It's not a desk job, but I wear a uniform. I work outdoors, in the streets. I don't work on the weekends or at holidays, and I always start working very early in the morning. My work is important for the community because I make sure the streets and sidewalks are clean. Can you guess what I do?

UNIT FOUR

Video Script 05

S: Sam **P:** Paula

S: Hey, Paula! What are you working on?

P: Oh! Hi Sam... I'm just reading something in the local news about our community. Some of our classmates and their families are having a hard time.

S: Really? What do you mean?

P: Well, you know, Rick, the tall boy? He's really friendly with everyone and always happy, but this morning he was very serious.

S: The blond boy, right? Yes, he is friendly. Is there something wrong with his family?

P: Well, things are more expensive than before, and many families are having a hard time to pay the bills or even buy food. I think Rick's family is having a hard time, too.

S: That's terrible! How can we help them?

P: I'm looking online to see what we can do, as a group. I think we can do better together, you know? I'm sure we can help some way.

S: Yeah, I think we can talk about this problem in class. If everybody knows about the problem of social inequality, we can think of a way to help people in need. We can talk to people about differences in opportunities and salaries.

P: You're right. The best way to help is to talk about this.

S: Sure! We can all try to be more generous.

Audio Scripts

Activity 6 30

1. **Paul:** When I am in my car, I prefer to listen to heavy metal music. It's stronger, more beautiful. Definitely the best.
2. **Niles:** Well, my favorite would be electronic music for sure. It's more interesting than K-Pop, in my opinion.
3. **Keiko:** No, no, I don't play tennis anymore. It's very expensive. I prefer running now, it's cheaper.
4. **Muriel:** Me? I'd rather do yoga for three hours than go swimming. I hate the water.
5. **Lilian:** I definitely prefer taekwondo to capoeira. It's more difficult, but it's so much fun!

Activities 2 and 3 32 and 33

P: Paula **R:** Raul

P: Hey, Raul, are you ready for tonight? You look so happy!

R: Hey, Paula! Yes, I am really excited for tonight. Wow, you look beautiful! Your dress is amazing.

P: Thanks! It was not easy to decide what to wear, but I prefer dresses to skirts and shirts. I feel more comfortable like this.

R: I know what you mean. It's our high school graduation, and we have to wear formal clothes. I wanted to wear a suit tonight, but it was too expensive. So I got into these pants and this shirt. They were cheaper! And it's easier to dance like this!

P: Haha, you're right. Tonight has to be fun. We have to be happy! We don't want to be sad and serious. We are 17, not 70, right?

R: Exactly. It's the most important night of our school lives. We're older now. Remember when we were new to the school?

P: Oh, I remember! I was the shortest kid in class.

R: And I was the tallest, haha. Good times.

P: True. I met some really kind and generous people here.

R: Not everybody was friendly, but most people were hard-working.

P: Yeah. Well, I guess it's time to go. Everyone is waiting for us! It's showtime!

UNIT FIVE

Video Script 06

P: Paula S: Sam

P: Sam! The media room is ready, it looks amazing! Look!

S: Wow, it does look amazing, Paula. There are places for us to sit, there's Wi-Fi, and snacks... It's like a café. I love it! We must take care of this place and keep it clean.

P: You're right. I'll make some signs with rules of what we can and cannot do in this room. For example, we can't leave cups on the tables.

S: Actually, students must not eat or drink near the computers. I think we should make a poster with all the rules.

P: You're right! Imagine if someone spilled juice on a new computer? No way!

S: Exactly!

P: Can we ask for some supplies?

S: Well, we should always talk to the principal first. We shouldn't do anyhting without permission.

P: Sure! This is a public school, resources are limited, I know.

S: Not bad for a public school. I know private schools that don't have a media room like this.

P: Public schools are very important to make good quality education accessible to everyone. Access to education is a universal right and governments must make sure kids are in school.

S: You're right. We're lucky to have good quality education. I can't wait to sit here and chat with everyone! Now let's make that poster.

Audio Scripts

Activities 5 and 6 38 and 39

1: When I finish school at the end of the day, I don't go home. I have a quick snack and go straight to the school library to study. In my country, we need to study a lot to get into university.

2: My dad has a schedule for my classes. I study three subjects a day, and my father is my tutor. I live on a farm in the countryside and going to a regular school is impossible because it's very far away.

3: I'm really excited because this year I'm going to have specialist classes at the school laboratories. I'm learning how to be an electrician to help the community with volunteer work.

Activity 11 40

P: Paul J: June

P: June, I've been looking for you. How are you?

J: Oh, hey, Paul. I'm great. Can I help you with something?

P: Ah, yes! I want to visit a school in France next year, and Professor Matt told me I have to take an exam. Now, I remember you are going to Italy for a semester, are you taking any exams?

J: Yes, I am. I have to take a language exam. I'm taking a test in Italian.

P: OK, then I have to pass a test in French. Anything else I have to do?

J: Hmm, you don't have to take a science test, but maybe you have to test for sports, like football or tennis, it depends on the sport you want to practice there.

P: Great, I don't want to test for a subject, a sport is always better.

J: You should take the test in your free time. You shouldn't miss classes to do it.

P: Right, OK...I hope I don't fail. I really have to pass the sports test.

J: Oh, I'm sure you will!

Activities 2 and 3 41 and 42

So, today I'm going to talk about the four levels of education in the United States: preschool, elementary school, middle school or junior high, and high school. All levels of school can and have to be fun for the students, with classes according to their age and interests. Let's start with preschool. This first level of education is the most fun! Students must use colors, paints, and games to learn. This is the only rule! The second level, elementary school, is when we start to study the basics. Students usually don't have to take tests at this level, but good behavior and good performance are important! The third level, middle school or junior high school, is the time when we learn about mathematics, science and language.

At this level, we have to take and pass exams. The rule here is simple: students must attend classes and study. Students shouldn't miss classes. The last level before university is high school. At this level, students have to study hard to get good grades and pass their exams.

UNIT SIX

Video Script 07

P: Paula **S:** Sam

P: Sam, were you at the game last night?

S: What game? Oh, the soccer game. I was. Very exciting, right?

P: It sure was! I watched it with my girlfriends. We loved it! Now we just want to know why there's no girls' soccer team. We girls like soccer, too!

S: I don't know why there's no soccer team for girls at school, Paula. I know you girls like soccer, and you play very well, too.

P: Maybe I can talk to the principal, and we can start a girls' soccer team this year.

S: Which other sports do you girls play at school?

P: Well, there's a handball team and a volleyball team. I know there was a gymnastics team in the past, too, for boys and girls, but not anymore. I'll definitely talk to the principal about that. I didn't talk to the girls about that last night because we all returned home when the game finished.

S: Playing sports is very important, Paula. I can't believe you and your friends don't exercise.

P: Well, we didn't. We are changing this. We just have to find a sport we like. And we like soccer very much. I'm sure the girls that are not part of the other teams will join the soccer team!

S: When we invited the boys for the soccer team, first we talked about it to the students who were not part of any other team, but then we decided everyone was welcome!

P: That was nice.

S: And remember: a healthy mind lives in a healthy body. Our mental health and physical health have a lot more in common than we can imagine. That's why choosing to play sports we really like is important: finding pleasure in sports is essential!

P: You're right, Sam. I'm meeting the girls after school so we can talk to the principal about that.

S: Great, Paula, let me know what you decide and how I can help you organize everything with the coach.

Audio Scripts

Activity 6 45

S1: Speaker 1 **S2:** Speaker 2 **S3:** Speaker 3

S1: It's a new sport world, only online. I'm a World of Warcraft player. I started playing Counter-Strike with my friends online and then changed into more complex games. I take it seriously and practice online for 3 hours every day.

S2: I go to practice every day. We exercise for several hours. It keeps most of us out of the streets. Doing sports helped many kids go to better schools and have a better education.

S3: I didn't want to go to school or leave the house. My parents were worried about me. Until one day one of my friends asked me to go running with her. You don't need any special equipment, just a pair of sneakers and off you go. We talked so much! Running changed my life. I get up every morning to run. It's great for my mental and physical health.

Activities 2, 3, and 4 47, 48, and 49

S1: Speaker 1 **S2:** Speaker 2 **S3:** Speaker 3

S1: First, my friend called me, and we talked about the tournament. Next, I turned on my PC and logged into the game. I asked if anyone needed help, and everyone was OK. Then I started to play, and the time passed fast. I didn't realize it was already midnight when my mom called me to turn off the lights and go to sleep.
The next day, I decided to go running with my dog and stay away from the computer.

S2: Lidia called very early on Sunday morning. It was the day we would go horse riding, and I was very excited. I didn't want to drive to the place, so I called a taxi.
Before I arrived, I asked the trainer to prepare my horse. Next, I put on my boots and called my horse. He was so beautiful. Finally, I headed home.

S3: The party was over, and we all started to clean and organize the space. We put the dirty cups in the recycling can and cleaned up the living room. Then Lin looked under the table and there it was, an old board game. We opened the box and started playing. Lin was very happy because she was winning, but then her luck changed. Mark was the winner.

Activity 8 52

L: Linda **D:** Dr. Alexander

L: How was our physical, mental, and emotional health in the past? Were teenagers happier then? Here's Dr. Alexander to answer all our questions.

D: Well, Linda, in the past, teenagers needed to ask their parents for permission to watch certain TV programs, to go out with their friends, etc. They danced in school parties and watched movies in drive-through movie theaters.

They played on the streets. Were they happier? I don't know, but they weren't afraid of violence, for example, and they celebrated even the smaller things.

L: How did teenagers deal with sports in the past?

D: Some teens did sports. The most common sports were soccer, volleyball, basketball, and tennis. But we didn't stop to think about these things back then. We just called our friends and arranged to meet outside to play soccer, for example. There weren't video games or streaming services. It was fantastic to be a teenager back then. We didn't need to worry about the future. It was a good life!

UNIT SEVEN

Video Script 08

P: Paula S: Sam

P: Sam! Over here! I knew I would see you! Big day today, right? Our vacation is starting.

S: Paula, nice to see you here. Are you catching a flight, too? Where are you going?

P: We're going to Brazil, to an ecological reserve called Bonito.

S: Brazil, how cool is that? I've never been to Brazil.

P: Oh yes, when we land in Campo Grande, the capital of Mato Grosso do Sul, we're going to rent a car to go to Bonito. Where are you going, Sam?

S: Well, my uncle Nate moved to Germany a few years ago, so my parents bought tickets and booked a hotel to visit him. We've been to Europe before but not to Germany. I'm excited to spend my vacation there and take loads of pictures.

P: Me too. My family chose the ecological reserve thinking about the damage that tourism is causing to the land and natural resources of the tourist destinations. Have you ever been to an ecological reserve, Sam?

S: No, I haven't, Paula. Take a lot of pictures to show me!

P: Sure, Sam! I'm going to hike and go sightseeing there.

S: Awesome! Oh, I have to go, Paula, I need to go to the gate and board the plane, they are calling our flight.

P: Have a safe trip, Sam!

S: You too, Paula, bye!

P: Bye!

Audio Scripts

Activities 6 and 7 55 and 56

Hi, I'm Sam! I spent my last vacation in Malaysia with my family. It was an awesome trip! I was surprised to see the diversity of animals and plants. We explored modern cities and old buildings, too. We relaxed on the most beautiful beaches, and I went hiking in amazing forests! We stayed at a hotel near an ecological reserve called Bukit Piton. I was a volunteer in a project to preserve life on land for the orangutan population and other species that live there. This project also taught us to minimize our carbon footprint. That is, what we can do to protect the environment in our daily life. Green areas are disappearing and the animals that live there, too. What can we do to help? I came back home more interested in finding simple ways to preserve life on land in my hometown. It's been the best vacation ever!

Activity 6 57

D: Davi R: Ross

D: I haven't been to a glacier before. What about you?

R: No, I haven't. I'm very curious to see it. Where was your last stop?

D: We were in Brazil and then went to Buenos Aires. How about you? Have you traveled to Brazil?

R: Yes, I have. I went to Brazil two years ago. I really liked it. Have you seen this much snow before?

D: Ha-ha, no, I haven't. I think the colors are amazing.

R: It is very sad that global warming is making the glaciers melt. We are lucky to see this.

Activities 3, 4, and 5 58, 59, and 60

S1: Speaker 1 S2: Speaker 2 S3: Speaker 3

S1: When I arrived at the airport, I showed my passport and got my boarding pass at the check-in. There were many people on my flight and a long line to board. Everything looked fine. I was anxious. Have you ever traveled alone?

S2: When we got on the platform, I started looking at the numbers. Imagine, I was in London, and the Harry Potter platform was there, between platforms 9 and 10! I wanted to run into the wall to be part of the world of magic! When we left the station, I called my best friend to tell her everything. Have you ever felt that kind of magic?

S3: We didn´t know we could use the river to go sightseeing in London. We bought our tickets and got on the boat. Can you believe we went under the bridge? I took a lot of pictures. The River Thames is beautiful! Have you ever enjoyed a boat ride?

Activity 9 62

R: Reporter – Pablo M: Mateo Sanchez

R: Welcome to Ibiza's Sustainability Report. Today, our guest is Mateo Sanchez, responsible for environmental actions in Ibiza. Welcome, Mateo!

M: Thank you, Pablo! Have you been to Ibiza? It's a very touristy Spanish island. More than four million people visit it every summer. The island is beautiful, but there are some problems, too. The sustainability report of Ibiza has shown low forest cover, which causes forest fires.

Temperatures have increased a lot, too and we have lost our biodiversity. Last year, a local school did an environmental project about what species mostly disappear when there are forest fires. Students and teachers made water tanks to store water in case there are forest fires and invited tourists to join in!

UNIT EIGHT

Video Script 09

P: Paula S: Sam

P: Sam! You're back!! How was your vacation? Did you have fun?

S: Hey, Paula! Yes, it was fantastic. We're going to go back for Christmas. It will be snowy, my uncle said. What about you, Paula? How was Bonito?

P: Amazing! There are so many rivers and lakes. The trees are so beautiful. The reserve has lots of animals that live underwater, such as turtles and fish. Let me show you the pictures...

S: Wow! This place looks impressive! How was the weather there?

P: It was mostly sunny. There was heavy rain one day, but the sky was clear and blue most days.

S: Great to hear that, Paula. I love the water. It's amazing to think how much life there is underwater, in the oceans and seas, like sharks, whales, and dolphins.

P: That's true. We're all responsible for keeping the oceans clean and preserving life below water.

S: What do you think about starting a new campaign, Paula? We are going to have a school meeting tomorrow to talk about future projects. We can talk about the lake at the foot of the mountain.

P: I'll be there, Sam. Then we can talk about sustainable solutions to preserve the lake and keep it clean.

S: Not only the lake, but the fish and other animals that live in it, too.

P: Yes, of course! Excellent idea!

S: Oh, I have to go now, Paula. Before it starts to rain.

P: Do you think it's going to rain, Sam?

S: Didn't you see the weather forecast? It will be cloudy and rainy all day. Bye!

Audio Scripts

Activities 6 and 7 64 and 65

S1: Speaker 1 S2: Speaker 2 S3:Speaker S4: Speaker 4

S1: The winters are more difficult because of the wind and the storms. Living in front of the ocean means winters are wet and noisy.

S2: Summer's my favorite season, you know? We go hiking and camping in the woods. The forests are green and full of animals.

S3: The best thing about living here is that in the winter the lake freezes and we can ice skate. The kids love it!

S4: My friends and I love to go rafting down the river on weekends. Living here is an adventure!

Activities 2 and 3 68 and 69

Every year in November, everyone starts thinking about their Christmas tree. But which Christmas tree is better for the environment? The real tree or a fake one? Real trees help fight climate change and are better for the environment than fake plastic trees. Fake trees are not recyclable, and their production causes a lot of carbon emission. Real trees can be recyclable and will become products made of wood. Now I know we aren't supposed to be cutting trees, but the National Christmas Tree Association says that for every real tree we buy, farmers plant three more! Also, when we buy a real tree, we are supporting the local farmers and helping to preserve healthy forests. Healthy forests are home for lots of animals and they also protect us from extreme weather conditions, such as storms, for example. Healthy forests fight climate change and extreme weather.

NOTES

NOTES

PICTURE CREDITS

Front cover (A) s_oleg/Shutterstock/Shutterstock / (B) Sebestyen Balint/ Shutterstock/Shutterstock / (C) 3dector/ Shutterstock/Shutterstock / (D) Doomu/ Shutterstock/Shutterstock / (E) Mix Tape/ Shutterstock/Shutterstock / (F) Oatawa/ Shutterstock/Shutterstock / (G) Natykach Nataliia/ Shutterstock/ Shutterstock; Page 9 Viacheslav Iakobchuk/123rf/123RF; Page 10olegdudko/123rf/123RF; Page (A) ShutterStockStudio/Shutterstock/Asset Library / (B) Wellford Tiller/Shutterstock/Asset Library / (C) Leigh Prather/Shutterstock/Asset Library / (D) wavebreakmedia/Shutterstock/Asset Library / (E) Patrick Guenette/123rf/Asset Library / (F) BlurryMe/Shutterstock/Asset Library / (G) Denis Tabler/Shutterstock/Asset Library / (H) Syda Productions/Shutterstock/ Asset Library; Page 12 (A) PUWADON SANG/Shutterstock/Asset Library / (B) Mark Bowden/123rf/123RF / (C) Jules Selmes. Pearson Education Ltd/Asset Library / (D) Shutterstock/Asset Library / (E) Cathy Yeulet/123rf/Asset Library; Page 13lightfieldstudios/123rf/123RF; Page 14 (A) Sergey Novikov/ Shutterstock/Asset Library / (B) Gareth Boden. Pearson Education Ltd/Asset Library / (C) Andrea Obzerova/123rf/Asset Library; Page 15 (A) Neal, C/O KJA Artists. Pearson Education Ltd/Asset Library / (B) pockygallery/Shutterstock/Asst Library / (C) Neal, C/O KJA Artists/ Pearson Education Ltd/Asset Library / (D) Filipe Laurentino/ Pearson Brasil/Asset Library; Page 16 (A) Rawpixel.com/Shutterstock/Asset Library / (B) Roman Stetsyk/123rf/123RF / (C) Mark Bowden/123rf/123RF; Page 17 (A) incamerastock / Alamy Stock Photo/Alamy / (B) Antonio Guillem/123rf/Asset Library / (C) GagliardiPhotography/ shutterstock/Shutterstock / (D) Sentavio/shutterstock/Shutterstock; Page 18 Sasha Ka/Shutterstock/Asset Library; Page 20 Elizaveta Galitckaia/123rf/123RF; Page 23 piksel/123rf/123RF; Page 25 (A) karelnoppe/Shutterstock/Asset Library / (B) Deklofenak/Shutterstock/Asset Library / (C) Dragon Images/ Shutterstock/Asset Library / (D) Motortion Films/Shutterstock/Asset Library / (E) Iakov Filimonov/123rf/Asset Library / (F) Pixel-Shot/Shutterstock/Asset Library / (G) Blend Images/Shutterstock/Asset Library / (H) David Tadevosian/ Shutterstock/Asset Library; Page 26 (A) Dean Drobot/123rf/123RF / (B) Photography/123rf/123RF / (C) Dmytro Flisak/Shutterstock/Asset Library; Page 27 Shutterstock/Asset Library; Page 29 (A) milkos/123rf/123RF / (B) Mark Bowden/123rf/123RF / (C) IKO-studio/Shutterstock/Asset Library; Page 30 (A) fizkes/Shutterstock/Asset Library / (B) bearmoney/Shutterstock/Asset Library / (C) Shutterstock/Asset Library; Page 31Jon Barlow/ Pearson Education Ltd/Asset Library / (B) Jörg Carstensen/ Pearson Education Ltd/Asset Library; Page 32 luckybusiness/123rf/Asset Library; Page Ponkrit Uthaikorn/123rf/Asset Library; Page 37 Chayantorn Tongmorn/shutterstock/Shutterstock; Page 38 (A) Joe Gough/Shutterstock/Asset Library / (B) hd connelly/ Shutterstock/Asset Library / (C) HandmadePictures/Shutterstock/Asset Library; Page 39 (A) Africa Studio/Shutterstock/Asset Library / (B) a9photo/Shutterstock/Asset Library / (C) vanillaechoes/Shutterstock/Asset Library / (D) AlexeiLogvinovich/ Shutterstock/Asset Library / (E) Krzysztof Slusarczyk/Shutterstock/Asset Library / (F) nblxer/123rf/Asset Library / (G) Dea e Bruno/Shutterstock/Asset Library / (H) Amarita/Shutterstock/Asset Library / (I) rimdream/123rf/Asset Library / (J) dnaveh/Shutterstock/Asset Library / (K) AJR_photo/Shutterstock/ Asset Library; Page 40 (A) Michael Warwick/shutterstock/Shutterstock / (B) dani3315/shutterstock/Shutterstock / (C) Vladimir Wrangel/Shutterstock/Asset Library; Page 41 Rawpixel.com/Shutterstock/Asset Library; Page 42 (A) iofoto/Shutterstock/Asset Library / (B) Dmitri Ma/Shutterstock/Asset Library; Page 43 (A) EVGENIYA68/Shutterstock/Asset Library / (B) magone/123rf/Asset Library / (C) victoriaKh/Shutterstock/Asset Library / (D) Peter Zvonar/Shutterstock/ Asset Library / (E) Glenn R. McGloughlin/Shutterstock/Asset Library; Page 44 (A) Viktor Bondar/123rf/Asset Library / (B) Kzenon/Shutterstock/Asset Library / (C) Billion Photos/Shutterstock/Asset Library / (D) Dmitrijs Gerciks/123rf/Asset Library / (E) Sergey Novikov/Shutterstock/Asset Library / (F) 187633/ Shutterstock/Asset Library; Page 45 BAZA Production/Shutterstock/Asset Library; Page 46 G-Stock Studio/Shutterstock/Asset Library; Page 48 (A) rarrarorro/ Shutterstock/Asset Library / (B) weedezign/123rf/Asset Library; Page 51 Paulus Rusyanto/123rf/123RF; Page 52 (A) NIKCOA/Shutterstock/Asset Library / (B) Pressmaster/Shutterstock/Asset Library / (C) Ian Wedgewood/Pearson Education Ltd/Asset Library / (D) Zurijeta/Shutterstock/Asset Library / (E) kurhan/ Shutterstock/Asset Library / (F) Lisa S./Shutterstock/Asset Library / (G) Andrey_Popov/Shutterstock/Asset Library / (H) Angelo Giampiccolo/Shutterstock/ Asset Library; Page 53 (A) lenetstan/Shutterstock/Asset Library / (B) piyaphun/Shutterstock/Asset Library / (C) Serdar Tibet/Shutterstock/Asset Library / (D) Lightspring/Shutterstock/Asset Library / (E) RTimages/Shutterstock/Asset Library / (F) Mark Vorobev/123rf.com/Asset Library / (G) phive/Shutterstock/ Asset Library / (H) kostasgr/Shutterstock/Asset Library / (I) zimmytws/Shutterstock/Asset Library / (J) PHENPHAYOM/Shutterstock/Asset Library / (K) wavebreakmedia/ Shutterstock/Asset Library; Page 54 (A) Allstar Picture Library Ltd./Alamy Stock Photo/Alamy Stock Photo / (B) gorodenkoff/123rf.com/ Asset Library / (C) Shutterstock/Asset Library; Page 55 EdBockStock/Shutterstock/Asset Library; Page Zentangle/Shutterstock/Asset Library; Page 57 KaptureHouse/Shutterstock/Asset Library; Page 58 (A) goodluz/Shutterstock/Asset Library / (B) BigBlueStudio/Shutterstock/Asset Library / (C) Bo1982/ Shutterstock/Asset Library; Page 59 theartofphoto/123rf.com/Asset Library; Page 60 (A) Jean-Marie Guyon/123rf.com/Asset Library / (B) Fona/Shutterstock/ Asset Library; Page 61 Andy Dean Photography/Shutterstock/Asset Library; Page 62 (A) presidenciamx/Alamy Stock Photo/Alamy Stock Photo / (B) SOPA Images Limited / Alamy Stock Photo/Alamy Stock Photo / (C) ART Collection/Alamy Stock Photo/Alamy Stock Photo / (D) Everett Historical/Shutterstock/Asset Library; Page 65 CarlosBarquero/shutterstock/Shutterstock; Page 66 Rawpixel.com/shutterstock/Shutterstock; Page 67 (A) TAGSTOCK1/shutterstock/ Shutterstock / (B) Bricolage/Shutterstock/Asset Library / (C) Olena Savytska/Shutterstock/Asset Library / (D) Alexander Maksimov/shutterstock/Shutterstock / (E) Diego Vito Cervo/123rf/Asset Library / (F) chatursunil/Shutterstock/Asset Library / (G) Amikishiyev/123rf/Asset Library / (H) Rob Judges/ Pearson Education Ltd/Asset Library; Page 68 (A) Torgado/Shutterstock/Asset Library / (B) xixinxing/123rf/123RF; Page 69 Kzenon/Shutterstock/Asset Library; Page 71 Arsgera / Shutterstock/Asset Library; Page 72 (A) kedrov/Shutterstock/Asset Library / (B) Chiyacat/Shutterstock/Asset Library / (C) elenovsky/Shutterstock/ Asset Library / (D) sagir/Shutterstock/Asset Library / (E) Karkas/Shutterstock/Asset Library / (F) Karkas/Shutterstock/Asset Library / (G) gogoiso/Shutterstock/ Asset Library / (H) Adisa/Shutterstock/Asset Library; Page 73 Syda Productions/shutterstock/Shutterstock; Page 74 (A) Happy Together/Shutterstock/Asset Library / (B) Ukki Studio/Shutterstock/Asset Library / (C) maxstockphoto/Shutterstock/Asset Library / (D) Lucie Drobna/Shutterstock/Asset Library; Page 76 (A) svkv/Shutterstock/Asset Library / (B) Jon Barlow/ Pearson Education Ltd/Asset Library; Page 79 shutterstock/Shutterstock; Page 80 shutterstock/ Shutterstock; Page 81 (A) asset library/Asset Library / (B) Greg Balfour Evans / Alamy Stock Photo/Alamy / (C) asset library/Asset Library / (D) Kzenon/ Shutterstock/Asset Library / (E) luckybusiness/123rf/Asset Library; Page 82 (A) industryviews/Shutterstock/Asset Library / (B) VGstockstudio/Shutterstock/ Asset Library / (C) KPG_Payless/Shutterstock/Asset Library; Page 83 James Martin/123rf/Asset Library; Page 84 (A) yusuf demirci/123rf/123RF / (B) OmaPhoto/Shutterstock/Asset Library / (C) 558148/Shutterstock/Asset Library / (D) majivecka/123rf/123RF / (E) arcady31/123rf/Asset Library; Page 85 (A) asset library/Asset Library / (B) Bram Janssens/123rf/Asset Library / (C) iqoncept/123rf/123RF; Page 86 (A) David Kostelnik/ Pearson Education, Inc./Asset Library / (B) Rawpixel.com/Shutterstock/Asset Library / (C) SpeedKingz/Shutterstock/Asset Library / (D) sirtravelalot/Shutterstock/Asset Library; Page 87 klee048/shutterstock/Shutterstock; Page 90 (A) RaZZeRs/Shutterstock/Asset Library / (B) vectorikart/123rf/Asset Library / (C) Wavebreak Media Ltd/123rf/123RF; Page 93Sergey Novikov/shutterstock/Shutterstock; Page 94 Saxsagan/Shutterstock/Asset Library; Page 96 (A) Sophie Bluy/ Pearson Education Ltd/Asset Library / (B) Volodymyr Melnyk/123rf/Asset Library / (C) DarioZg/shutterstock/Shutterstock; Page 97 Friends Stock/Shutterstock/Asset Library; Page 99 rsndetre/123rf/Asset Library; Page 100 (A) alvinge/123rf/Asset Library / (B) Svyatoslav Lypynskyy/123rf/Asset Library / (C) Inspirestock

International - Exclusive Contributor/123rf/Asset Library; Page 101 Tefi/Shutterstock/Asset Library; Page 102 (A) Hasan Shaheed/Shutterstock/Asset Library / (B) Melinda Nagy/Shutterstock/Asset Library / (C) A_Lesik/Shutterstock/Asset Library / (D) Thomas Bullock/123rf/Asset Library / (E) WinWin artlab/ shutterstock/Shutterstock; Page 103 solarseven/123rf/Asset Library; Page 104 Gustavo Frazao/Shutterstock/Asset Library / (B) marekuliasz/ Shutterstock/ Asset Library / (C) Denis Pepin/Shutterstock/Asset Library; Page 107 Marmolejos/shutterstock/Shutterstock; Page 108 rawpixe/123rf/123RF; Page 109 (A) PhotoSunnyDays/Shutterstock/Asset Library / (B) Weerapat Wattanapichayakul/123rf/Asset Library / (C) varuna/Shutterstock/Asset Library / (D) yvon52/ Shutterstock/Asset Library / (E) Cathy Yeulet/123rf/Asset Library / (F) Stock-Asso/Shutterstock/Asset Library / (G) David Prado/123rf/Asset Library / (H) Yasar Turanli/Shutterstock/Asset Library / (I) Africa Studio/Shutterstock/Asset Library / (J) THANANIT SUNTIVIRIYANON/123rf/Asset Library / (K) e2dan/ Shutterstock/Asset Library / (L) JCVStock/Shutterstock/Asset Library / (M) Early Spring/Shutterstock/Asset Library / (N) Mostovyi Sergii Igorevich/Shutterstock/ Asset Library; Page 110 (A) Dudarev Mikhail/Shutterstock/Asset Library / (B) Beer5020/Shutterstock/Asset Library / (C) Tokelau/Shutterstock/Asset Library; Page 111 wavebreakmedia/Shutterstock/Asset Library; Page 113 (A) Elnur/Shutterstock/Asset Library / (B) Matt Gibson/Shutterstock/Asset Library / (C) SJ Travel Photo and Video/Shutterstock/Asset Library / (D) elnavegante/Shutterstock/Asset Library / (E) Kudriavtsevy/Shutterstock/Asset Library; Page 114 (A) Snvv18870020330/Shutterstock/Asset Library / (B) encierro/123rf/Asset Library / (C) Kite_rin/Shutterstock/Asset Library; Page 115 Karol Kozlowski/ Shutterstock/Asset Library; Page 118 (A) snegok13/Shutterstock/Asset Library / (B) Robert Ciprian Lupu/123rf/Asset Library / (C) Ljupco Smokovski/ Shutterstock/Asset Library / (D) S.Borisov/Shutterstock/Asset Library / (E) DUSAN ZIDAR/Shutterstock/Asset Library; Page 121 Cantuaria/shutterstock/ Shutterstock; Page 122 Stephen Moehle/ Shutterstock/Asset Library; Page 123 (A) Viacheslav Lopatin/shutterstock/Shutterstock / (B) wessam Noufal / Shutterstock/Asset Library / (C) Marcus Brown/Shutterstock/Asset Library / (D) Chon Kit Leong/123rf/Asset Library / (E) Ruslan Suseynov/Shutterstock/Asset Library / (F) Natalia Siiatovskaia/shutterstock/Shutterstock / (G) TTphoto/Shutterstock/Asset Library / (H) Nikita Burdenkov/Shutterstock/Asset Library; Page 124 Volodymyr Goinyk/Shutterstock/Asset Library / (B) gangoo/Shutterstock/Asset Library; Page 125 (A) mirco1/123rf/Asset Library / (B) silvae / Shutterstock/Asset Library; Page 126 (A) Aleksandr Lupin/Shutterstock/Asset Library / (B) Neyman Kseniya/Shutterstock/Asset Library / (C) Rawpixel.com/ Shutterstock/Asset Library; Page 128 (A) Sandra Kemppainen/Shutterstock/Asset Library / (B) Asha Berezutskaya/Shutterstock/Asset Library / (C) Wojciech Wrzesien/Shutterstock/Asset Library / (D) misszin/Shutterstock/Asset Library / (E) Kamira/shutterstock/Shutterstock / (F) Gray wall studio/Shutterstock/ Asset Library; Page 129 Shutterstock/Asset Library; Page 130 (A) lekstuntkite/123rf/123RF / (B) ky123/123rf/123RF / (C) Anastacia - azzzya/Shutterstock/ Asset Library / (D) Tomas Griger/123rf/Asset Library / (E) Roman Doroshenko/123rf/123RF / (F) Olga Kositskaya/123rf/123RF; Page 132 Albachiaraa/ Shutterstock/Asset Library; Page 137 AiVectors/Shutterstock/Asset Library; Page 138 (A) kanin abhiromsawat/123rf/123RF / (B) IM_photo/Shutterstock/ Asset Library; Page 139 scusi/123rf/Asset Library; Page 140 Pavel Voinau/123rf/Asset Library; Page 141 MaraZe/Shutterstock/Asset Library; Page 142 (A) giedre vaitekune/Shutterstock/Asset Library / (B) SARYMSAKOV ANDREY/Shutterstock/Asset Library / (C) THANANIT SUNTIVIRIYANON/123rf/Asset Library / (D) Jasminko Ibrakovic/Shutterstock/Asset Library / (E) dragoscondrea/123rf/123RF / (F) BearFotos/shutterstock/Shutterstock; Page 143 Tom Wang/ Shutterstock/Asset Library; Page 144 aratehortua/123rf/123RF; Page 145 Helder Almeida/Shutterstock/Asset Library; Page 147 nicoelnino/123rf/Asset Library; Page 148 (A) harunatsukobo/123rf/Asset Library / (B) Lorelyn Medina/Shutterstock/Asset Library; Page 149 Denis Pepin/Shutterstock/Asset Library; Page 150 PILart/Shutterstock/Asset Library; Page 151 Somchai Siriwanarangson/Shutterstock/Asset Library; Page 153 grafner/123rf/Asset Library